# THE MODEL ARAB LEAGUE MANUAL

Manchester University Press

# THE MODEL ARAB LEAGUE MANUAL

A guide to preparation and performance

*Philip A. D'Agati and Holly A. Jordan*

MANCHESTER UNIVERSITY PRESS

Published by Manchester University Press
Altrincham Street, Manchester M1 7JA
www.manchesteruniversitypress.co.uk

British Library Cataloguing-in-Publication Data
A catalogue record for this book is available from the British Library

Library of Congress Cataloguing-in-Publication Data applied for

ISBN 978 1 7849 9339 9 paperback

First published 2016

Typeset by Out of House Publishing
Printed and bound by CPI Group (UK) Ltd, Croydon, CR0 4YY

This textbook is dedicated to several individuals who have been key players in the growth and development of the Model Arab League program. Among the most noteworthy is the founding and current President of the National Council on U.S.-Arab Relations (NCUSAR), Dr. John Duke Anthony. His dedication to the study of the Arab World and the promotion of understanding of Arab culture in the United States is a testament to his career and the founding principles of the present Model Arab League program. Additionally, the entire staff of the NCUSAR – most of whom are or have been alumni of the Model Arab League program – have contributed tireless hours of time and care to the promotion and betterment of the event. Some, but not all, of these include Melissa Matthews, Megan Geissler, Salim Furth, Scott McIntosh, Kaylee Boalt, Shawn Romer, Josh Hilbrand, Mark Morozink, and Patrick Mancino. Lastly, this book is also dedicated to those individuals recognized as Lifetime Achievement winners by the NCUSAR for their contributions to the Model Arab League program:

1st – Michael Nwanze of Howard University

2nd – Dean Bergeron of University of Massachusetts Lowell

3rd – Smokey Ardisson of Berry College

4th – Philip A. D'Agati of Northeastern University

5th – Joe P. Dunn of Converse College

6th – Linda Morrisson of Kennesaw State University

7th – Holly A. Jordan of Virginia Polytechnic Institute and State University

# Contents

# Tables

# Preface

Twelve years ago a timid student, who was unaware of the Arab World beyond the ability to find six of the twenty-two members of the League of Arab States on a map, joined my Model Arab League team. She was afraid of public speaking – terrified would be a more accurate but less kind way of describing her situation. She joined out of pressure from two of her friends and with the promise that my program could "fix her," to quote her friend's description of the situation to me. It took both of her friends and me working with her an entire semester to get her to speak even once. Some members of my team insisted that she would never be a strong delegate and would never get past her fears. I reminded them that our program was not just for those students who could perform, but for those who wanted to perform. Thus began what some would consider a hopeless task.

The beauty of the Model Arab League (MAL) program is that it provides a flexible opportunity to shape the learning experience to meet the needs of the individual student. In the hands of an advisor and team leadership that are skilled in the program, an MAL experience can provide endless opportunities for growth and learning. My program provided this for a timid student who could not find Morocco on a map in her first year. By her junior year, the student had become a capable member of my team and would speak often. At the National Conference one year, she was debating in the Joint Defense Council (JDC). Something happened in committee prompting my head delegate to come running to find me and inform me that I was needed in JDC immediately. All my head delegate knew was that there was an altercation in a moderated caucus, that my delegate was in a conversation with the other delegate in question in the hall, and that there was crying involved.

Upon arrival at the JDC committee, my delegate was standing in the hallway trying to calm a delegate from another committee. She looked up at me and said, "She said something wrong in committee and I tried to help ... she just started crying ... and I can't make her stop." My delegate, who at this point still saw herself as that timid, quiet delegate, had no idea of the power that her tone and poise in committee had conveyed. She had no idea that she was no longer the freshman delegate she had started as. The situation was resolved to the satisfaction of everyone involved and my delegate became the mentor of the student from the other school. By the end of conference, both won awards in JDC that year and I could not have been prouder. Three years after graduation from Northeastern University, she graduated from law school and is now a litigator for a law firm recognized for its record of excellence.

The MAL program has been a part of my life for approaching two decades. It is a program I have grown to cherish over these years and that I promote to any student and professor whom I think may have an interest in becoming part of the MAL family.

The program offers so many opportunities for learning, leadership development, and public speaking. As a student participant, I had the opportunity to experience the program in debate as a member of both the Lower Secretariat (Chair, Chief Justice) and the Upper Secretariat (JCC Coordinator, Secretary-General). I performed each of these roles more than once and found value, learning, and personal growth every time. Once I had transitioned in my studies from the status of student to that of doctoral candidate, I took up the mantle of faculty advisor and discovered the joy and enrichment one gets from being a mentor and guide to the dozens of students each year in my program.

This book was conceived by myself, an editor from Bloomsbury Press, and a representative of the National Council on U.S.-Arab Relations – all of whom were delegates in the Model Arab League at one point – as a means of making initial and continued participation in the MAL program easier and friendlier for students and faculty advisors. Without some means of support or guidance, starting a team and maintaining it can be a daunting task. The downside of this reality is that it has the effect of inhibiting new schools from taking the plunge into the MAL world and it has stunted the growth of teams that have started but have yet to see success or stability in their programs. This text provides the details necessary for a faculty advisor, a student leader, or a student to successfully become part of or create an MAL team.

Each year, new schools and new students join the MAL family. Some teams have been proactive in reaching out to and supporting fledgling programs, as we all see the expansion of the MAL program as an investment in the future success and stability of this learning experience. The better each delegate becomes – and by extension each delegation – the better the overall debate experience will be for every student participant. In that spirit, this text provides all the necessary tips, skills, tricks, and policies used by some of the most successful teams in the history of the MAL program for the betterment of any team or student wishing to enhance their learning experience in the program.

Compiling this text was quite the process and quite the stroll down memory lane. It is based on documents, guides, histories, personal experiences, best practices, and course syllabi that stretch from 1999 to 2014. The text represents the most comprehensive collection of knowledge and history of the MAL program ever assembled and contains the most successful strategies and best examples of the use of rules and procedures from those fifteen years. It draws on my own and others' experiences and expertise, and attempts to be a readable introduction to MAL for novice and intermediate participants. For expert participants, it serves as a reference guide and as a collection of alternative solutions to common problems in committee and on an MAL team.

Philip A. D'Agati

# Acknowledgments

This book would not have been possible without several key individuals, including our two Model Arab League advisors: Denis Sullivan and Joe Dunn. For Philip, Denis was the person who first instilled in him a love of the Arab World and the Model Arab League (MAL) program and who served as Philip's MAL advisor at Northeastern University. For Holly, Joe took a gamble on her in the spring of 2004 and asked her to join Converse College's MAL program. Joe then went on to mentor both Philip and Holly, first as students and then as team leaders, and then as coaches and advisors of their own MAL teams. We owe them both for instilling in us the love of mentorship and we owe them a great debt of gratitude for our careers and for the accomplishment of this text.

The MAL program has been a source of many long-term friendships in our lives, including, of course, our close friendship with each other, which began in 2004 at the National University Conference. MAL friendships are the kind of friendships that contribute to one's quality of life for years far beyond our contributions as students of the program. The process of writing this textbook proved once again the strength of the bonds of friendship that MAL can create. We were particularly touched by our friends' willingness to support and assist us in the process of collecting and writing the various parts of this text, especially Jon Barcus, Daniel Quintal, Zach Hrynowski, and Benjamin Schneider. In support of this endeavor, other current and former members of our programs, including William Joyce, Kat Teebagy, Matt Cournoyer, Brandy Blanton, and Victoria Ball, provided insights, suggestions, information, fact checking, and other assistance in the process of drafting this text. Lastly, Josh Hilbrand, a current NCUSAR representative, provided invaluable time and comment on the process of writing the textbook in order to maintain its accuracy in accordance with current MAL policies and language in the official Handbook.

We would also like to take this opportunity to thank both the many National Council representatives and the NCUSAR founder and president, Dr. John Duke Anthony, for their continued dedication to, support of, and maintenance of the MAL program. Their commitment to the program and the endless opportunities they have created for my and others' students have provided tens of thousands of participants with an unparalleled learning experience that has changed the lives of many of them.

**A note from Philip:** This text would not have been possible without the lineage of student leaders who have contributed to the development and evolution of my team and to the history of Northeastern University's student membership of the National Secretariat; many of them have been responsible for the major changes in the MAL program. A complete list of these students would be impossible, but some students who contributed to the development of team policies and the learning environment are individuals I wish to mention here. They include Jonathan Barcus, Lara Cole, Matt Cournoyer, William Joyce, Noreen Leahy, Laura Mueller-Soppart, Daniel Quintal, Daniel Rothschild, Benjamin Schneider, Catia Sharp, and Jared Simons.

**A note from Holly:** For me, this text would never have happened without two key groups of people: the brilliant young women of Converse College and my current and former students on the Virginia Tech MAL team. Being a member of the Converse College MAL team has shaped me as a teacher, a mentor, and a researcher, and I still look to these women for support as I lead my own team of students, especially to former Converse College MAL members Josie Fingerhut Shaheen and Victoria Ball. Additionally, in the four years I have had to work with them, my Virginia Tech students have been my inspiration to continue advising for MAL programs. In 2012, our fledgling team consisted of three women attending the Southeast Regional Model Arab League: Rachel Kirk, Elizabeth Womack, and myself. Their commitment to beginning and sustaining a successful MAL team led to the recruitment of additional students, the creation of the Regional International Organizations club, and the founding of the Appalachia Regional Model Arab League (ARMAL). Thank you, especially, to Meghan Oakes, Marquis Reynolds, Rasika Pande, Matthew Jordan, and Andrew Lindsay for your leadership at our first ARMAL and for helping me achieve my dreams of sharing MAL with Virginia Tech and our region.

# 1

# Introduction to the League and the Model League

This chapter provides the reader with a history of the Model Arab League program and the League of Arab States, also known as the Arab League (see the section below on "What is the League of Arab States?"). The history of the program provides context on where the program came from and the purpose behind its perpetuation by the National Council on U.S.-Arab Relations (NCUSAR) and the recent growth and expansion of the program. From there, the chapter provides the reader with a list of current conferences, their locations, and the approximate times of year when they are held.

The chapter also provides an introduction to the League itself through a brief synopsis of its history and some of its successes. It provides the reader with details on the current structure of the League, noting the purpose of some of its main bodies, and the history of the growth of its membership. The chapter is not intended to be a comprehensive history of the League; rather, its goal is to provide the reader with enough background to effectively participate in a Model Arab League learning experience.

## History of the program

The Model Arab League (MAL) program is a series of competitive high school and collegiate conferences held throughout the United States, Europe, and the Middle East. The primary syndicate of conferences is a collection of regionals across the United States and a national conference held in Washington, DC, each spring. The MAL program, which was created in 1981 by Dr. Michael Nwanze of Howard University, was adopted by the NCUSAR in 1983 and quickly became its flagship program. The program soon grew from only a handful of conferences to twenty-five as of 2015 and the potential for further expansion in the next few years.

As a leadership, diplomacy, and public-speaking development program, MAL is a key learning opportunity in the development of college and high-school students, as it provides a unique learning environment that is not duplicable in a traditional classroom context. The program was originally developed to promote an active learning environment that encouraged students to hone research, public speaking, problem solving, and teamwork skills and to receive feedback from advisors and judges on their performance. Students who excel in their performance may also win awards to take back to their school.

Over the past thirty years, the MAL program has seen two phases of growth. First, an increasing number of schools has prompted growth in the number of conferences being offered. This growth, occurring at both high-school and collegiate levels, has been a testament to the quality of program offered by the NCUSAR and to the quality of students participating in debate year after year. Second, individual conferences have grown in student capacity over thirty years. From 1983 to 2002, all conferences featured only five committees. The original five committees were Political Affairs, Economic Affairs, Security Affairs (now Joint Defense Council), Social Affairs, and Palestinian Affairs. In 2002, the program saw the first expansion of committees, spearheaded by representatives of the NCUSAR: the Gulf Cooperation Council and the Arab Economic Unity Forum. In 2003, the program the Gulf Cooperation Council was removed[1] and the Arab Court of Justice (ACJ)[2] was created as a hypothetical committee based around proposed language in the Charter of the League of Arab States and the Statute of the International Court of Justice. In 2004, the Arab Economic Unity Council, which only involved twelve of the twenty-two members, was replaced by the Economic Affairs Council. By the end of 2004, the National Conference and two regionals (Northeast and Southeast) featured six standing committees and the Arab Court of Justice.

In 2005, the NCUSAR experimented with the addition of a special rotating committee, the topic of which would differ from year to year. One of these committees, the Heads of State Committee, was so successful that it became a permanent committee in 2013. The Council continues to host a special topics committee each year. The final expansion, which occurred in 2014, was the addition of the Joint Cabinet Crisis, which is a dynamic quasi real-time crisis simulation involving at a minimum two committee rooms acting as individual governments. The 2014 National Conference, Southeast Regional, and Northeast Regional were the three largest conferences in MAL history, featuring ten committees and a capacity for over 200 student participants. That was double the capacity of the 2002 Nationals, which had room for only 110 student participants.

---

[1]  A committee of only six countries was unrealistic for a three- or four-day conference in a student centric environment.

[2]  Two representatives of Northeastern University (Daniel Quintal and Philip D'Agati) and one representative of Converse College (Maria Perry) met in Boston and proposed the creation of the ACJ.

The various changes in the learning opportunities represent growth in interest and diversity of the MAL program. Some aspects of the program, therefore, have evolved to meet the dynamic needs of the Model Arab League and are less indicative of the structure of the real League. It is important to understand that the rules, organization, and functions of an MAL conference are structured to boil down weeks' worth of negotiation in the real League to a three- to four-day simulation. MAL rules are based in large part on *Robert's Rules of Order Newly Revised* and other sources unaffiliated with the League. The rules are meant to facilitate quick debate with short speaking times, allowing for draft resolutions of reasonable quality to be written, debated and voted on during a total conference debate period of 15–30 hours. Real-world League debate occurs on many levels, encompassing staff as well as League diplomats, formally and informally, and of course is not subject to nearly the same time restrictions. MAL generally intends to be a substantive approximation and makes significant procedural compromises to accommodate time and personnel constraints inherent to the conference format.

Similarly, the existence of the ACJ is intended to be a hypothetical learning experience that allows students to explore international law in a more hands-on approach while simultaneously exploring intra-Arab conflicts that do not fit the topical agenda of any one committee. It is, therefore, an excellent learning experience that has successfully enthralled student and faculty participants for over a decade.

## NCUSAR'S Model Arab League conference program

MAL conferences fall into one of five broad categories: collegiate conferences, hybrid conferences, high-school conferences, special conferences, and international conferences. Hybrid MAL conferences are open to both collegiate and high-school students. Potential participant schools should inquire of the NCUSAR whether the conference features separate high-school and collegiate committees or if the conference has committees in which high-school and college students participate together. Special conferences are run by the NCUSAR or another organization in partnership with the NCUSAR and feature a unique structure, set of committees, or are open only to specific participants.

As of 2015, the MAL conferences are:

### Collegiate MAL conferences
National University Model Arab League (NUMAL)

- Host: NCUSAR
- Location: Washington, DC
- Time of year: March/April

Appalachia Regional Model Arab League (ARMAL)

- Host: Virginia Polytechnic Institute and State University
- Location: Blacksburg, Virginia
- Time of year: Mid to late November

Bilateral U.S.-Arab Chamber of Commerce University Model Arab League

- Host: University of Houston, Honors College
- Location: Houston, Texas
- Time of year: Spring semester

Capital Area Regional Model Arab League (CARMAL)

- Host: NCUSAR/Georgetown University
- Location: Washington, DC
- Time of year: Mid November

Michigan Regional Model Arab League

- Host: Grand Valley State University
- Location: Allendale, Michigan
- Time of year: Mid February

Northeast Regional Model Arab League (NERMAL)

- Host: Northeastern University
- Location: Boston, Massachusetts
- Time of year: First week of November

Northern California Regional Model Arab League

- Host: University of California, Berkeley
- Location: Berkeley, California
- Time of year: April

Ohio Valley Regional Model Arab League

- Host: Miami University
- Location: Oxford, Ohio
- Time of year: Mid February

Rocky Mountain Regional Model Arab League

- Host: Variable
- Location: Utah or Colorado
- Time of year: Mid February

Southern California Regional Model Arab League

- Host: University of La Verne
- Location: La Verne, California
- Time of year: March

Southwest Regional Model Arab League

- Host: Texas A & M University
- Location: Commerce, Texas
- Time of year: April

Upper Midwest Regional Model Arab League

- Host: University of North Dakota
- Location: Grand Forks, ND
- Time of year: Mid to late October

### Hybrid MAL conferences
Florida Regional Model Arab League

- Host: University Area CDC
- Location: Tampa, Florida
- Time of year: March

Northern Rockies Regional Model Arab League

- Host: Montana State University
- Location: Missoula, Montana
- Time of year: April

Southeast Regional Model Arab League (SERMAL)

- Host: Converse College
- Location: Spartanburg, South Carolina
- Time of year: Mid March

### High-school MAL conferences
National High School Model Arab League

- Host: NCUSAR
- Location: Washington, DC
- Time of year: April

Atlanta High School Model Arab League

- Host: Marist High School
- Location: Atlanta, Georgia
- Time of year: January

Chicago High School Model Arab League

- Host: Variable
- Location: Chicago, Illinois
- Time of year: Fall Semester

Columbia Model United Nations Conference & Exposition – Model Arab League Committee(s)

- Host: Columbia University
- Location: New York City, New York
- Time of year: January

Little Rock High School Model Arab League

- Host: University of Arkansas at Little Rock
- Location: Little Rock, Arkansas
- Time of year: Florida

North Texas High School Model Arab League

- Host: Variable
- Location: Denton, Texas
- Time of year: Fall semester

### Special conferences
Boston Model Arab League (BOSMAL)

- Host: Northeastern University
- Location: Boston, Massachusetts
- Time of year: March/April
- Note: Traditional councils for high-school students and Joint Cabinet Crisis cabinets for college students

Summer Intern Model Arab League (SIMAL)

- Host: NCUSAR
- Location: Washington, DC
- Time of year: July
- Note: Open only to college students on internship programs throughout DC.

### International conferences
Cairo International Model Arab League

- Host: American University in Cairo
- Location: Cairo, Egypt
- Time of year: November

Corinth Model Arab League

- Host: Variable
- Location: Corinth, Greece
- Time of year: No traditional time period for the conference

University of Birmingham Model Arab League

- Host: University of Birmingham
- Location: Birmingham, United Kingdom
- Time of year: Spring semester

## What is the League of Arab States?

The League of Arab States, or Arab League, is a regional intergovernmental organization made up of Arab states and exists both to foster relations and cooperation among its members and to protect individual state sovereignty. Resolutions that are passed by the League are binding only on the members that vote for them. The League was founded on 22 March 1945 with the adoption of the Charter of the League of Arab States (see Appendix B for the text). The membership at its founding consisted of Egypt, Iraq, Jordan, Lebanon, Saudi Arabia, Syria, and Yemen. Over the next fifty years, the remainder of the current twenty-two members joined, with 1971 seeing the greatest annual membership increase since the League's inception. Its current membership total of twenty-two was attained in 1993 when Comoros joined the League.

Over time, the League grew in membership and purpose. Comparatively, the League is still a relatively small organization with less than one thousand staff at its headquarters and around the world (Toffolo 2008: 45). The League's modest size has not, however, dissuaded it from developing a complex structure and a broad area of topical governance. As it expanded, it began solidifying means of cooperation in various areas of policy, requiring increasing layers of infrastructure to manage its various areas of interest. Today, the League is a multifaceted organization with many layers of committees and subcommittees. Among the most important governing bodies and committees of the League are the following:

- **League Council:** The Council is the leading body within the League made up of the member states where each state receives one vote. The September session of the League Council is a session of the foreign ministers while the March session, usually referred to as the Summit of the League, is a session of the heads of state and foreign ministers of the League.
- **General Secretariat:** Headed by the Secretary-General, the Secretariat is responsible for the administration of the League as well as implementing the measures approved by the League Council. In total, the Secretariat

"consists of a [Secretary-General], an undefined number of assistants and an adequate number of clerks" (Hätinger 2006: 11). There is a Secretariat member, often along with staff, for each major committee, organization, and body of the League.

- **Joint Defense Council (JDC):** Made up of the foreign affairs and defense ministers from the League's member states, the JDC focuses on defense issues. The creation of this committee, which occurred in 1950, signified a critical shift in the overall purpose and future governance of the League. It was established by the Joint Defense and Economic Cooperation (JDEC) Treaty, the text of which can be found in Appendix C.
- **Economic and Social Council (ESC):** The ESC was created for the discussion of economic and social development within the Arab region. Established in 1950 in the JDEC Treaty, the ESC along with the JDC set the precedence for all future committees of the League.
- **Ministerial councils:** Ministerial councils are official meetings of corresponding ministers of all members of the League for the purpose of formulating common policies and responding to pan-League issues within their policy jurisdiction. In the case where a state does not have a corresponding minister, the member state sends either the foreign minister, a minister with similar portfolio (for example, the environmental and energy ministers interchangeably), or a minister without portfolio. Fourteen ministerial councils currently exist in the League of Arab States:[3]
  - o Energy and Electricity Council
  - o Environmental Affairs Council
  - o Council of Health Ministers
  - o Housing Affairs Council
  - o Information Affairs Council
  - o Council of Interior Ministers
  - o Joint Defense Council
  - o Justice Affairs Council
  - o Social Affairs Council
  - o Telecommunications Council
  - o Tourism Council
  - o Council of Transportation Ministers
  - o Youth and Sports Council
- **Specialized organizations:** The League of Arab States has a series of specialized organizations that member states may be party to (see Table 1.1). Which states are members of each is contingent on each organization's purpose, membership guidelines, and the interests of each League member.

---

[3] This list of current ministerial councils was established through materials from the NCUSAR and Hätinger (2006: 11).

The total list of specialized organizations is uncertain, but the following organizations – categorized as financial and non-financial agencies – are illustrative:[4]

o Financial agencies
  • Arab Authority for Agricultural Investment and Development (AAAID)
  • Arab Bank for Economic Development in Africa (BADEA)
  • Arab Economic Unity Council (AEUC)
  • Arab Fund for Economic and Social Development (AFESD)
  • Arab Monetary Fund (AMF)
  • Inter-Arab Investment Guarantee Corporation (IAIGC)
o Non-financial agencies
  • Arab Academy for Science, Technology and Maritime Transport (AASTMT)
  • Arab Administrative Development Organization (ARADO)
  • Arab Atomic Energy Board (AAEA)
  • Arab Center for the Studies of Arid Zones and Dry Lands (ACSAD)
  • Arab Civil Aviation Association (ACAA)
  • Arab Educational, Cultural, and Scientific Organization (ALECSO)
  • Arab Industrial Development and Mining Organization (AIDMO)
  • Arab Labor Organization (ALO)
  • Arab Organization for Agricultural Development (AOAD)
  • Arab Satellite Communications Organization (ARBSAT)
  • Arab States Broadcasting Union (ABSU)
  • Organization of Arab Petroleum Exporting Countries (OAPEC)

## League successes

During the League's over sixty-year history, the organization has seen many successes and failures. There is no agreed upon list of the greatest successes of the League, besides perhaps the very fact that it continues to endure, so creating any set list of League accomplishments is inherently subjective. Below are a few facts or events that are considered noteworthy by many MAL experts.

### First successful international organization

The League of Arab States has the distinction of being the oldest extant sovereign-state membership organization, being founded before the United Nations, the Organization of American States, the North Atlantic Treaty

---

4  This list of specialized agencies was established through materials from the NCUSAR and Hätinger (2006: 11–12).

TABLE 1.1: Memberships of League specialized organizations

| | Algeria | Bahrain | Comoros | Djibouti | Egypt | Iraq | Jordan | Kuwait | Lebanon | Libya |
|---|---|---|---|---|---|---|---|---|---|---|
| AAAID | X | X | X | X | X | X | X | X | X | |
| BADEA | X | X | | | X | X | X | X | X | X |
| AEUC | X | X | | | H | X | X | X | X | X |
| AFESD | X | X | X | X | X | X | X | H | X | X |
| AMF | X | X | X | X | X | X | X | X | X | X |
| IAIGC | X | X | | X | X | X | X | H | X | X |
| AASTMT* | | | | | H | | | | | |
| ARADO | X | X | X | X | H | X | X | X | X | X |
| AAEA | X | X | X | X | X | X | X | X | X | X |
| ACSAD | X | X | X | X | X | X | X | X | X | X |
| ACAA | X | X | X | X | X | X | X | X | X | X |
| ALECSO | X | X | X | X | X | X | X | X | X | X |
| AIDMO | X | X | X | X | X | X | X | X | X | X |
| ALO | X | X | | X | H | X | X | X | X | X |
| AOAD | X | X | X | X | X | X | X | X | X | X |
| ARBSAT | X | X | | X | X | X | X | X | X | X |
| ABSU | X | X | X | X | X | X | X | X | X | X |
| OAPEC | X | X | | | X | X | | H | | X |

Notes: H indicates that the state is the location of the headquarters of the organization. X indicates that the state is a member of the organization. The AASTMT (Arab Academy for Science, Technology and Maritime Transport) is an institute of higher education and does not have state-based membership.

Organization, and all other existing regional bodies. Furthermore, it has *continuous* history. Since its inception, the League has operated without interruption and has weathered several major events that could have destroyed the League. These include three major conflicts between many of its members and Israel, the expulsion of Egypt, the Iraqi invasion of Kuwait, and the Arab Spring.

### Egypt's readmission while recognizing Israel

The League's decision to readmit Egypt in 1988 demonstrated a key turning point in the policy of the organization as a whole and was a demonstration of courage in the face of some of its less diplomatic members. In 1978, Egypt entered into a unilateral peace treaty with the State of Israel that included recognition of the state. The League at that time responded by expelling it from the organization. In 1987, the League restored diplomatic relations with Egypt and then readmitted the country as a member the following year, despite relations with Israel. In 1994, a peace treaty between Jordan and Israel did not result in any action by the League against Jordan. Through these policies on Egypt and Jordan, the League removed itself as an obstacle to peace with Israel

| Mauritania | Morocco | Oman | Palestine | Qatar | Saudi Arabia | Somalia | Sudan | Syria | Tunisia | UAE | Yemen |
|---|---|---|---|---|---|---|---|---|---|---|---|
| X | X | X | X | X | X | X | H | X | X | X | X |
| X | X | X | X | X | X |   | H | X | X | X |   |
|   | X | X | X | X | X |   | X | X | X | X | X |
| X | X | X | X | X | X | X | X | X | X | X | X |
| X | X | X | X | X | X | X | X | X | X | H | X |
| X | X | X | X | X | X |   | X | X | X | X | X |
| X | X | X | X | X | X | X | X | X | X | H | X |
| X | X | X | X | X | X | X | X | X | H | X | X |
| X | X | X | X | X | X | X | X | H | X | X | X |
| X | H | X | X | X | X | X | X | X | X | X | X |
| X | X | X | X | X | X | X | X | X | H | X | X |
| X | H | X | X | X | X | X | X | X | X | X | X |
| X | X | X | X | X | X | X | X | X | X | X | X |
| X | X | X | X | X | X | X | H | X | X | X | X |
| X | X | X | X | X | H | X | X | X | X | X | X |
| X | X | X | X | X | X | X | X | X | H | X | X |
|   |   |   |   | X | X |   |   | X |   | X |   |

and signaled a continued movement toward a moderate policy on various regional issues.

### *Libya and Syria, 2011*

In 2011, the Arab Spring saw the League take an active role in international affairs, notably over Libya and Syria. The League suspended the membership of Libya after President Muammar Gadaffi ordered the use of force against civilian protesters. The League proceeded to take action that was integral to authorizing air strikes over Libya by NATO forces to help protect civilians. With Syria, the League took similar action, suspending membership after the Syrian government responded with force against protesters. Unanimously, the League approached the United Nations Security Council, seeking international assistance to protect Arab civilians within Syria. These are critical decisions of the League and demonstrate the increasing relevance of the regional organization to current major issues in the Arab World, as well as its future involvement in the future of its member states.

### *Relationships with other regional and international organizations*

The League has relations with non-member states and other regional and international bodies, and sometimes will grant observer status to such groups and non-members to bring valuable perspective to the topics being debated.

The following are a couple of examples, but are by no means the only relationships that the League maintains.

One such relationship has been the continued association between the African Union (AU) and the League that was formalized in 1977 and continues to see cooperation between the two organizations today. They have held joint summits and, recently, the League sent a delegation to the AU headquarters to gain experience with some organs that the League was considering implementing within its structure.

Another relationship the League maintains is with the European Union (EU), a relationship that saw increasing levels of traction as the EU grew into a more political organization. League relations with the EU culminated in 2008 with a summit of foreign ministers from all of the then twenty-seven EU member states and all twenty-two Arab League members. The resulting Malta Communiqué paved the way for future cooperation between the two organizations.

### Summary

The League of Arab States is a dynamic regional and international organization that has been shaping foreign policy in the Middle East for over six decades. Its role in recent events in the region, most notably during the Arab Spring in Libya and Syria, has shown the relevance and impact of the League on current events and on the lives of Arabs across the Middle East and North Africa. The MAL has been successfully simulating the League for over thirty years, providing students from around the United States and from several other countries with a unique opportunity to understand the League through a hands-on, experiential learning conference.

Student participants in the MAL can expect to broaden their understanding of the Arab World and broaden their understanding of foreign policy, international relations, and politics in the Middle East and North Africa. Student participants can also develop valuable skills in research, public speaking, writing, and leadership. The MAL program is thus one of the most valuable learning experiences for students with a broad range of academic interests.

# 2

# Conference structure
## *Councils, leadership, and guidelines*

This chapter introduces the basic structure and organizational factors of a Model Arab League (MAL) conference. It provides new and returning participants all the details necessary to understand the types of councils, select the right council for them, and also understand the roles of each participant and the jobs they do. Lastly, the chapter introduces the reader to three specialized MAL learning experiences (Joint Cabinet Crisis, Arab Court of Justice, and Press Corps) that are not available at all conferences.

## Councils: types of councils

Model Arab League provides a wide variety of opportunities that both appeal to a variety of personalities and approximate some of the role diversity within the League of Arab States. Primarily, the various councils differ topically but there are less rigid and official differences in terms of committee dynamic and council tone. Broadly speaking, the councils can be broken up into two categories: standard councils and specialized councils.

Five of the seven standard councils run at the vast majority of conferences. Every League member state is a voting member on these committees and observer states are invited to attend their meetings. The Rules of Procedure are designed for these councils, and these councils are where most students who are new to MAL will start. The standard councils are: Joint Defense Council, Council on Palestinian Affairs, Council on Political Affairs, Council of Arab Social Affairs Ministers, Council of Arab Environmental Affairs Ministers, Council of Arab Economic Affairs Ministers, and Council of Arab Heads of State.

### *Joint Defense Council*

*Joint Defense Council (JD)[1] coordinates common defense policies of the member states in an attempt to maintain regional peace and stability. It can adopt*

---

[1]  These brief descriptions in italics for each council are taken from the official *Model Arab League Handbook* (NCUSAR 2014).

*any measures it deems necessary to repel an act of aggression against any of the member states.*

The Joint Defense Council, typically referred to by its participants as the "JDC," is the principal League body on security. The committee manages the defense policy of the League and typically deals with topics related to mutual security cooperation, policies related to weapons, small arms, and cross-border security, and those related to issues of instability in member states and the region that have a military dynamic. More recently, the role and response of the League as it pertains to terrorism, extremism, and other destabilizing facets is an area of broad topical interest for this committee.

Student participants will find an aggressive debate, in comparison to other committees, and a diplomacy style that is very fluid and hard to predict. The JDC often sees crises mid conference and rarely attains unanimity in the course of its negotiations. In short, the JDC is a dynamic committee that is best served by a delegate with similar enthusiasm and experience.

### Council on Palestinian Affairs

*Council on Palestinian Affairs (PA) is concerned with all Palestine-related matters, with special emphasis on issues pertaining to defense, economics, politics, and social conditions. This council has the permanent mission of working for the establishment of a viable, independent Palestinian State.*

Palestinian Affairs is a council by special request of the League of Arab States. It invites students to immerse themselves in a deeper appreciation for the complexities of the Arab–Israeli conflict and the question of Palestine's status in the international community. The committee features a very unique dynamic as some members of the League recognize Israel, while others have a tangential policy of appeasement toward Israel, and still others have no formal recognition of Israel and may even take a boisterous and aggressive tone toward the state.

The tenor of discussion in Palestinian Affairs is hard to predict and often ebbs or flows with the situation in the Middle East. Topics range from the status of Palestine to relations with Israel with regard to the Palestinian question, to topics in social, cultural, and refugee matters, and issues related to Palestine's needs and interests. The committee can tend toward an aggressive debate with loud and impassioned speeches or toward a softer and more amiable tone that can even result in unanimous consent for council resolutions. The council is best served by delegates capable of a versatile skill and tone in session, as it is hard to predict the nature of this council from conference to conference.

Advisors and head delegates should take care to refrain from assigning a student to Palestinian Affairs with personal or emotional ties to the

Arab–Israeli conflict. Such students have found the council to be a stressful and emotional experience that rarely results in a positive participatory experience. Furthermore, advisors and head delegates should be mindful of the tone of participants in this committee. Phraseology that involves the term "Zionism" and "Zionist" is completely inappropriate and off policy for twenty of the twenty-two League members, and the remaining two – Syria and Mauritania – rarely use the language as a matter of foreign policy. No observers to the League consider it appropriate for use in their foreign policy either.

### Council on Political Affairs

*Council on Political Affairs (PO) addresses broad political issues that exist both around the Arab world and within the League of Arab States. Issues can range from broad concerns dealing with the Arab world as a whole to addressing situations in specific member countries.*

The Political Affairs council has topics that meet one of three broad categories. First, the focus can be on inter-Arab policies, politics, and relations. The second area focuses on the relations of the League and its members to non-member states and other international organizations. Topics involving relations with the African Union, the United Nations, and other regional organizations or relations with a specific state, such as Iran, Turkey, the United States, or China, are all potential examples of this category. Third, topics can cover the establishment of pan-Arab policies on domestic issues. In this case, the Council on Political Affairs discusses the establishment of a common policy across the League for the benefit of League relations and Arabs everywhere.

Student participants in this council will find a debate very similar to the JDC, but with a bit less bluster. The Council often uses draft language that is broad in scope and thematic in nature, and often also produces draft language that is very precise, detail oriented, and systematic. Students interested in a committee with many dynamics and many avenues for relevant topical interest will find a great home in this council.

### Council of Arab Social Affairs Ministers

*Council of Arab Social Affairs Ministers (SA) coordinates common social policies of the member states, with special emphasis on issues pertaining to education, women and children, historical preservation, and culture.*

The Social Affairs council plays a key part in satisfying one of the critical roles of the League: the preservation and promotion of Arab culture. The Council focuses on topics in relation to societal issues that are matters of pan-Arab domestic policy or matters of inter-Arab policy. Topics in relation to the status of women, children, and minorities are commonplace as well as topics on the preservation of Arab history, language, culture, and heritage.

Student participants in Social Affairs will find a dynamic committee that focuses on the nuts and bolts of policy instead of on broad strokes and philosophies. Building on a general agreement on the importance of culture, traditions, and faith in Arab society, the Council focuses more on the details of its preservation and promotion. While the Council often features detailed and spirited debate, it is not uncommon for broad consensus to develop and a tone of cooperation to govern the majority of its proceedings.

### Council of Arab Environmental Affairs Ministers

*Council of Arab Environmental Affairs Ministers (EN) coordinates common policies with regard to management, conservation, and protection of ecosystems, natural resources, and related environmental concerns.*

The Environmental Affairs council has three areas of topic jurisdiction that become the foci of its agenda. These areas are energy and energy resources, preservation of the environment and natural wonders, and natural resource extraction, use, management, and so on. The Council primarily handles cross-border and multi-state cooperatist endeavors. In a fashion similar to Social Affairs, the Council tends to work on the details of policy instead of broad concepts or legal arguments.

Furthermore, the Council carries a tone similar to that of Social Affairs and is a great experience for delegates who want to develop and then detail policy as part of their debate environment. The committee differs in tone from Social Affairs in that the dynamics of poor versus wealthy and of resource rich versus resource starved create different sets of allies from the more socially and politically focused councils.

### Council of Arab Economic Affairs Ministers

*Council of Arab Economic Affairs Ministers (EC) coordinates international, inter-regional, and domestic policies on trade, labor, development, and other economic matters in order to ensure the maximum economic benefit to all member states.*

The Economic Affairs council is the most straightforward in its topical jurisdiction. Quite simply, the Council fulfills the League's economic obligations defined in the Joint Defense and Economic Cooperation (JDEC) Treaty. Economic Affairs has a reputation for being highly detail oriented and quick to utilize key words and concepts in economic studies, and for featuring a very unique and interesting divide in terms of coalitions of states fostering policies of common interest.

While an economics background is not considered a requirement for participation in this committee, it is wise to place students on Economic Affairs who have, at a minimum, encountered concepts in micro/macro finance, foreign direct investment, international banking, and international trade. Student participants in Economic Affairs with no background or understanding in economics often find themselves marginalized from the discussion and withdraw as debate becomes increasingly technical.

## Council of Arab Heads of State

*Council of Arab Heads of State (HoS) is a fictional council attended by the head of state of each member of the Arab League. The agenda varies widely but often concerns the most pressing issues of the day.*

The Heads of State council is an attempt to mimic the various meetings of heads of state during summits, in which state leaders instead of state diplomats discuss policy. The students represent the official heads of state of their governments. In circumstances where two students are partnered together, the student speaking is considered to have the authority and title of the head of state, and that "title" simply swaps between them when one or the other speaks.

Students on the Heads of State council discuss a wide range of topics that have consequences in multiple policy areas. The room has a unique and fun environment where titles of "Your Highness" and "Your Excellency" are among the designations by which speakers are recognized. Given the broadness of topical jurisdictions and the occasional complex roles in crises, students that welcome a dynamic and fluid debate environment find a good home in this council.

## Specialized councils

Specialized councils follow the same rules as the standard councils, but the councils that meet will vary from year to year. For example, a "Council on Arab Youth" may meet one year and may be replaced the next with a "Council on the Status of Women and Children."

The specialized councils provide the MAL program and its participants with a chance to explore topics that either do not fit within any regular committee, that allow the program to look at a subtopic of a committee (such as the Status of Women) through the lens of multiple topics and areas of focus, or that are based on exceptional current events. The specialized councils typically include all member states, but sometimes have a smaller subset of states or even a larger one with additional observer states.

Debate in the specialized councils tends to be much more focused, substantive and technical, and enforcement of the rules is often relaxed, allowing for a much freer flowing discussion. Newer delegates may find these councils challenging and if there is a question on whether a specialized council is appropriate for a newer delegate it is advisable to discuss it in advance with conference organizers.

### Arab Court of Justice

*Arab Court of Justice (ACJ) mimics the procedures used by similar international judicial bodies, i.e., the International Court of Justice, not domestic courts. The ACJ hears legal disputes between member states and parties – participants present one side of a case on behalf of their country, and alternate as Justices when other Court participants present cases. The ACJ is governed by the rules not laid out in this Handbook, but rather the ACJ Statute.*

The ACJ is a fictional court based in large part on the International Court of Justice. The Charter of the League of Arab States initially mentioned an Arab court of justice, but it was later amended out and the League has never actually had a court. The Model Arab League's ACJ gives each student the opportunity to represent a state and argue a case on behalf of that state. Each student also has the chance to act as a justice. There are significant written arguments that are compiled before the conference and the ACJ is a very intense experience both before and during the conference. As such, it tends to attract experienced delegates. The ACJ does not meet at most conferences.

The ACJ involves significant research and writing pre-conference. At conference, student participants act as justices on the Court until their case is up on the docket, at which point they act as advocates for their government. The Court's deliberative sessions are a free-flowing discussion of the relevancy and veracity of law, the facts of the case, and the competing interpretations of law, history, and treaties. While acting as an advocate, student participants must present for up to twenty minutes, take questions from justices and from the other advocate(s), and provide concluding remarks. Some students find the experience to be the best MAL learning opportunity, while others find they have a distaste for the Court's styles of debate.

It is important to note that students must be timely in their paperwork prior to conference. Not submitting a memorial or counter-memorial on time creates many problems for the Court and is unfair to the student(s) on the other side of the case. Students should also take the research and writing of their memorial or counter-memorial seriously.

### Joint Cabinet Crisis

In a Joint Cabinet Crisis (JCC), each delegate represents a named individual in a simulation of a national government's cabinet. JCCs require a minimum of two governments and have no maximum, limited only by available space and number of student participants. Typically, there will be two or three governments, each with a "cabinet" of officials. These cabinets will work through a crisis situation that impacts the states represented in the JCC, communicating with the other cabinets as needed. These councils are very technical and each individual has a very specific role to play; there are no bystanders or minimal contributors. JCCs tend to attract the most experienced delegates, those who are very comfortable with informal debate and have a broad general knowledge of the Arab World, the regions beyond the Arab states, and international relations.

## The Press Corps

*The Press Corps reports on the events of the conference and councils in the form of a daily newspaper and various online media.*

Student participants in the Press Corps work with the Editor-in-Chief, who coordinates the research and production of the newspaper, online media, and social media for the duration of the conference. The Press Corps currently only operates at the National University MAL (NUMAL).

## Players at the conference

### Delegations

A delegation comprises the students representing a single country on each of the councils held at the conference, a head delegate, and a faculty advisor. If a school is representing more than one state, then the school has more than one delegation and may opt to bring a head delegate and even a faculty advisor for each. Ultimately, it is up to each team to decide how much support staff it brings to a conference and how it builds and designs its team. The one rule of thumb that all teams should follow is that the first delegation should have at a minimum one student representing their country on each council before the school takes a second country. It is preferable to not have partners unless all councils have at least one student as well.

Each state may be represented by up to two **delegates** on each of the councils whose meetings the state is entitled to attend. If numbers allow, it is always beneficial to have two delegates sitting on each council – any delegation should be able to improve its efficiency when there are two people to share the workload. Often, one delegate will take the lead on formal speaking and debate while the other will work behind the scenes to build relationships and collaborate on resolution writing. There are many other ways to divide the work, but, inevitably, two delegates who work well together will be a benefit and not a hindrance compared to a single delegate representing a state.

Each delegation (not each school) may have one **head delegate** at the conference. The head delegate will usually (but not always) also represent his or her state on a council. In addition, the head delegate leads his or her national delegation, serving as the primary conduit between the delegation and the conference secretariat/staff, representing the delegation at head delegate meetings, advising the less experienced members of the delegation, and so on.

Generally, every school at the conference will bring at least one **faculty advisor**. Advisors are encouraged to circulate among the council rooms and advise delegates in a non-disruptive manner. At times, advisors may not have access to the ACJ, but no restrictions exist for other councils. Advisors also participate in faculty meetings along with conference staff and secretariat, and many use the time at the conference as a chance to catch up with advisors from other schools on MAL best practices, and so on. In the absence of a faculty advisor, many of these functions will be performed by the head delegate.

### National Council on U.S.-Arab Relations (NCUSAR) staff

MAL conferences are organized by the National Council on U.S.-Arab Relations (NCUSAR) in collaboration with local organizers. The **NCUSAR staff** present at the conference serves no substantive role during the normal functioning of the conference; at a successful conference, the NCUSAR representatives work behind the scenes and have no apparent influence on debate in any council. NCUSAR does, however, ultimately have final say over all conference activities and in extreme situations may intervene in substantive matters.

### Conference director

At conferences hosted in partnership with another organization, there will be a conference director. The titles **conference director** and **local coordinator** are used rather interchangeably and refer to the same general position at the conference. The conference director is responsible for facilitating organization of the conference on their campus or similar facility that plays host to the conference. Once conference begins, the conference director works with the NCUSAR staff on location to manage the conference and respond to participant concerns. Most conference directors work out an amenable relationship with the NCUSAR representatives and come to consensus on issues that need to be settled. In case of disagreement, the NCUSAR representative has final say over substantive and procedural matters pertaining to the conference while the conference director has final say over logistical matters relevant to the delivery of the conference and its various elements.

### Secretariat

There are a variety of substantive roles at conference, ranging from the people responsible for moderating council debates to those who manage the overall operation of the conference. These positions comprise the Secretariat. The Secretariat is divided into two categories: Upper and Lower. The Upper Secretariat, sometimes referred to as the "Senior Secretariat," includes the Secretary-General, the Assistant Secretary-General, and the Chief of Staff. The

Lower Secretariat includes the council chairs, the Chief Justice of the Arab Court of Justice, the JCC Coordinator, and the Editor-in-Chief of the Press Corps.

## Upper Secretariat

The most senior student position at the conference is **Secretary-General (SG)**. The SG is responsible for the overall operation of the conference. The SG chairs the opening plenary meeting and the closing summit, leads the Secretariat, and is the point of escalation above the council chairs. The SG's job begins long before the conference, as they are a key decision maker on most aspects of conference planning. As such, the SG is often selected a full year in advance.

The SG is assisted by an **Assistant Secretary-General (ASG)**, who is available to assist with any of the SG's responsibilities in a backup capacity or as requested by the SG. Many larger conferences will also have a **Chief of Staff** available to take on operational tasks delegated by the SG while the ASG focuses primarily on substantive/topical matters. Some of the largest conferences will have two ASGs to help divide the workload between four students instead of just three. Along with the SG, the ASG(s) and Chief of Staff are often selected a full year in advance.

## Lower Secretariat

The most common position in the Lower Secretariat is that of the **council chair.** Each council will have a council chair who is responsible for fairly moderating debate, interpreting rules, and coordinating delegation awards within the council. The chair position is normally appointed well before the conference, often a full year in advance. The Chief Justice and the Editor-in-Chief perform the equivalent function of the council chair for their respective bodies. Specifics on their position and role can be found later in this chapter in sections devoted to both of these participation options.

The Joint Cabinet Crisis (JCC) Coordinator is also a member of the Lower Secretariat, but performs a role similar to that of Upper Secretariat, but only for the JCC. The structure of the JCC and the roles of various players in it is a topic of significant consideration and afforded its own section toward the end of this chapter.

## Council officers

In addition to the chair, the council officers are the vice-chair, the rapporteur, and the parliamentarian. During the first council session, the chair will preside over elections for the additional committee officers. The delegates that fill these positions will continue to represent their delegations in addition to the position's duties. The **vice-chair** is responsible for the operation of the council in the chair's absence or at the direction of the chair. The **rapporteur** is responsible for maintaining speakers lists and performing other administrative duties. This is a great leadership position for less experienced delegates. The **parliamentarian** is a person with extensive knowledge of the Rules of Procedure who is available to assist the chair and vice-chair with points of parliamentary inquiry. Commonly, the parliamentarian has previous council chairing experience.

## Judges

Larger conferences will also have **judges** who observe council sessions and participate in the awards selection process. Judges are normally academic or industry professionals, with a significant knowledge of the region, member states, and relevant topics, or are laureate alumni of the program with a long history in the MAL program. Often, the keynote speakers from the opening and closing ceremonies will also serve as judges at conferences that employ judges. Specific details of the use of judges in the awards process are discussed later in the chapter.

## What to expect at conference

Upon arrival at the conference, the faculty advisor or head delegate should report to the registration desk. Conference staff will confirm the names of those on the delegation, so it is useful to have a roster to cross-check. The delegation will receive a name badge and a conference agenda booklet for each delegate. Both are critically important throughout the conference and delegates should know before arriving that they will be required to wear a name badge at all times. Conference staff will also confirm the financial status of the delegation at check-in. Registration is also a good time to ask any specific questions about conference logistics, amenities, and so on.

Normally, after registration, there will be some downtime before the opening ceremonies begin. The delegation should find an area to assemble and all delegates and advisors should fill out At-Model Registration forms (provided by the NCUSAR) and name tags according to the format prescribed by conference staff. Additionally, students should use this time to find other members of their committee to introduce themselves and to begin strategizing the order of the agenda and possible resolution ideas.

Once the delegation enters the room where the opening ceremonies are to occur, the delegates should sit together. The meeting will take a couple hours and will include at least one substantive keynote address. At the end of the opening ceremony, the Secretary-General will introduce all of the council chairs, and delegates will follow their chairs to their councils' meeting rooms. This transition tends to be somewhat chaotic and it is helpful if delegates are prepared to stand up and follow their councils' chairs as soon as the opening ceremony adjourns.

At the first council session, the chair will first introduce themselves and usually give a brief background on their chairing style and expectations for decorum in the room. Then the chair will lead an election process for the vice-chair, rapporteur, and parliamentarian positions (occasionally these might be appointed instead). After the election, the council will enter a plenary session and will debate the contents and ordering of the agenda. Only after the agenda is finalized will the core substantive work of the committee begin. Appendix J has a scripted council session to provide a bit more detail on how council sessions begin and then flow into the speakers.

From there, council sessions continue through the process of proposing and discussing ideas. Discussions eventually result in enough consensus on some ideas for a group of delegates to begin drafting language. Once language is drafted, sponsored/signed, and introduced, the primary work of the committee is to amend the introduced language or propose new language until such time as a document is amenable to a majority of the committee. Once delegates believe they have arrived at that point, the debate is closed and the document(s) are voted on.

Over the course of an entire conference, one to four topics will be discussed and potentially many drafts of language will be introduced, amended, and voted upon. Council sessions continue through topics, subtopics, resolutions, and amendments in an order and at a pace determined by committee members through parliamentary procedures. Chapters 3 and 4 provide details on how all of this works and should help in preparing delegates for this experience.

## Awards: what they are and how they work[2]

After the conclusion of the summit session, students will be presented with awards based on a number of factors: preparation, debate, caucusing, accurate country representation, teamwork, diplomatic leadership, and overall positive contribution to the work of their council. In addition to the formal awards, chairs, at their discretion, reserve the right to give verbal commendations[3] both at the end of their final council session and during the awards ceremony.

---

[2] The descriptions of each award in italics are taken from the *Model Arab League Handbook* (NCUSAR 2014). The regular text is explanative.

[3] The tradition of in-committee verbal commendations began with David Valente of Kennesaw State University, who presented an empty soda bottle as an award to a delegate in his council who had provided a significant and valuable contribution to the council but was not among the award winners.

*Processing awards*

*The National Council representative(s) shall count and record all votes cast and issue awards based solely on those tabulations. Certain unbreakable ties may alter the total number of awards given. All decisions regarding awards are made at the sole discretion of the National Council. Any errors in printing will be corrected as soon as possible. Problems or concerns with awards will only be addressed with Faculty Advisors after the conclusion of the Summit Session.*

In practice, the NCUSAR often invites the assistance of further staff or faculty advisors to assist in the awards processing. This used to be commonplace at the National Conference but has fallen out of standard practice now that the final committee session is the evening before the awards are given. At many regional conferences, the timing between the last session (and therefore voting on awards) and the summit session is only a few hours at most, so others have assisted to make production of awards realistic. At some regionals, awards are tabulated by the conference director as a matter of tradition at that conference or a matter of feasibility due to timing and logistics of the conference and its awards ceremony.

*Delegate Awards*

*Delegate Awards are presented to the students who exhibit the highest degree of excellence in preparation, debate, caucusing, accurate country representation, teamwork, diplomatic leadership, and overall positive contribution to the work of their Council. Two types of awards are typically given, Outstanding Delegate Awards for the top performers and Honorable Mention Awards for those falling into a secondary tier of high performers. In some instances at larger conferences, other categories may be added at the discretion of the National Council representative and/or local coordinators.*

*Delegate Awards are determined through balloted peer evaluation, Chair evaluation, and at some conferences, third-party Judges. All participating delegates are eligible for awards, including observers. If a school has multiple country delegations present, those delegations should be considered as independent from each other. Two-person delegations receive the same award. The number of awards given varies at the discretion of the National Council representative(s). Any student who violates the rules of award voting will be ineligible to receive any award and may be subject to additional disciplinary actions.*

The total number of awards given in a council is contingent on two factors: number of countries represented and the spread of votes in the balloting. Councils with a large number of delegations will have more awards than councils with smaller numbers of delegations. In addition, in the instances of ties or near ties, the conference director and the National Council representative(s) may decide to give an extra award in a specific council. In short, the awards are a fluid system that is responsive to the dynamic of the committee. In the instance of additional award categories for much larger conferences, the spread of the awards and how many in each category is equally fluid and also up to the conference director and the National Council representative(s).

The JCC and the ACJ follow similar procedures for conference awards, but the awards are titled differently to account for the reality in those committees. For the JCC, for each cabinet there are two awards: Outstanding Cabinet Member and Honorable Mention Cabinet Member. Additionally, the JCC Coordinator and facilitators give an Outstanding Cabinet Leader award to the cabinet leader who most effectively advanced their cabinet's goals and policies and most accurately represented their cabinet's position. For the ACJ, two sets of awards are given: Outstanding/Honorable Mention Justice and Outstanding/Honorable Mention Advocate.

*Overall Delegation Awards*

*Overall Delegation Awards are issued to country teams for overall superior performance throughout the entire Model. These awards are based on the collective performance of a country delegation across all Councils. Two types of awards are given, Overall Outstanding Delegation Awards for top delegations, and Overall Honorable Mention Awards for those falling into a secondary tier of high performing delegations. Other award categories may be added at certain conferences at the discretion of the National Council representative and/or local coordinators. The number of awards given varies at the discretion of the National Council representative(s).*

Similar to the delegate awards, the exact number of awards, categories of awards, and number of awards per category is a fluid system that fluctuates based on the number of delegations present and the overall performance of these delegations in comparison to each other. The method of determining the Overall Delegation Awards is not rigid and different conferences are free to employ the method preferred by the National Council representative and the conference director. Whatever the specific system, the logic always remains the same: Overall Delegation Awards are contingent on performance in all councils at the conference. It is important to note that teams that do not put at least one delegate on each standard council are often at a disadvantage in the overall awards, as they have few opportunities to score points toward best delegation. That being said, the specialized committees operate differently.

Since multiple awards are possible in some specialized committees (JCC and ACJ), delegations participating in these committees are allowed to earn points toward Overall Delegation equivalent in maximum value to one standard council. If there is only a JCC, this is true for the JCC. If there is a JCC and an ACJ, this is true across the two committees combined. If there is only an

ACJ, then performance in the Court is omitted from the Overall Delegation Awards and considered only in the event of a tie between two schools that participated in the ACJ. The reason for the difference between ACJ and JCC is due to an issue of capacity. Only ten delegations can participate in the ACJ, so it is an unfair advantage for those delegations when only an ACJ exists. The JCC, however, can be expanded to accommodate at least one student from every delegation and therefore participation in the JCC does not create an unfair advantage.

### Chair Awards

*Chair Awards are presented to the Chairs who manage their Councils efficiently and smoothly, have a strong grasp of the rules, and best facilitate the work of the delegates. All Chairs are eligible to receive these awards. Chair Awards are determined by a vote of the faculty advisors present at the conference, in consultation with the National Council Representative(s). At most conferences, one Outstanding Chair Award and one Honorable Mention Chair Award will be presented, but the number of awards given is at the discretion of the National Council representative(s).*

Faculty advisors attending conferences should remain aware of this requirement of their position at conference. The advisor should spend time in every committee every day in order to observe and assist their delegations. As a result of that fact, they are in a prime position to see the performance of every chair. The advisors do not need to worry about observing the ACJ in this manner as the "chair" of the Court is ineligible for the award. A separate award is given for JCC cabinet leaders, so they are similarly ineligible for the Chair Award.

## Joint Cabinet Crisis simulation

### Introduction

The Joint Cabinet Crisis (JCC) is a real-time simulation of a crisis situation between two or more governments. In the simulation, students represent members of a government's cabinet, ambassadorial staff, military staff, and other relevant offices/agencies working together to guide policy during the crisis. The crisis is a compelling and in-depth look at crisis diplomacy and strategic bargaining through the perspective of actors immersed in the moments of the crisis. Students arrive at the conference with very little detail of the committee's topic, often only knowing the list of governments and cabinet positions on each government until the first crisis update by the JCC Coordinator(s).

Student participants should be aware that the JCC crisis exists in its own bubble of reality at the conference. Events of the crisis do not affect other councils. Student participants should feel free to share the experience and the events of the JCC with anyone, but just remember that those events are not open for discussion in other councils. On occasion, the Secretary-General may deem an aspect of the JCC or a question sent (see later in this section) to be worth inclusion as a crisis in one of the regular councils. Such a decision is not under the purview of the JCC participants and attempts to interject the crisis into other councils is highly frowned upon.

### Structure of the cabinet and the crisis

The JCC comprises two or more cabinets, which usually contain high-ranking members of the government or organization that it represents. At the beginning of conference, the JCC Coordinator will present the crisis topic to the cabinets, which will connect and involve them all in some way. It will then be the job of the cabinets to work with – or against – one another to resolve the crisis and advance their own goals, however each cabinet defines them.

All cabinets are physically separated from one another, with each having its own room. Each room is presumed to be located in the headquarters that the organization is based in; that is to say, a cabinet representing the League of Arab States would be located in Cairo. As a result, participants – other than ambassadors – are expected to maintain geographic reality and not walk from their cabinet to another as it is presumed that cabinets are meeting in the capital city of their state. Cabinet rooms are closed-door meetings that are open only to cabinet members, secretariat, faculty advisors, and any representatives of other governments that are invited by the cabinet and approved by the Coordinator.

Instead of a country, each participant in the JCC will represent a specific member of the cabinet. In a standard government cabinet, members will include the heads of state and government, ministers of defense, state, and finance, as well as various ambassadorial posts. The participant will then be responsible for carrying out all the various duties of his assigned office. For instance, a defense minister would be responsible for informing the cabinet of the state's military capabilities, while the finance minister is the primary resource when assessing the fiscal feasibility of a proposal. Therefore, it is critical that each member of the cabinet is intimately familiar will all the capabilities and responsibilities of his or her office, so that he or she may quickly and efficiently make decisions when called upon.

### Crisis procedure

#### The cabinet room

With the entire cabinet, including ambassadors to other countries, assembled together in one room, the cabinet conducts a discussion of their state's options in the crisis. The manner in which the cabinet runs is at the discretion of the cabinet leader – generally the head of government – and will vary based on the atmosphere and status of the crisis. The format of this discussion typically takes one of two forms:

1.  A permanent moderated caucus format where the cabinet leader chairs their cabinet and calls on members to speak. The cabinet leader may use a strict moderated caucus format with a set speaking time or allow cabinet members a more informal structure where time is not kept.
2.  A permanent unmoderated roundtable discussion where cabinet members inject their comments without being called on by the chair. In this format, the cabinet leader may opt to regulate debate in the aforementioned format when the discussion becomes unproductive.

The purpose of these debate structures is to allow for a fluid and dynamic debate environment that can quickly respond to the changing atmosphere of a JCC while also not allowing the debate to descend into an unproductive environment where multiple people are talking over each other and no one is really listening. In the end, intra-cabinet discussions are flexible and will be shaped and reshaped mid conference based on numerous factors present in the room.

*Communication*

In order to maintain the simulation of restricted communication in a crisis scenario, official communication is strictly managed through the cabinet leader. Only the cabinet leader may send official communications on behalf of their government. Cabinet leaders will write or email communiqués and give/send them to the JCC Coordinator for delivery. Unofficial communications are messages outside official channels of the cabinet leadership. While they do not carry the weight of official state policy they can still be an effective vehicle for advancing the state's policy, for example, when a member of the cabinet opts to send a message to their counterpart in another cabinet or the cabinet decides to use an unofficial communication as a means of "leaking" information to the press. Whether official or unofficial, the communication must still go through the JCC Coordinator for delivery to the other cabinet. Another aspect of official communication is through ambassadors, which is covered in the next section.

In addition to official and unofficial communication, cabinets have a few other options for communication. These are through press releases, high-level negotiation, and directives. Press releases may be released by a government at any time. Press releases are distributed to all participants of the JCC by the Coordinator. They should be written from the perspective of the press and are usually labeled as coming from a legitimate news source. High-level negotiation occurs when one government requests and at least one other government accepts said request for direct negotiations between cabinet members of two or more governments. Most commonly, this will involve a minister from each cabinet meeting to discuss the current situation. The JCC Coordinator arranges for the applicable students to meet in a separate location (usually a hallway outside of committee rooms) to conduct the negotiation. Directives are internal communications, usually including instructions or orders, to a facet of a cabinet's own government. These include, but are not limited to, instructions to intelligence agencies to provide information, instructions to military assets to take some action, and instructions to local bureaucracy to respond logistically to a situation occurring on the ground. These directives are sent to the JCC Coordinator, who then determines the plausibility of the action taking place and the outcome, if necessary, of said action.

*Role of ambassadors*

Each cabinet includes ambassadors to other relevant states involved in the crisis. Ambassadors will sit in the cabinet of the state of origin but may go to the cabinet of the government they are ambassador to at any time, subject to the consent of that cabinet. So, for example, the Egyptian ambassador to Sudan sits with the Egyptians by default and discusses strategy, policy, and decision-making with that cabinet. He may also walk to the Sudanese cabinet at any time to speak with the Sudanese government. This simulates the reality that ambassadors are the only member of the cabinet that are on location in the capital city of another government but are still in regular communication with their home government during most crises. In similar fashion, the receiving government (in this example, Sudan) is free to refuse admittance of an ambassador at any time and for any reason, though it should be noted that this will often have diplomatic consequences. Alternatively, a receiving government may also instruct an ambassador to appear. This request is most commonly sent electronically to the JCC Coordinator, who then informs the cabinet leader of the request.

One complication in the role of ambassadors is that not all states have formal relations with each other in a crisis. It is also possible the ambassador is unavailable for whatever reason or the role is simply unassigned due to absence of a student participant. In either case, the realm of diplomatic relations must continue and relations are passed through other ambassadors. In the event that a state is missing an ambassador, ambassadors may communicate with each other to bring a message from one government to another. For example, let us say:

1.  Egypt has an ambassador to Sudan, but not one to Libya;
2.  Libya has an ambassador to Sudan, but not one to Egypt;

3.  the Egyptian ambassador in Khartoum may speak with the Libyan ambassador in Khartoum in order to establish an ambassadorial information channel between Egypt and Libya during the crisis.

Ambassadors carry with them the power of official communication and also can conduct the only form of communication that does not go through the JCC Coordinator. They only conduct official communication when sent or summoned by a cabinet leader. Any other communication the ambassador conducts is unofficial in nature and governed by those rules.

*Communication beyond represented cabinets*

Cabinets are free to communicate with governments, international organizations, non-governmental organizations, and others not present or represented in the JCC. Any such communication is sent to the JCC Coordinator who then determines the appropriate response to the communication and sends it back. Cabinet members should be aware that responses to these requests can be time-consuming and are sometimes delayed or denied based on conference logistics; therefore, requests that require action from the JCC Coordinator should not be made frivolously. Faculty advisors, National Council representatives, and the Upper Secretariat are all potential sources for responses to these requests and are often tapped to assist the JCC Coordinator on an as-needed basis. This is handled differently when the request is for the League of Arab States.

In the event a cabinet is asking for the input of the League, the request is sent to the JCC Coordinator, who then takes it to the Secretary-General (SG) for the conference. The SG, with the input of the JCC Coordinator, National Council representatives, and any advisors assisting the JCC, has the sole discretion on how the request is handled, noting the following:

1.  If it is beneficial to the conference, the SG may opt to "task" a committee and have them debate League responses/actions given the crisis and the Cabinet's request. In that event, all cabinets are informed of the tasking by the Secretariat. Furthermore, the JCC Coordinator and an ambassador or minister of foreign relations of relevant cabinets may be asked to visit a committee session to brief in a Q&A session format.
2.  If it is not beneficial to the conference, then the SG and faculty leadership of the JCC determine the appropriate response of the League to the Cabinet's request and act on the League's behalf in future communication relevant to the initial request.

*Crisis tactics*

In the event a cabinet wishes to take a decisive act against another government, the cabinet leader must inform the JCC Coordinator of the government's decision. Cabinets are in full control of all their state capabilities and may utilize them at any time. The JCC Coordinator and his support staff determine the outcomes of actions/events where the outcome is uncertain. Cabinets and cabinet leaders are not in control of fate, random chance, or luck at any time and therefore cannot make statements that imply the success or failure of any outcome they make. This does not, however, restrict a government from using propaganda to embellish the success or failure of any action by any cabinet at any time.

## Capabilities

Cabinets should be aware of the full potential of the capabilities their state possesses. These include political, social/cultural, geographic, environmental, economic, military, technological, and resource capabilities. In a JCC, it is easy to resort to military force as a tactic for attaining state objectives in the crisis, but that is often a mediocre plan at best. The best cabinet members are those members who can find tactics that may include, but are not limited to, military action to advance the policy of their state.

## Intrigue

Cabinets are encouraged to think outside the box and employ intrigues as part of their efforts to advance state policy. Using deception, espionage, red herrings, the fabrication of information, and the engagement of questionably relevant governments or agencies into the simulation is an effective means of confounding other cabinets and gaining a significant advantage in the JCC.

## *Examples of communication and documents*

### Sample Press Release

DATE HERE

**PRESS RELEASE**

TO: All States Present

FROM: Khalifa Al Nahyan

SUBJECT: Iranian Invasion of the UAE

The recent occupation of both the United Arab Emirates and Oman by the Islamic Republic of Iran is considered to be an act of aggression that is illegal under international law. This unilateral movement presents a clear danger to all states, as it shuts off all trade coming in and out of the Strait of Hormuz.

Furthermore, the Emirati intelligence community has intercepted Iranian cables that imply the possible use of fully enriched uranium.

We implore all states to condemn these actions and offer military aid in the event that this situation escalates.

**Sample Directive**

DATE HERE

**DIRECTIVE**

To: Syrian Army Assets in Aleppo

From: Head of Military Intelligence Abdul Fatah Qudsiya

In light of its recent victory, Syrian Army forces around Aleppo are to launch a counteroffensive to destroy the depleted Syrian National Coalition forces in the area.

This attack should focus on killing or capturing the remaining forces as they regroup from their defeat.

**Sample Communiqué**

DATE HERE

**OFFICIAL COMMUNIQUÉ**

To: President Vladimir Putin

From: President Bashar al-Assad

The Syrian Arab Republic is grateful for the increased Russian military response at the port of Tartus. We greatly appreciate their timely response to our requests for augmented military assistance when combating the terrorism that is rampantly destroying our land. We hope to keep the channels of communication open between our joint military efforts. The Syrian Arab Republic looks forward to continued cooperation with the Russian Federation in restoring and emboldening our territorial sovereignty and legitimacy.

**Sample Treaty/Agreement**

Treaties/agreements can take the form of a resolution (see Appendix K) or any formal treaty, including the Charter of the League of Arab States (see Appendix B), or other treaties in the appendices to this textbook.

## JCC awards

Two categories of awards are given in the JCC: Cabinet Leader Awards and Cabinet Member Awards. The Cabinet Leader Awards are chosen from among the heads of state in the crisis. There is one head of state per government, so typically only one of these awards is ever given at a conference. The recipient(s) of the Cabinet Leader Awards are selected by the JCC Coordinator in consultation with any faculty advisors or National Council representatives that were involved with the management of the JCC. Cabinet Member Awards are the awards that the rest of the cabinet members are eligible to receive. They are voted on in cabinet just like awards in the regular councils. Normally, only one Outstanding Cabinet Member and one Honorable Mention Cabinet Member award is given per cabinet. As with the regular council awards, the number of awards is subject to the size of the cabinet, the outcome of voting, and similar factors that are all at the discretion of the National Council representatives and the conference director.

## Arab Court of Justice

### Introduction

The Arab Court of Justice (ACJ) was first introduced to the MAL program in 2003 as a special committee at the National University MAL (NUMAL). Since then, the ACJ has run at every NUMAL in addition to sessions at the Northeast Regional MAL, the Southeast Regional MAL, and the Michigan Regional MAL. The Court is a smaller committee, generally represented by no more than ten countries. The Court is chaired by a Chief Justice, who is assigned to no case and presides over the proceedings. The rules of the Court are enforced by the Bailiff, whose description can be found in the Statute of the Arab Court of Justice in Appendix I.

The primary purpose of the ACJ is to provide a simulation-based opportunity to learn about international conflict and international law through the lens of a current or dormant dispute between representatives of two Arab states. The ACJ functions with rules similar to those of the International Court of Justice and provides student participants with the opportunity to act as a judge – hear a case, question advocates, and then rule on the matter at hand – and to act as an advocate – representing one side of a case by submitting a formal claim, presenting evidence, responding to justice and advocate questions, and state a nature of their state's claim in the case.

### Swearing in

At Opening Ceremonies, the Secretary-General swears in the Chief Justice of the ACJ. The Chief Justice then swears in all the members of the ACJ as formal justices of the court. The text of the swearing in can be found in the Statute of the Arab Court of Justice, Article 3, Section 3.03(b). It reads: "I solemnly declare that I will perform my duties and exercise my powers as judge honorably, faithfully, impartially, and conscientiously."

### Structure of the ACJ

The bench is represented by eight countries – each with one to two representatives – in addition to the Chief Justice, who presides over the Court's proceedings. The Chief Justice represents no country in particular and is a representative of the League of Arab States. The Chief Justice may break procedural ties but may not vote in substantive matters; therefore, justices must come to a majority on any Opinion of the Court. Additionally, an Assistant

Chief Justice is elected from the pool of available justices prior to the commencement of hearings. The Assistant Chief Justice is responsible for fulfilling the duties of the Chief Justice should he or she be unable or unavailable to do so; as a result, nominees for the position of Assistant Chief Justice should be intimately familiar with the statute and procedure of the Court.

Students on the ACJ prepare to fulfill two primary roles: advocate and justice. As advocates, students represent prosecuting and defense attorneys who present formal cases before a body of Arab justices. Advocates can represent a person, a country, a regional body, and so on, as long as the petition is brought to the Court by a country. As justices, students hear cases, are involved in cross-examination of the advocates, and deliberate on cases coming to a majority opinion of the Court.

Note that, as students fulfill two roles, they must also assume two personas. As an advocate, students must zealously present their arguments as just that: an advocate for the interests and policies of the state that they represent. As a justice, however, students must relinquish their affiliations with any particular state, instead representing objective arbiters of the law. They must favor no particular outcome of a case on the basis of personal preference, positive or negative relations with the states which are party to the case, or any rationale not related to the legal reasoning presented.

### Responsibilities prior to conference

All advocates are required to prepare a number of materials for use during the presentation of their case. The first and most important item is the Memorial (for petitioners) or Counter-Memorial (for respondents). This document contains the facts and background of your case, your argument for your position, the legal grounds on which your case rests, and a request for remedy from the Court. Each side must email their Memorials and Counter-Memorials to the Chief Justice and any other parties that the Chief Justice may request by the prescribed deadline. Failure to adhere to these dates may jeopardize your (as well as your opponent's) ability to present your case at conference, and will very commonly impact eligibility for awards; as such, it is of paramount importance that your materials are received by these dates.

Following the submission of the Counter-Memorials, petitioners will have the opportunity (if they so choose) to submit a Reply to the respondent's Counter-Memorial; upon submission of a Reply, respondents may respond to that with a Rejoinder. While this is optional, it provides both sides a good opportunity to get their objections to the other side's points in writing, before taking them on at oral argument. For examples of Memorials and Counter-Memorials, please refer to Appendices L and M.

Aside from your Memorial, you must also prepare a binder containing printed copies of all the legal materials used to support your argument, including (but not limited to) those that you specifically reference in your Memorial. This is primarily for the benefit of the justices during deliberations, when they may review your legal documents to determine whether they truly apply to and support your case in the manner that you suggest. It would serve you well to make this information as easy to access and assess as possible, and to reference the documents in your Memorial, so that justices may easily know which documents to reference when weighing each portion of your argument. Failure to provide appropriate documentation may harm your ability to convince the justices of your position.

Finally, you must prepare your oral presentation to the Court. You may present your argument in any manner and order that you wish; however, it would be to your benefit not to simply read from your brief. While your brief's information and format should be used as a guide, the most compelling oral arguments are those which demonstrate a strong grasp of your case and its facts, as well as your legal argument regarding it. The justices are just as capable of reading your brief as you are – use your available time to explain it to them and not read it to them. The format and elements of your presentation will be further explained below.

Please note: any information that does not appear in your Memorial will not be permitted to be presented at oral argument. This is to prevent any "surprise arguments" that the other side was not afforded the opportunity to prepare for. Just as real-world attorneys are required to submit to discovery and present all their evidence and witnesses to opposing counsel prior to trial, you must also allow your opponent the opportunity to adequately prepare themselves.

## Court procedure

Though eligible to be run in the same fashion as a normal committee, in practice the procedure of the ACJ tends to run much differently. In some ways, the Court is much more regimented; in others, it is more informal. While this is largely left to the discretion of the Chief Justice, there is a certain amount of the procedure that is mandated by the Statute of the Arab Court of Justice (see Appendix I).

A typical case runs as follows:

(a) The Plaintiff shall present its case first and shall be allotted twenty minutes to do so;

(b) The Court shall question the Plaintiff on the merits of its case for twenty minutes;

(c) The Defendant shall then present its case and respond to the questions of the Court in the same manner and within the same time allotments as the Plaintiff;

(d) If deemed prudent by the Court, and time allows, the Court may enter into a question period between the Plaintiff and the Defendant. The Court shall have discretion as to the length of time, but both sides must be granted equal time to ask and to respond to questions. The Chief Justice may bring such period to an end if it becomes unproductive for the proceedings of the Court;

(e) The Plaintiff, followed by the Defendant, shall make a five minute closing remark;

(f) Should the Plaintiff find the Defendant's closing remark grossly offensive or inaccurate, it may rise to a Right of Reply, which may be granted at the discretion of the Court and shall not exceed one minute;

(g) The time restrictions imposed by Section 18.04 may be extended at any time at the discretion of the Court.

In rare instances, the Chief Justice may, at his or her discretion, allow for testimony by expert witnesses. The purpose of such testimony is to call upon a person who is well-versed in a particularly complicated facet of the case – be it law, science, or policy based – to aid the justices' understanding of it. It should only be utilized in cases where such clarification is deemed necessary, either by advocates (who must determine the incorporation of such a witness prior to their presentation) or by justices (who may call for such testimony, subject to its availability, during the proceedings); it should not be used to simply repeat information presented during arguments, nor should it be used as a means of wasting time. Furthermore, the expert witness should be a true expert, not simply an actor masquerading as one. For instance, a faculty advisor with an international law degree or a student studying environmental science would both be appropriate candidates to testify as an expert witness regarding certain provisions of the United Nations Convention on the Laws of the Sea.

### Deliberations

Following the presentation of both sides' cases, the advocates will be asked to leave the room while the justices deliberate. The Court will be sealed for the duration of deliberations, during which only justices, National Council representatives (or their designee), and the conference director will be permitted in the committee room. This is to reinforce the objectivity and fairness of any rendered decision: the presence of an advocate, their faculty advisor, or other unnecessary party presents the risk of justices avoiding an honest expression of their opinion for fear of offending the advocate in question, or invoking said advocate's retribution during the justice's own case. Advocates of the case being decided may choose to obtain refreshments, observe other committees, or simply take advantage of the well-earned (and often, much-needed) break to relax until deliberations are finished.

During deliberations, the members of the Court will be allowed to discuss the case among themselves, including strong arguments, conflicting facts, and questions regarding legal support. There is no strict time limit for deliberations, though they may have to be expedited in order to give all cases their fair share of time. It should be reiterated that only facts and arguments that are legally relevant to the case should be discussed during deliberations. Arguments not presented should not be considered and *ad hominem* arguments should be avoided; however, flaws in presentation are permissible considerations (in instances where an advocate's argument was unclear, or appeared to contradict itself).

Once all the justices have decided whether they support the petitioners or the respondents, they must draft written opinions. The group of justices whose reasoning garners the most votes will draft the majority opinion and the remainder will draft one (or more) dissenting opinions. Each side must outline the reasons they arrived at their decision, including the most compelling arguments, as well as the legal documentation that supported them. Although these are generally the only two opinions filed, individual justices may draft concurring opinions (agreeing with the decision of the majority, but disagreeing with its reasoning) or separate dissents (agreeing with the decision of the dissent, but disagreeing with their reasoning). At the summit session, members of the Court will read the majority opinions to the entire conference. The decisions of the Court are kept secret until the opinions are read at Summit.

## Press Corps

### Introduction

The Press Corps provides media coverage of the MAL through a newsletter released periodically during the conference. The Press Corps also commonly utilizes social media, primarily Twitter and Facebook, to promote its newsletter, the conference, and share real-time coverage of events of the MAL. The best Press Corps has a team of students able to disseminate throughout the conference and gather information of interest, interview delegates, advisors, and conference staff, and provide fun and interesting stories throughout the weekend. Because the Press Corps requires a great deal of work upon the start of the conference, it is important that students on the Press Corps keep a few best practices in mind.

### Press Corps has its own version of pre-conference preparation

Get started early. Before the conference begins, create all the social media accounts that you may want to use over the course of the weekend. That way, you can begin to reach out to other people who will be attending before

NUMAL even begins. If possible, try to contact the leader of the Press Corps from the year before to see if you can gain access to any social media accounts they may have used. That way, you will not have to start from scratch when building a Model Arab League community. If you plan on publishing the first print paper on the first day of conference, starting it early is a must.

### Interact with conference participants

Be present. It might be easy to hide behind a Twitter handle, but it will be far easier for you to get material for the paper by interacting with delegates. Not only should you try and connect with as many of them through social media as possible, you should also reach out to delegates in person. Do not be afraid to let them know who you are. See if they have any ideas about things they might want you to cover both online or in print.

### Balancing information and infotainment

Be entertaining. Conference is a fun time for everyone, but sometimes all the debate starts to blend together. The Press Corps should strive to be as entertaining as possible without being too distracting. Try to mix up the serious with the silly in the print paper and come up with some amusing hashtags for use online. Examples that have had much success in the past include "#MALproblems," "#OverheardAtNUMAL," and "#HotatNUMAL."

### Be imaginative; be creative

Be creative. Try to come up with as many new and interesting ways to use social media as possible. Use these ways both to entertain and to problem solve. One problem that delegates sometimes complain about is not knowing what is going on in other committees. A solution to this is using the Notes feature on Facebook to publish short press releases anytime a committee passes a new draft language or has a heated debate.

### Importance of photography

Take lots and lots of pictures. People love to look at pictures of themselves and you can use this to your advantage. Posting tons of photos is the best way to draw people to look at your social media accounts. While you may not have posted a photo of them yet, they will keep looking out to see if you do (and possibly give you a few new interactions in the process). Group pictures are also a great way to make people want to pick up your newspaper and read it. If there is a chance their face might be featured, they will definitely want a copy.

## Summary

At large conferences, there are many moving parts with their own structures, rules, governing documents, and best practices. Upward of 300 students may be in various positions in council sessions, the ACJ, the Press Corps, the JCC, and the Secretariat. Understanding the basic structures and rules that you will be interacting with is a critical piece to being an effective conference participant. Being aware of the various opportunities for participation in a conference your school will be attending will help you to better understand your options for participation and understand the various leadership roles of students, faculty, and staff that you may interact with at any given conference.

This chapter provided the shell of an MAL conference, including all the various councils and committees, and all the roles and details of the participants in the conference. The next chapter provides details on how to be a delegate in a standard council. It also provides some best practices for representing a country and being a diplomat. This chapter and the next combined provide all the basic information for successful participation.

# 3

# Representing a country

Chapter 3 provides tips and information on how to be an effective delegate in committee. The chapter starts with a look at the proper use of language and tone needed to stay in character during committee. It also provides information on common mistakes and how to avoid making them. From there, the chapter provides details on being a diplomat, which includes tone and public speaking, bargaining strategies, theoretical understandings of diplomacy and how to apply them to committee, and tips on promoting your state's policy. Part of the trick of being effective in committee is approaching committee correctly in view of the state you are representing. Details on the different types of states in committee and how to effectively handle them round out this half of the chapter. The second half of the chapter focuses primarily on resolution writing. Resolution structure and effective writing are explained. Strategies for getting others to sign up to your ideas while also avoiding common mistakes in language will be a primary feature of the section. (Proper format is explained and demonstrated in Appendix K.) Amendments are also covered as part of this section. The chapter concludes with a brief discussion on awards and tips for being a competitive delegate.

## Staying in character

Staying in character can be one of the most important things a delegate can do during conference. Separating any personal feelings a delegate may have from the positions of the country that they are representing is of the utmost importance. The more delegates conform to this rule, the more likely that the conference's proceedings will feel and look authentic to a real Arab-centered discussion. The further away from policy a delegate is the less likely the rest of the room will respect their position or that their policy will make sense, causing the learning experience to be less valuable.

Delegates should focus on playing the role of a representative of their country and vehemently support the policies of their government. When they fail to do so, they become vulnerable to other delegates who may call them out for being off topic and/or speaking off policy for the country they are representing, which can damage the delegate's credibility for the remainder of the conference.

Staying in character can be achieved through practice and is greatly helped by avoiding use of the first-person singular pronoun, "I," during debates, be it formal debate or during a suspension of the rules for the purpose of a moderated caucus. As an alternative, delegates should state "my government" or, in the case of a monarchy, use the language "His/Her Majesty's government." In informal discussion, delegates often return to a more personal touch and use "I." While it is generally more acceptable in this setting, it is still generally frowned upon as being less professional.

The normal preparation for conference/committee that a delegate engages in will help to establish comfort in the role they will be "playing." Developing a thorough understanding of their country's history, facts, and current state of affairs (as basic as population, how to spell the capital city, etc., and as complicated as recent laws being passed within the country or economic treaties that have been entered into) will help provide the delegate with a basis of confidence when presented with contention during committee that could lead to a break in their role.

## Being a diplomat

Being a good diplomat and being a good politician are not necessarily the same thing. While politics can be important and many times essential in committee, diplomacy is always of the utmost importance. Diplomacy is what will allow a delegate to take a leadership role within the committee and drive debate in a productive manner (and often times in the direction that the delegate's country's policies would like).

### Keys to being a successful diplomat

- Have a thorough understanding of the country being represented. Commanding knowledge of the country will make responding to statements, questions, and other (items) much easier and helps avoid moments where a delegate might feel flustered in front of the committee.
- Be familiar and comfortable with the Rules of Procedure. Knowing the rules and how/when to use them can put a delegate in a positive position within the committee and among the other delegates as well as elevate the delegate to a position of leadership within committee. Using the rules can be done to both facilitate/lead the discussion/debate and sometimes help a delegate bring focus to debate on issues that are important to their country. Misuse

or abuse of the rules can have a negative effect on a delegate, however, so it is essential that the delegate be familiar and comfortable with the rules.

- Always be respectful of conference staff and other delegates. Treating each other with respect at conference is essential to being a good diplomat (besides important for being a good human being). Making personal attacks inside or outside of committee and failing to act with good decorum can destroy a delegate's credibility in the committee and damage not just their own reputation but also their school's. Being respectful and proper will also help foster trust between the delegate and their counterparts in the committee.

- Maintain a level of formality at all times. Not using the first-person singular pronoun "I" is very important to staying in character as well as to being a good diplomat. It reinforces the delegate's role as a representative of their country speaking in support of their country's policies.

- Listen to other delegates speak and take notes on what they say. Active listening is very important, is recognized by chairs, your fellow delegates, as well as the staff and faculty that floats in and out of the committees during the conference. Taking notes on other delegates' speeches during committee sessions can help a delegate keep track of where other countries stand on various issues, which is invaluable throughout the remainder of the conference.

- Reference other delegates' statements in formal and informal debate. This is key in building relationships in committee. Delegates recognize and appreciate it when their ideas/positions/comments are recognized on the floor and doing so during debate will help build the relationship as well as make other delegates more attentive to the delegate's floor speeches.

## Representing challenging states

### Big states versus small states

Newer delegates often assume that success in conference is contingent on the state they represent. This is untrue. In the past ten years, students on states perceived to be stronger – such as Egypt, Saudi Arabia, and Jordan – have won awards as well as students on states perceived to be weaker – such as Comoros, Yemen, and Mauritania. Even states in transition, discussed in the next section, have been among the top delegations. While any state can win an award, the representation of a small state poses some challenges that need to be addressed.

### Small state challenges

Small states tend to pose two challenges of which the student representing them should be aware. The first challenge is that some student participants tend to assume states such as Comoros, Djibouti, or Somalia have no value and can largely be ignored in debate. It is important to remember that on resolutions it is one state one vote. It is also important to remember that it takes one-fourth of a committee to introduce a resolution. Assuming all twenty-two members are present, that means the states most commonly and unfairly marginalized – Comoros, Djibouti, Somalia, Mauritania, Oman, and Sudan – can together introduce their own resolution. That is also a significant voting bloc for the passage of a resolution. Observers often face a similar problem, but have other options to consider. They are discussed in the next section of this chapter.

The second challenge in representing a small state is that they lack capabilities to influence debate. They often have little or no military assets, little by way of economic power, and inadequate political or economic ties to other members, as well as a shorter list of issue areas where they have a relevant policy. Relevant policy is its own issue and a topic for all states, regardless of status in debate, so it will be discussed separately from this subsection. The most desirable states for delegations tend to have a long list of capabilities that provide a significant arsenal for debate tactics. This does not mean that the small states cannot provide valuable insights, options, or resources for a resolution.

First, the intelligence and skill behind effective resolution writing is not contingent on the delegation, it is contingent on the delegate. Second, resolutions are often about establishing new plans and policies for enhanced cooperation. Some states will offer money to pay for it, while others may offer infrastructure to house or maintain it, while still others will provide human resources to manage it. What can your state provide? There is not a single League member or observer that has nothing to provide the instruments of enhanced cooperation.

While you can rank capabilities provided to the League in terms of their value or desirability, you cannot dismiss as necessary the lower ranked needs. Because all states have an equal voice in the drafting of a document, that equality places the state that offers millions in dollars and the state that offers hundreds of hours in manpower on the same plain. All that matters then is for the student on the smaller state to become active in debate with the options that that state has to offer. Even then, if the state has nothing to offer that can be written into the resolution, the student on the state can still offer his or her expertise and skills as valuable resources to the committee for the drafting, amending, and ultimate passage of a document.

## Relevancy

Most students like to assume that relevancy is only an issue for the smaller states. This is not true. For any given topic, the list of states that are or are not immediately relevant will be different. Even some of the most active League members – states highly sought after to represent by most teams – find themselves trapped in a topic where they have little interest to push forward. In these circumstances, the skilled delegate can still be part of the topic because of the irrelevancy of their policy.

Student participants too quickly dismiss the power of being the state with the most fluid policy. Having no direct policy on the topic allows the student the greatest latitude to pursue policy options. This makes these delegations the strongest voice for compromise and committee unity possible. Delegates representing a country with a strong policy on the topic at hand are restricted to what extent they are able to flex on that policy. States with no official policy on a topic are able to balance policies on other similar issue areas with the best interests of their state in general and with the best interests of the League as a whole. This allows for a fun and dynamic role in committee.

Identifying the right policy when the government you are representing has no official policy is a challenge, but one that is easily solved if a few steps are followed. The first of these steps is to find an area of policy that is very similar and is something your state has an official policy on. For example, if your state has no policy on desalination and its impact on the environment, consider looking for the state's policy on the impact of oil or fishing on the environment. Once you find the right policy area, you then need to draw lines between similar issues, similar policy consequences, and other similar realities between the two. Once done, you will see the specific, and usually minor, details of the policy on the agenda. Possibly you will find a solution, along the lines given above, in a third policy area. Possibly you will find no guidance at all. At this point, the process is simple and twofold.

1. For those aspects of the topic where you were able to draw a line to a similar policy, follow that policy position for the basics of your state's policy on the topic. Utilize the other policy area and the information/facts about it to justify your position if asked by another attendee at the conference.
2. For those aspects of the topic where you were unable to draw a line to a similar policy, fashion the state's policy based on your knowledge of the state and how it responds to issues in that category of international law and policy.

### States in transition

A state in transition is a state where the government has either been removed, replaced, or is in the midst of a significant revisioning and restructuring (in recent years, Syria). For states in transition, the question is simple and rooted solely in the source of your state's policy at this time. The options are twofold. First, policy can be based on the previous government that is no longer in power. This is common when the status of transition is due to the death of a leader, where the main instruments of authority are maintained but the state and its policies are somewhat in flux. This often makes sense early in the transition period because the diplomatic infrastructure abroad is typically unchanged until transition is well under way. The second option is to identify the direction in which the state is moving and base policy either on the political authority moving the state in that direction or on the stated goals of the transition. What type of state is it becoming? Which state's political alignment is closest to what the state is in the process of becoming?

Two important things should be remembered when making a decision. First, what would be closest to the actual situation on the ground in the state you represent? Second, what position or opinion does the National Council on U.S.-Arab Relations (NCUSAR) have on the options you have in making this decision? For the good of the conference and potential outcomes of debate, the NCUSAR may ask states to take on a specific role for representation in conference. For example, during the time of Syria's suspension due to the unrest with Bashar al-Assad in power, all Syrian delegations have represented the Syrian National Council (SNC) instead of the Syrian Arab Republic. In the end, whatever decision is made needs to be supported by the delegation's advisor and head delegate because it is a team-wide decision. It is completely inappropriate for, in the above instance, Syria to represent al-Assad on some councils and the SNC on others.[1]

## Observer states

In order to provide additional opportunities for student participation, larger Model Arab League (MAL) conferences incorporate observer states into the list of countries. Instead of offering slots for only twenty-two delegations, the addition of observers allows an MAL conference to provide slots for up to twenty-five delegations. Different conferences include different observers, taken from the following list: Brazil (2003), Eritrea (2003), Armenia (2004), Chad (2005), Turkey (2005), Venezuela (2006), India (2007), and Uzbekistan (2007).[2] Typically, the observers are either Chad, Eritrea, or Turkey because

---

[1] The exceptions to this are the JCC, which exists in its own universe while at conference, and the ACJ, at which the case itself determines which version of a state is represented at any given time. In both cases, the decision is in the hands of the NCUSAR.

[2] Armenia, Brazil, Venezuela, Eritrea, and India are all current official observers of the League of Arab States. Turkey is a candidate for official observer status. Chad and Uzbekistan have enhanced cooperation with the League and have observed some proceedings. They are potential future observer states. Dates in parenthesis indicate the year the state became an observer or established enhanced cooperation with the League.

their geographic proximity to League members makes it easier to integrate them into discussion in all committees at any given conference.

As observers are not full members of the League, they are governed by a few different rules. Students representing either full members or observer members should be familiar with these rule differences as it allows them to strategically maximize cooperation with observer states. These rule differences are noted in the Rules of Procedure section of this text, but are collected below for your convenience:

- In a roll-call, observers should not answer as "present and voting" they should only respond as "present."
- Observers must vote on *all* procedural motions. Observers do not vote on any substantive motions. (See Chapter 4 for a list of procedural and substantive motions.)
- Observers may object to an Adoption by Consent, because this motion is a procedural and substantive motion simultaneously. Their objection is on the procedure of taking the vote as an Adoption by Consent only.
- Observers may sponsor a resolution or amendment.
- Observers may be signatories to a resolution or amendment.

It is easy to assume that observers are less relevant than full members, as they cannot vote on the final passage of any document, but this is a poor view of the role of the observer. Observer states participate to provide a broader or different perspective on the agenda. To that end, they contribute to all discussions and procedures of the committee other than voting. As they can author a resolution, observers can provide a significant level of contribution to any document that is ultimately passed. Additionally, observers are free to negotiate with any state in the room and therefore can be powerful allies who conduct diplomacy on behalf of partner states in the room. For example, while Eritrea may not be able to vote on a resolution, they can convince voting members in the room to change their votes in favor of or against a document, based on the policy of Eritrea and her allies on the topic.

One area of significant relevance for observer states is any topic where the League is discussing relations or cooperation with non-member states or organizations. An observer is the only state in the room with the perspective of the non-League side of these relations and can easily shape debate by providing that point of view. Observer states can also add a non-member cooperatist element to any topic by encouraging league partnership or cooperation with the observer state or with other non-member states depending on the topic and how the student wishes to conduct their state's policy on that topic.

Lastly, it is important to know that from a conference management perspective, the observer state and its student representatives are not different in any way from any other participating delegation. All students, no matter what state they are representing, have equal access to conference services, equal opportunity to win awards, and equal opportunity to participate in all aspects of the conference program.

## Resolution writing

Resolutions are the culmination of your committee's debate and represent the official binding actions that the committee has determined to take. They are what transform circuitous discussions into concrete declarations of the body and are therefore a critical aspect of the committee's function (and often a measure of its success). As such, a significant amount of time should be dedicated to the creation, debate, and amendment of resolutions.

### *Procedural guidelines*

In the League of Arab States, resolutions require a simple majority of those members who are present and voting to support it in order to pass; however, only those who vote in favor of the resolution are bound by it, should it pass. These distinctions are important both in the way that resolutions are written as well as in how states vote on them. As certain resolutions may not have any bearing on many member states, member states should vote yes as an act of solidarity with the League if they agree to the language of the resolution and it is on policy. They should abstain from resolutions that do not affect them specifically and they wish not to be bound by it, or if they disagree with the document but do not consider the document harmful to the League or their fellow Arab states. A resolution that is harmful to the League, even if irrelevant to a member state, requires a no vote from the state.

It is important to note that in order to pass, a resolution needs a simple majority of those voting yes or no. Abstentions do not count toward this. Therefore, a resolution can pass with three in favor, two opposed, and fifteen abstentions, with the resolution itself being binding only on those voting yes.

### *Turning talk into action*

Because of the frequent differentiation in policies between a committee's members, it is often difficult to quickly formulate a coherent unified position on a topic; this is acceptable. There are, however, a number of strategies to reconcile diverging policies within a committee.

The first approach, which should almost always be utilized early in the debate of a topic, is to gauge the general policies of the body's members. Knowing early in the debate which elements of a topic the committee can agree on – and which will be most difficult to resolve – will ensure that the body makes the most efficient use of its time. This can be achieved through a combination of formal and informal discussion and will be a productive use of time, irrespective of the level of consensus it achieves: it will either create a unified stance within the committee or identify the different camps that exist. The level of consensus that exists will determine how to proceed in the second stage. Once considerable work has been done on an introduced resolution, holding a straw poll on the document as a whole or on specific parts of it allows the committee to gauge the next steps in the finalization of a resolution.

In those rare cases of near unanimity, resolution writing becomes a unified effort with most members of the body contributing their thoughts to a single document. Formal debate allows for the refinement of ideas and avoidance of repetition; informal debate allows for the expedition of the writing and editing process. Compromise becomes more about wording and specifics than large-scale ideals.

In all likelihood, however, there will be differing opinions on a given topic, resulting in two or more blocs in the committee and, sometimes, two or more active resolutions. In this case, both formal and informal avenues can serve different roles in the resolution-writing process. Formal debate serves as a way for the camps to communicate their goals to their opposition and allows the opposition to comment on those positions. Informal debate will still accelerate the writing process, though it will generally see the blocs segregate themselves to edit their respective resolutions and incorporate the sentiments of prior formal debates, which can then be presented in subsequent caucuses. This process repeats until the sponsors of the resolutions achieve the necessary support to introduce a resolution, or decide that the resolution will not garner it.

### *Introducing, limiting, and amending resolutions; voting procedure*

Once initial debate and policy statements have concluded and the resolution's first draft has been completed, the formal resolution procedure begins in earnest. There are generally four stages in the debate of a resolution. The first stage is the introduction of the resolution, which allows it to be debated officially on the floor of the committee. Before a resolution is eligible to be introduced, it requires at least one-fourth of the present members to be either sponsors or signatories. It can then be introduced by a motion, which only requires multiple seconds to pass.

Once the resolution has been introduced, the body may then vote to limit debate to the resolution, which will then curb any debate not directly related to that resolution. When the document is limited, the authors can invoke "Author's Rights," sometimes referred to as "Sponsor's Rights," during which time the floor is yielded to the authors to make a statement and take questions. Typically, authors make a brief statement or no statement at all and yield to questions. This is an excellent time for delegations to seek clarification on the document or ask the authors to explain the purpose of specific facets of the language.

During debate, members may wish to introduce amendments to the resolution, which reflect the changes that one or more states want to make. These amendments must have at least one-eighth of the body as sponsors or signatories before they can be introduced. Upon introduction, the sponsors of the resolution to be amended will be asked whether the amendment is friendly or unfriendly. A "friendly" response indicates that the sponsor endorses the immediate incorporation of the amendment into the resolution, while an "unfriendly" response prevents automatic inclusion into the document and forces it to be voted on separately by the entire body during voting procedure on the resolution as a whole. Amendments whose sponsors and signatories parallel the sponsors and signatories of the resolution automatically pass as friendly.

The final stage of debate on a resolution is the closure of debate and voting procedure. Once the committee feels that the document has been sufficiently amended, or a deadlock has been reached, a motion to close debate on the resolution can be made. At this time, speakers will be afforded the opportunity to advocate for or against the closure of debate. If the motion passes, the committee immediately moves into voting procedure on all unfriendly amendments, followed by the resolution itself.

During voting procedure, there are a number of changes to decorum: there is no entering or exiting the room, there is no talking or passing of notes, and all laptops and electronics must be put away. All states which are present and voting will be given the opportunity to vote on all unfriendly amendments and the resolution as amended. Voting on resolutions and unfriendly amendments may be done in one of three formats: placard vote, roll-call vote, and adoption by consent.

In a simple placard vote, the chair will ask for those who are in favor of, opposed to, or abstaining from the document. This method of voting is automatic and does not require a motion. When the chair offers each option, all states of that opinion will raise their placards. The three voting options indicate the following:

1. Yes: the state is in favor of the resolution and will be bound by it if it passes.
2. No: the state is opposed to the resolution and will not be bound by it if it passes.
3. Abstain: the state is neither in favor of nor opposed to the resolution and will not be bound by it if it passes; furthermore, the state is not counted toward the required majority.

The second option for voting procedures is by roll-call vote. If a motion is made for a roll-call vote, each state will vote individually on the resolution. The chair will start at a random point on the roll-call list and proceed alphabetically, asking each state how they vote on the resolution. In this procedure, states have two additional options to choose from:

1. No with Rights: the details of the resolution are within the policy interests of the state, but there is some reason or situation compelling the state to vote no when it would otherwise vote yes. At the close of voting procedure, states that vote No with Rights will be afforded a short amount of time to explain the reason for a no vote to the body. (Further details of a "No with Rights" are explained in Chapter 4.)
2. Pass: the state would like to delay its vote until all other states have been afforded the opportunity, at which time the chair will once again ask the state how it votes. (Note: a state may only pass during a roll-call vote, and may only pass once per vote.)

The third option for voting procedures is adoption by consent. If a motion is made to adopt by consent, the body will attempt to vote unanimously for the document. The chair will bang the gavel three times, each time stating "without objection." Any state that would not vote for the document should verbally object at this time. If there are no objections, the document will pass as if all states voted in favor of it. Delegations may object because they disagree with the resolution on a substantive level or they may object to the procedure of the adoption by consent for the language. As such, all delegations – including observers who otherwise cannot vote on a resolution or an amendment – can object.

### Special rule for voting

#### Division of the Question

Division of the Question is the final opportunity a delegate has to amend a resolution prior to closing debate on the resolution. After closure of debate but prior to voting-specific motions, a delegate can move to divide the question. A Motion to Divide the Question allows a council to vote on pieces of a draft resolution separately. The delegate making this motion must specify which pieces are to be voted upon separately, each piece being at least one full clause. This motion begins a two-part process of votes: one procedural and one substantive. The first procedural motion is simply on whether to divide out the clause(s) in question. If this passes, two resolutions are created, both with the same preambulatory clauses. The second substantive vote is on the separated language and passes or fails in the same way as any resolution (see Chapter 4 for more on Division of the Question).

### What do I include?

Resolutions are a very long sentence. A resolution is made up of two sections: the preambulatory clauses and the operative clauses. The preamble of a draft resolution describes the problem, recalls past actions relating to it, and explains the rationale behind the actions that the draft resolution proposes. The preamble does not prescribe action. It may not be amended after the draft resolution has been introduced, so delegates should take special precaution when drafting it. Preambulatory clauses generally begin with "-ing" verbs. Operative clauses make up the latter part of the draft resolution. They are action statements, beginning with present tense active verbs, that express how the council will address the issue as described in the topic and preamble. Operative clauses may be modified using amendments during the debate process. The preamble and the operative sections are separated by a single line that states, "Be it Hereby Resolved by the League of Arab States:". The line acts as an introduction to the list of actions (operatives) to be taken by the League. See Appendix R for a list of preamble and operative clause starting words.

The content and specificity of resolutions will vary based on the atmosphere of the committee and the results of debate; however, there are a few rules that almost always apply. First, the resolution must contain a minimum of two preambulatory and three operative clauses, which should be formatted according to the guidelines set forth in the *Model Arab League Handbook*. There is no typical length to a resolution, but a standard practice is that there should always be more operative clauses than preambulatory clauses and the number of preambles should be sufficient to provide some balance in the document between preambles and operatives.

Appendix K has a copy of a properly formatted resolution, annotated to point out all the important aspects of the format of a resolution. On the next pages are samples of a poorly written and a well-written resolution to allow for a comparative analysis to illustrate common errors, best practices, and strategic writing in a resolution. Since any particulars in regard to well-written resolutions are topic-based, it is easiest to provide examples of mistakes in resolution writing followed by an explanation of why the document is wrong.

### Sample of a Poorly Written Resolution

RESOLUTION: 1/
COMMITTEE: Political Affairs
TOPIC: Iranian Nuclear Development
SPONSORS: Egypt, Saudi Arabia
SIGNATORIES: Jordan, Qatar, Palestine
**Acknowledges** the inherent danger of nuclear proliferation,
**Urging** the continued acknowledgment of this,
**Understanding and Recognizing** that iran has been a fundamental cause of increasing tensions,
**Beleving** that the NPT should be binding to all states,

**Be it Hereby Resolved by the League of Arab States:**

1) **Condemns** any state actively seeking to develop Nuclear energy with the intent of pursuing weapons programs;
2) **Instructs** the United Nations Security Council to ensure that the Islamic Nation of Iran does not acquire Nuclear materials,
3) **Calls Upon** the United Nations to establish a special committee to oversee any and all Iranian nuclear facilities, inspect and determine their potential use for the creation of weapons of mass destructiveness, inspect Iranian borders to ensure nuclear material is not being smuggled in by other hostile nations, ensure that no peaceful energy are being converted into weapons materials, to inspect civilian facilities and ensure they are not being used for military purposes, and to monitor for human rights abuses at such facilities.
4) **Demands** that all League member states sanction the Islamic Republic of Iran until it cooperates with inspections and proves that no effort toward creating nuclear weapons has occurred,
5) The sovereignty and territorial integrity of all nations involved must be respected at all times by during the carrying out of these policies by the League and by the UN
6) **Believes** that these relations be convened with all possible haste, while respecting the needs for all parties to adequately prepare.

### Sample of a Well-Written Resolution

RESOLUTION: 1/
COMMITTEE: Political Affairs
TOPIC: Iranian Nuclear Development
SPONSORS: Egypt, Saudi Arabia
SIGNATORIES: Jordan, Qatar, Palestine
**Acknowledging** the inherent danger of nuclear proliferation,
**Urging** all states to attest to this fact,
**Recognizing** that Iran's interest in developing Nuclear Technology is a source of Tensions in the region, and
**Further recognizing** that universal compliance with International Bans on Proliferation and testing of Nuclear weapons is essential for Peace, and
**Believing** that the NPT should be binding to all states,

### Be it Hereby Resolved by the League of Arab States:

1) **Calls Upon** all states to immediately cease trading of Nuclear materials and other items necessary for the development of a Nuclear Program with the Islamic Republic of Iran;
2) **Requests** that the United Nations Security Council take necessary steps to ensure a swift response should Iran develop any form of Nuclear Technology;

3) **Calls Upon** the United Nations to establish a special committee to oversee any and all Iranian nuclear facilities, which will:
   a) Inspect and determine their potential use for the creation of weapons of mass destructiveness,
   b) Inspect Iranian borders to ensure nuclear material is not being smuggled in by other entities,
   c) Ensure any existing Iranian nuclear-energy facilities have not been used for military purposes, and
   d) Monitor for human rights abuses at such facilities;
4) **Invites** member states to take domestic action on Iran through cessations of trade and other agreements with Iran until such time as their immediate and continuing compliance with UN Resolutions and the IAEA;
5) **Reaffirms** the importance of the sovereignty and territorial integrity of all nations involved, especially that of Iran; and
6) **Requires** all international Agencies and State Governments involved report regularly as to their progress with this situation to the UN General Assembly, the UN Security Council, and the IAEA.

Some of the errors in the poorly written resolution are obvious. There is a spelling error in the fourth preambulatory clause ("Beleving"), the fifth operative clause does not start with an action verb, and the punctuation is incorrect after operative clauses 2, 3, 4, and 5. Most students can avoid these kinds of mistakes by simply comparing their document with the template in Appendix K. The rest of the errors are either stylistic or strategic and therefore require a bit more of an explanation.

Preambulatory clause 3, starting "Understanding and Recognizing" has two errors. First, it is generally inadvisable to use two perambulatory clause openers in one clause. Either state "understanding" or "recognizing," but not both. Second, the language is accusatory in a preamble, which should never happen. The purpose of the preamble is to provide the history leading up to the actions being taken. Any statements that are easily disputed by member states only complicate passage of the document. In general, resolutions should avoid language that is harsh, as the tone pressures some states into abstentions or no votes.

For example, operative clause 1 and operative clause 4 use unnecessarily aggressive language as action verbs. It is best never to use the word "condemns," or similar verbs, to start a clause. The first operative clause does nothing, provides no solutions, and just weakens the document. The fourth clause is better served, as demonstrated in the well-written resolution, by "inviting" states to take an action instead of "demanding" it. States unwilling to comply with the demand will vote no on the document while they will more likely vote yes on a document inviting, but not requiring, compliance with the action.

Another formatting issue can be found in operative clause 3. The poorly written document has language formatted in a manner that makes it hard to read and hard to reference in committee. The well-written document uses the exact same text, but formatted into subclauses, as is expected in proper resolution format. Another formatting error is obvious in operative clause 5, which has been written as its own sentence and is missing the "; and" which is required at the end of the second-to-last operative clause.

One other common mistake to make note of is the extent of authority a body has when writing a resolution. The League of Arab States does not have the authority to "instruct" the United Nations Security Council (UNSC), as noted in operative clause 2, to do anything. It does, however, have the authority to "request" that the UNSC take a particular action.

This brief analysis shows some issues to be mindful of when writing a resolution by illustrating a properly and improperly done approach to the same basic document. Spend some time comparing other differences in the language of the two documents and note how the tone of the well-written document meets all the policy goals of the poorly written document but in a manner that is more professional and more likely to pass a vote of the council.

### Creating committees

Another common issue in resolution writing is the creation of committees, agencies, or other bureaucratic infrastructures to carry out some task the states drafting the resolution consider important. There is a right way and a wrong way to creating committees and other elements of bureaucracy, the first step of which is to ensure that an agency does not already exist for the exact proposed purpose. If not, then delegates should keep in mind a few details on the process of creating committees and remember to include all the necessary information.

When creating a committee in a resolution, always remember that the resolution is basically the committee's bylaws. Make sure you include the following details:

- Committee name and acronym
- Committee objectives:
  - What are the goals of the committee?
  - How and when will it report the progress of attaining these goals?
  - Where will the committee be based and is there any important infrastructure it should have?
- Committee membership (including who/how countries may become members, potential length of term, how the committee will be led)
- When, where, and how often the committee will meet

- Whether any specific rules govern the committee. If so, what are they? How does the committee make decisions?
- Committee powers (these must be within the overall powers of the League of Arab States)
- If the committee is separate from the regular infrastructure of the League, how the committee will be funded (e.g., is there a membership fee?).

In addition, you should think about any unique aspects of this committee that are required elements but are outside the standard list noted above. For example, you may want to include a sunset clause on the committee (e.g., it stops working after two years unless it is reauthorized). Below is an example of a set of clauses for a resolution properly creating a committee:

1. **Establishes** the Bureau of Arab Foreign Labor (BAFL), for the purpose of:
   (a) Monitoring the treatment of Arab nationals performing labor in states where they do not hold citizenship,
   (b) Establishing a common policy on the rights of citizens of member states living and working in other League member states, and
   (c) Providing a forum for the discussion of foreign labor rights, including the handling of passports, work papers, and other forms of documentation;
2. **Declares** that BAFL shall consist of one representative from every League Member and shall meet twice a year in Cairo, and may meet additionally upon the request of two members of the League of Arab States;
3. **Further declares** that BAFL shall:
   (a) Establish its own rules, but all members shall have an equal say in the decision processes of BAFL and non-member states may only be extended observer status at the discretion of BAFL,
   (b) Report to the Political Affairs Council and the Economic Affairs Council biannually on the work of the committee, and
   (c) May make recommendations on policy to the Summit of the League of Arab States; and
4. **Notes** that BAFL shall not have the authority to impose policy of any kind on a member state and may only investigate allegations of unfair treatment of Arab foreign labor with the express consent of the member states in question.

## Strategies for success and winning awards

Each participating team defines "success" at conference in terms that meet their purpose in attending the conference. For some teams, success is contingent upon winning awards at conference. To that end, this section introduces students to some strategies for winning awards while placing awards into their proper context. To start, not everyone wins awards and the most deserving are not always the ones who win. Typically, awards go to only approximately twenty-five percent of the committee, so in highly competitive conferences not all students deserving of recognition will receive it. Additionally, as awards are determined primarily by a vote of participants, there is the potential of popularity or politics clouding the judgment of voters and the wrong individuals being recognized. There are, however, tricks to avoid these problems and be in award contention by the end of the conference.

Students who want to win an award should be mindful of three key things: meaningful participation, polite/respectful participation, and committee leadership. Meaningful participation is key because students who do not participate are not noticed in the room (and often do not receive the full educational benefit of the conference). Every award-minded student should have their placard up more than ninety percent of the time when the chair calls for speakers. They should also be prepared to provide intelligent, helpful, and comprehensive solutions to the committee when they speak. A common and effective strategy for this is to build off a previous speaker by stating whether their state agrees or disagrees and why. Follow up "why" with the next step in the discussion by proposing something as an alternative, an addendum, or an addition to the ideas just brought up. This demonstrates that a student is actively involved, is paying attention to others, and is working toward the final resolution.

Polite and respectful participation is not only a requirement of the conference rules, but it is also a key strategy for winning an award. Participants should use a polite tone that offers criticism of ideas, but does not criticize the delegation or the state. Loud, disrespectful participation that creates a spectacle undermines a student's credibility and will stop other participants from taking them and their points seriously. Another surefire way to violate this condition of excellence as a delegate is to become emotional about a topic and speak from that emotion instead of in a calm and rational manner. In the event that a stronger tone becomes necessary, there are rules of procedure – such as the Right of Reply and a Suspension of the Meeting – that allow other ways to respond to a situation created by another delegate without sinking to their level of behavior.

Committee leadership is the third and critical part of the formula for in-committee success. Committee leadership involves guiding the committee to productive solutions for the agenda. Most commonly, committee leadership is demonstrated through authoring a resolution and then guiding that resolution to an ultimate vote. By authoring the resolution, the student places him or herself in the center of the discussion and therefore is expected to respond to delegations with questions on the upcoming flow of debate. Authoring also provides the delegate with several opportunities for meaningful participation that no one else has. For example, "Author's Rights" gives the author(s) the chance to stand in front of the committee and directly interact – in a question and answer format – with the entire committee. As the resolution authors have direct control over whether an amendment is considered "friendly" or "unfriendly," it is common to seek out the original authors as sponsors for amendments.

While resolution writing is a very effective means of award seeking, it is not the only way to establish a leadership role in committee. Once a resolution is written, acting as primary opposition to a document or acting as the primary facilitator for amendments can establish leadership in committee. This functions much the same way as being an author with the key exception that you have to be more proactive at injecting yourself into debate than if you were the author. Either way, this requires both active participation in the discussion of the resolution and contribution to the language of a document that will ultimately be voted on.

Lastly, another very effective method of winning awards is through the facilitation of debate within the Rules of Procedure. Many delegates have a poor understanding of the rules and as such are resistant to use them. Delegates who learn how to use and manipulate the Rules of Procedure appear more active in committee than those who either do not use them or are reticent to use them due to discomfort with the rules. As a result, delegates that can facilitate debate by appearing to be an expert on the rules automatically carries the appearance of an active and quality delegate in comparison with those delegates who wait for others to rise to motions.

## Summary

Representing a country is a complicated process that involves accuracy in state policy, accuracy in presenting yourself as an Arab diplomat, and wielding the rules of council sessions effectively to allow for your participation fully in council sessions. When approached as one massive learning curve, it is impossible and leads to delegate failure. When it is compartmentalized into steps to take to become prepared for representing a country, it becomes more logical and easier to approach. This chapter has presented everything a participating student needs to know to get started on representing a country, being a diplomat, drafting the documents used in council sessions to formulate policy, and being competitive in the awards. The next two chapters provide other areas of information necessary to be a successful delegate, including how to use, understand, and interpret the rules, and how to research your state's policy and your council's agenda.

# 4

# The Rules of Procedure

The rules of procedure of any deliberative body are put into place to most fairly expedite debate among peers. The MAL Rules of Procedure are meant to provide a vehicle for debate to occur while protecting the rights of the participants of the debate. They can be used to compartmentalize committee discussions and direct debate to focus on specific subtopics, documents, or crises. Rules are an equalizer in committee in that they apply to all states by providing the same rights and the same obligations to voting members of the League regardless of their influence, power, or prestige. In practice, the rules provide a significant level of influence and control of committee for the few students who truly understand their logic.

## The logic of the Rules of Procedure

The rules are set in order of precedence, meaning from most important to least important based on one of two logics. Understanding these logics is a key facet to understanding the rules. The first logic is that the rules protect the rights of the member states prior to any other possible action being undertaken. In that endeavor, they guarantee courtesy and justice to all participant states. Therefore, the highest level of precedence is a point. The second logic is that rules that are more destructive to debate (a measure based on how much it can pull the committee away from making a binding decision on some or all of its members) come in precedence before rules that are less destructive. Thus, the chair, prior to considering motions lower on the list, must entertain points or motions higher in the order of precedence. It is a necessary logic of having a clear organizational structure that meets a collective goal.

For the student who has never used *Robert's Rules of Order Newly Revised* (or similar forms of parliamentary procedure), the Rules of Procedure can at first be overwhelming. We suggest beginning with a few rules that will be most helpful for quickly joining debate (detailed explanations on these rules are found in the next section and in Appendix H):

- Point of Order
- Point of Parliamentary Inquiry
- Point of Personal Privilege
- Motion to Limit Debate
- Suspension of the Meeting
- Suspension of the Rules (Moderated Caucus)
- Closure of Debate
- Yield to Another Country
- Yield to the Chair
- Yield to Points of Information

Each of these rules may require one of the following: seconds, speakers for/against, a placard vote. Some of these points and motions require a half (or simple) majority to pass, while others require a two-thirds (or super) majority to pass. Ultimately, all votes will come down to one of the following:

- simple majority: requires a yes vote from 50% +1 of the members of the committee, in which abstentions – if allowed – are not counted in the vote;
- supermajority: requires a yes vote from 67% of the members of the committee, in which abstentions – if allowed – are not counted in the vote;
- absolute supermajority: requires a yes vote from 67% of the members of the League, in which abstentions – if allowed – are counted as no votes and any absent state is considered to have abstained and therefore also voted no.

Please see Appendix Q, entitled "One-half and two-thirds voting chart," for any questions regarding these numbers.

Students should note that a simple majority is 50% of the committee plus one: if there are twenty members present, a simple majority would be eleven members. In most cases, the more destructive to debate the point or motion, the higher a majority it will require to pass. Furthermore, the most destructive points and motions require speakers for and against the motion; this allows for the committee to reflect upon the severe motion and allows each individual member to properly determine their best course of action.

## Alphabetical listing of the Rules of Procedure with detailed explanations

### 1. Motion to Add, Delete, or Amend a Topic

*The Motion to Add, Delete, or Amend a Topic changes the language of an Agenda topic, adds a new topic, or deletes an existing topic.*

IN ORDER: Plenary (which takes place in the first session of each committee)

REQUIRES: Second | 2+/2– | >50% Vote

DETAILS:

1. Proposed changes must be submitted to the Chair in writing.
2. All changes to the Agenda must be reported to the Secretariat.

## 2. Motion to Adjourn the Meeting

*The Motion to Adjourn the Meeting concludes a Council or Summit Session until the following year.*

IN ORDER: Conclusions of Council Sessions, Conclusion of Summit

REQUIRES: Second | >50% Vote

DETAILS:

1. Councils may not adjourn before the scheduled end of the conference, unless by express permission from the Secretariat, National Council representative(s), or Local Coordinator.

## 3. Motion to Adopt by Consent

*The Motion to Adopt by Consent signifies a unanimous "yes" vote on a draft resolution/amendment if no objections are raised. This motion is generally used to speed up the voting process. It is inadvisable to move to adopt by consent when the delegate knows there is objection. States wishing to abstain must object.*

IN ORDER: Voting Procedure – Council Sessions, Summit

REQUIRES: N/A

DETAILS:

1. Immediately after the motion is made, the Chair will say "without objection" and bang the gavel three times; if no objection is raised in this time the measure is considered passed by unanimous vote.
2. If an objection is raised during this time, voting procedure continues.

## 4. Motion to Adopt the Agenda

*The Motion to Adopt the Agenda accepts the current language of the Agenda topics and ends the Plenary Session.*

IN ORDER: Plenary (which takes place in the first session of each committee)

REQUIRES: Second | >50% Vote

DETAILS:

1. No changes to topic language may be made after Agenda is adopted.
2. Immediately after the Agenda is adopted, the Chair must open the General Speakers List.

## 5. Motion to Amend the Speaking Time

*The Motion to Amend the Speaking Time changes the length of time each speaker is allowed during formal debate.*

IN ORDER: Plenary, Council Sessions

REQUIRES: Second | >50% Vote

DETAILS:

1. The Chair sets the initial speaking time at the establishment of the General Speakers List.
2. Speaking time remains the same unless amended.
3. Applies only to speeches made during formal debate, during which a speakers list is used to determine the order of speakers.

## 6. Motion to Appeal the Decision of the Chair

*A Motion to Appeal the Decision of the Chair challenges a decision made by the Chair. It is nearly impossible for a Chair to rule this motion dilatory; however, the entire committee will be affected if the motion is in fact dilatory. This is not a motion to be made lightly. The purpose of the motion is to change the decision of a Chair that was made within the rules but is at the detriment of the committee, in the view of the motioner and those voting and speaking in favor.*

IN ORDER: Council Sessions, Summit

REQUIRES: Second | 2+/2− | ≥2/3 Vote

DETAILS:

1. Not to be used in cases where the rules of the Handbook have been breached; a Point of Order may be used in such cases.
2. The Chair must accept the outcome if the appeal is successful.

## 7. Motion to Change a Topic's Assignment

*A Motion to Change a Topic's Assignment removes a topic from a Council's Agenda and sends it to another Council for consideration.*

IN ORDER: Plenary

REQUIRES: Second | 2+/2− | >50% Vote

DETAILS:

1. Changes must be submitted to the Secretariat immediately.
2. Secretary-General proposes a topic be added to the Agenda of the receiving Council, regardless of whether receiving Council has adopted its own Agenda at that time.
3. Receiving Council must take majority vote on whether to add new topic.

### 8. Motion to Change the Order of the Agenda

*A Motion to Change the Order of the Agenda changes the order in which Agenda topics are to be considered.*

IN ORDER: Council Sessions

REQUIRES: Second | 2+/2– | ≥2/3 Vote

DETAILS:

1. Only to be used after a Motion to Set the Order of the Agenda passes.
2. Topics retain the number originally listed on the Agenda, a detail particularly important to the Chair for giving draft resolution designations.
3. Changes to the Agenda order must be reported to the Secretariat.

### 9. Motion to Close Debate

*A Motion to Close Debate ends discussion on an item, initiates voting procedure on that item and all subsidiary items and discards any speakers lists for said items. A Chair may often rule this motion dilatory if they do not feel that enough debate has been had on the topic or that there are currently still resolutions or amendments on the floor. A Motion to Close Debate can be moved on an amendment, a resolution, or a topic.*

IN ORDER: Council Sessions

REQUIRES: Second | 2+/2– | ≥2/3 Vote

DETAILS:

1. Debate cannot be closed on items broader in scope than the subject of the current speakers list.
2. Should a speakers list expire and no delegate wishes to be added or offer pertinent motions, the Council enters voting procedure as if a Motion to Close Debate has passed.

### 10. Motion to Close the Speakers List

*A Motion to Close the Speakers List ends discussion on an item after allowing the current speakers list to expire, after which voting procedure is initiated in the same manner as a closure of debate. At any time, this motion may be reversed using a Motion to Re-Open the Speakers List (which takes precedence over a Motion to Close Debate even if the motion is automatic due to the depletion of a closed speakers list).*

IN ORDER: Council Sessions

REQUIRES: Second | >50% Vote

DETAILS:

1. No new countries may be added to the speakers list.
2. Not in order during the initial establishment of a speakers list.

## 11. Motion to Divide the Question

*A Motion to Divide the Question allows the Council to vote on pieces of a draft resolution separately. The delegate making this motion must specify which pieces are to be voted upon separately, each piece being at least one full clause. This motion begins a two-part process of votes: one procedural and one substantive. The first procedural motion is simply on whether to divide out the operative clause(s) in question (please note that Division of the Question may not be used to divide out preambulatory clauses). If this passes, the committee proceeds to take substantive votes on each piece of the resolution divided out. The second substantive vote is on the separated language and passes or fails in the same way as any resolution. (Keep in mind that regardless of the number of parts that are divided out, there will always be an additional "remainder" part that comprises everything which was not divided out. Thus there will always be one more round of substantive voting than the number of parts divided out.)*

IN ORDER: Voting Procedure – Council Sessions

REQUIRES: Second | 2+/2– | >50% Vote

DETAILS:

1. Voting on draft resolutions may be divided into multiple parts, each part being at least one full clause.
2. After a procedural vote on the motion, separate substantive votes are taken on each piece divided out and the remainder.
3. A final vote is taken on the draft resolution's language as it reads as a result of the previous piecemeal votes.

## 12. Motion to Expand Debate

*A Motion to Expand Debate broadens the scope of debate and returns the Council to the previous speakers list. This motion happens most frequently when debate has been limited to a resolution and a second resolution has been submitted that the committee wishes to discuss simultaneously. This motion also is in order if the committee has been tasked with a crisis situation and needs to quickly change topics without closing debate.*

IN ORDER: Council Sessions

REQUIRES: Second | 2+/2– | >50% Vote

DETAILS:

1. No substantive vote taken, items "tabled."
2. Speakers list saved so debate may again be limited to that item later.

## 13. Motion to Hear Speakers' Rights

*A Motion to Hear Speakers' Rights allows limited substantive debate on a draft resolution.*

IN ORDER: Voting Procedure – Summit

REQUIRES: Multiple Seconds

DETAILS:

1. The Secretary-General takes up to two speakers against a draft resolution, then as many speakers in favor as there are against, up to two.
2. Speakers are granted 30 seconds each.

### 14. Motion to Introduce an Amendment

*A Motion to Introduce an Amendment brings a proposed amendment before the Council for consideration.*

IN ORDER: Council Sessions

REQUIRES: Second

DETAILS:

1. Amendments must be written on official amendment forms and have Sponsors totaling at least 1/8 of the countries present (minimum two).
2. The Chair must approve amendments before they may be introduced and will give them number designations.
3. Amendments may only modify operative clauses, not preambulatory ones.
4. The Chair will immediately verify if the amendment is friendly or unfriendly; friendly amendments are automatically accepted; unfriendly amendments remain on the floor to be debated and must be voted upon.

### 15. Motion to Introduce a Draft Resolution

*A Motion to Introduce a Draft Resolution brings a draft resolution before the Council for consideration.*

IN ORDER: Council Sessions

REQUIRES: Second

DETAILS:

1. Draft resolutions must comply with standard formatting rules and have Sponsors and Signatories totaling at least 1/4 of the countries present, minimum three.
2. The Chair must approve draft resolutions before they may be introduced and will give designation labels.
3. Digital or paper copies of draft resolutions are distributed after introduction.
4. Sponsors read operative clauses after copies are distributed.
5. Multiple resolutions may be introduced simultaneously, all of which may be discussed until debate is limited to just one.

### 16. Motion to Introduce a Right of Reply

*A Motion to Introduce a Right of Reply provides delegates the opportunity to respond to slanderous statements made by another delegation or to correct information presented in committee by another delegation that inaccurately presents facts about, or the policy of their state.*

IN ORDER: Council Sessions, Summit Session

REQUIRES: Chair Acceptance

DETAILS:

1. The Reply must be submitted in writing to the Chair, who may choose to read the Reply to the body at his or her discretion, not subject to appeal.
2. Reciprocal Replies are never in order.
3. A Reply can only be accorded in response to a speech made in formal or informal debate, and may be granted only to a delegate or delegate's government directly mentioned in the offending speech.
4. Delegates may state the intent to introduce a Right of Reply at the moment the offense is made, but the Reply will not be entertained until submitted in writing to the Chair.

### 17. Motion to Limit Debate

*A Motion to Limit Debate narrows the scope of debate, which immediately opens a new speakers list.*

IN ORDER: Council Sessions

REQUIRES: Second | >50% Vote

DETAILS:

1. Debate may be limited many times, narrowing the debate from the General Speakers List to topics, resolutions, or even amendments.
2. Limiting debate to a draft resolution triggers Author's Rights.
3. Other than limiting debate to a single topic, it is not necessary to limit debate in order to pass resolutions or otherwise conduct the work of the council. Limiting debate is a tool to add structure to the debate, but is entirely optional once within a topic area.

### 18. Motion to Read the Resolution

*A Motion to Read the Resolution calls for the operative clauses of a draft resolution to be read out loud before a vote.*

IN ORDER: Voting Procedure – Summit

REQUIRES: Multiple Seconds

DETAILS: N/A

### 19. Motion to Reconsider the Vote

*The Motion to Reconsider the Vote takes a re-vote on a substantive or procedural matter immediately after the initial vote concludes.*

IN ORDER: Voting Procedure – Council Sessions, Summit

REQUIRES: Second | 2+/2– | >50% Vote

DETAILS:

1. The motion must be made after a vote has taken place and prior to the committee moving on to further business. The motion to reconsider a procedural motion must occur before any other procedural or substantive matters are taken up by the committee. The motion to reconsider a substantive motion takes place after the Chair announces the outcome of the vote unless the substantive motion was voted on by means of a roll-call vote. In that case, the motion is considered only after rights have been entertained by the Chair.
2. If the motion passes, the vote is nullified and the Chair will entertain points or motions that take precedence before repeating the vote, including another motion to reconsider the action of the committee just taken, a motion to re-open debate, etc.
3. If more than one Motion to Reconsider occurs in a row, it is considered to be Cascading Reconsiderations and has the utility of backing a committee up through several motions the committee wishes to nullify. (Note that there are often simpler and thus more preferable ways to accomplish this.)
4. A Motion to Reconsider may only be used if a country believes the committee voted in error, misunderstood the vote being taken, or there was an aberration in the Rules of Procedure pertaining to voting such that the outcome of the vote is suspect.

### 20. Motion to Remove an Officer

*A Motion to Remove an Officer, also known as a Motion to Impeach, removes a negligent officer (Secretary-General, Assistant Secretary-General, Chair, Vice-Chair, or Parliamentarian) and replaces with a subordinate or by election.*

IN ORDER: Council Sessions, Summit

REQUIRES: Second | 2+/2– | ≥2/3 Vote

DETAILS:

1. Only in extreme cases of officer misconduct or inability to perform the required duties may this motion be used.
2. Immediately recess, inform the Secretariat or National Council representative(s), who will moderate the motion.

## 21. Motion to Re-Open the Speakers List

*A Motion to Re-Open the Speakers List nullifies a Motion to Close the Speakers List.*

IN ORDER: Council Sessions

REQUIRES: Second | >50% Vote

DETAILS:

1. May be made any time between the passage of a Motion to Close the Speakers List and before the speakers list is exhausted (including immediately following the final speaker).

## 22. Motion to Vote by Roll-Call

*The Motion to Vote by Roll-Call allows countries to vote one-by-one and allows more voting options.*

IN ORDER: Voting Procedure – Council Sessions, Summit

REQUIRES: Multiple Seconds

DETAILS:

1. The Chair calls each country, starting at a random place on the roster.
2. Countries may vote "Pass" to be added to the end of the voting roster, after which they must vote "Yes," "No," or "Abstain" (they may not vote No with Rights).
3. Countries may vote "No with Rights" to be given a thirty-second speech after the vote to explain their position if the item passes. A "No with Rights" is only to be used to explain a country's reasoning if it unexpectedly must vote "No."

## 23. Motion to Set the Order of the Agenda

*The Motion to Set the Order of the Agenda establishes the order in which Agenda topics will be discussed throughout Council Sessions.*

IN ORDER: Council Sessions

REQUIRES: Second | >50% Vote

DETAILS:

1. Council remains on the General Speakers List until this motion passes.
2. Topics retain the number originally listed on the Agenda, a detail particularly important to the Chair for giving draft resolution designations.
3. Changes to the Agenda order must be reported to the Secretariat.

## 24. Motion to Suspend the Meeting

*The Motion to Suspend the Meeting recesses the Council for an unmoderated caucus or scheduled break.*

IN ORDER: Plenary, Council Sessions

REQUIRES: Second | >50% Vote

DETAILS:

1. A time limit must be specified for un-moderated caucuses, with a maximum ten minutes, with a possible extension of five additional minutes (with the exception of scheduled breaks).

### 25. Motion to Suspend the Rules

*The Motion to Suspend the Rules engages in actions and debate styles not sanctioned by normal parliamentary procedure. The Motion to Suspend the Rules is most often used to allow the committee to enter a Moderated Caucus.*

IN ORDER: Council Sessions

REQUIRES: Second | ≥2/3 Vote

DETAILS:

1. Proposed action or debate style (including Moderated Caucus, Popcorn, Q&A, Round Robin, and Straw Poll votes) must be specified in the motion, as well as a time limit when applicable.
2. Typically used for a Moderated Caucus, wherein the Chair may call on delegates at will without using a speakers list.
3. The rules may not be suspended in order to take an action that can be achieved through formal debate.
4. No new motions may be made during a Suspension of the Rules.
   (i) *Standard options for Suspension of the Rules*
   In most cases, the Suspension of the Rules is used to move the committee away from formal debate into a Moderated Caucus (see the "Alphabetical listing of the Rules of Procedure with detailed explanations" for more information on Moderated Caucuses). Generally, any suspension of the rules will not exceed fifteen minutes including extensions.
   (ii) *Non-standard options for Suspension of the Rules*
   A Suspension of the Rules can be used to create other, alternative, structures for delegates to shape debate.
   (a) *Popcorn debate*
   A popcorn debate is used to facilitate a quick discussion between delegates that is directed primarily by the delegates themselves. A delegate wishing to enter into popcorn debate "moves for a five minute suspension of the rules for the purpose of popcorn debate" or "moves for a five minute suspension of the rules for the purpose of popcorn debate with a 30 second speaking time." Unlike a moderated caucus, a specified length of speaking time is not required; thus, a popcorn debate can have many or just a few speakers. In popcorn debate, the

Chair asks the delegate who made the motion for the Suspension of the Rules to name the first speaker. They may name any delegation in the room including themselves. From there, each speaker names the next speaker during the suspension. This differs from a Moderated Caucus in which the Chair chooses the next speaker from a show of placards. Popcorn debate is especially useful in airing out last minute grievances over draft language prior to a closure of debate.

(b) Question and answer (Q&A)

Q&A is a more relaxed form of a Yield to Questions. As yields are not appropriate during Suspension of the Rules, the Q&A has its own set of guidelines to govern the suspension. The following rules must be observed by the Council when it enters into a Q&A session. The proper motion is "moves for a five-minute suspension of the rules for the purpose of a Q&A session with <<Name Respondents here>>." The respondents can be any delegate, an expert witness, or another guest to the committee.

Once it begins, the Chair will ask the Council "Do any delegations have any questions for <<Names the type of respondent in front of the room>>." Delegates wishing to ask a question raise their placards at this time. When called upon by the Chair, the delegate directs their question to the Chair by saying "Would the chair ask <<name individual(s) you wish to answer the question>> <<state your question here>>." The Chair will ask the respondent(s) if they accept the question. If they do, the Chair begins to keep time and the question is responded to. If they do not, the Chair moves on to the next question in the room. The Chair keeps time for the Q&A session by timing only the responses to questions, but not the questions as they are being asked. Follow-up questions are at the sole discretion of the Chair.

(c) *Round robin*

Round robin debate generally begins when a delegate moves for a Suspension of the Rules to talk about a specific topic. In a round robin debate, every country speaks, beginning with the country making the motion. From there, countries speak in clockwise order around the Council until every country has made one comment. Round robin debate is a great way to start the conversation on a new topic or to quickly state delegation opinions on a crisis situation. In a round robin, all delegations must speak. To motion for a round robin, a delegate states "Moves for a suspension of the rules for five minutes for the purpose of a round robin to discuss <<state topic here>>."

(d) *Straw poll vote*

Moving for a Suspension of the Rules for the purposes of a straw poll vote allows the Council a way to quickly take the temperature of the room on anything: a piece of draft language, the willingness of the council to move on from a topic, etc. All countries are asked to vote

"Yes," "No," or "Abstain," but are not required to participate. The vote is not binding (countries may actually vote the opposite of how they voted in the straw poll should the action being polled actually come to a vote). A procedure for a straw poll vote is as follows:

A delegate wishing for a straw poll vote states the following: "moves for a suspension of the rules for the purpose of a straw poll vote on <state what you want the committee to voting on.>>" If it is in order, the Chair takes the vote to have the straw poll vote first. If the vote to have the straw poll vote passes, the chair then states the question posed to the committee and asks all votes to indicate if they would vote "Yes," then "No," then "Abstain" on the question.

While creative delegates may attempt to suspend the rules for any reason, the four additional suspensions listed above are common at MAL conferences: popcorn, Q&A, round robin, and straw poll.

### 26. Motion to Temporarily Revoke Delegate Rights

*A Motion to Temporarily Revoke Delegate Rights temporarily prevents a disruptive delegate from speaking or taking part in procedural votes.*

IN ORDER: Council Sessions

REQUIRES: Second | 2+/2– | ≥2/3 Vote

DETAILS:

1. Only in extreme cases of repeated disruptive behavior, after multiple warnings, may this motion be used.
2. A Chair must initiate it.
3. A time limit must be specified, with a maximum of twenty minutes.
4. If his or her rights are revoked, a delegate must stay in the Council room until the time expires and rights are returned, but he or she maintains the right to vote on substantive matters.

### 27. Point of Order

*A Point of Order brings improper usage of parliamentary procedures to the attention of the Chair.*

IN ORDER: Plenary Session, Council Sessions, Summit Session

REQUIRES: N/A

DETAILS:

1. A Point of Order may interrupt a speaker.

### 28. Point of Parliamentary Inquiry

*A Point of Parliamentary Inquiry asks for clarification from the Chair on a procedural matter.*

IN ORDER: Plenary Session, Council Sessions, Summit Session

REQUIRES: N/A

DETAILS:

1. A Point of Parliamentary Inquiry may not interrupt a speaker.

### 29. Point of Personal Privilege

*A Point of Personal Privilege allows a delegate to complain of unfair distractions.*

IN ORDER: Plenary Session, Council Sessions, Summit Session

REQUIRES: N/A

DETAILS:

1. A Point of Personal Privilege may interrupt a speaker.

### 30. Point of Reconsideration

*A Point of Reconsideration is used for the purpose of informing the Chair that the state rising to the point wishes to change their vote. The Chair will record the change and announce if it alters the outcome of the vote. In a case where the Chair is uncertain as to how the state voted previously or to the new final outcome, the Chair may opt to take the vote a second time for the sake of accuracy.*

IN ORDER: Plenary Session, Council Sessions, Summit Session

REQUIRES: N/A

DETAILS:

1. In order only after a procedural or substantive vote has occurred during which the state rising to the point voted "Yes," "No," "Abstain," or "No with Rights." It is not in order during a straw poll vote.
2. Chairs should retake the vote if they are unsure how the state(s) voted prior to making the Point and if the number of states making points of reconsideration is larger than the difference between the "Yes" and "No" votes.

### 31. Yield to Another Country

*A Yield to Another Country gives remaining speaking time to another country, which may not be yielded again.*

IN ORDER: After concluding a speech in formal debate

REQUIRES: N/A

DETAILS:

1. Delegates may yield remaining time to any delegation present in the room. The receiving state may speak for up to the amount of time remaining. Once finished, they do not yield, as the time was already yielded.

## 32. Yield to the Chair

*A Yield to the Chair ends the speaker's speaking time and returns the floor to the Chair.*

IN ORDER: After concluding a speech in formal debate

REQUIRES: N/A

DETAILS:

1. Delegates must yield to the Chair if their speaking time elapses.

## 33. Yield to Points of Information

*A Yield to Points of Information allows for a question-and-answer period until time elapses, with only answers being counted against time.*

IN ORDER: After concluding a speech in formal debate

REQUIRES: N/A

DETAILS:

1. When a delegate yields to Points of Information, the Chair informs the Council of that fact and then asks the Council "Are there any points of information?" Delegates wishing to ask a question raise their placards and the Chair selects one. That delegate then says, "Would the Chair ask the delegate?" and states their question. The Chair asks the speaker "Do you accept the question?" If not, the Chair calls on the next delegate to raise a Point of Information. If so, the Chair keeps time while the speaker responds to the question. Questions are taken until the time elapses.
2. Once a delegate concludes their speech and yields to the Chair, another delegation may rise to a Point of Personal Privilege and ask if the previous speaker would instead yield to Points of Information. It is at the Chair's discretion if they will allow the previous speaker to change their yield.
3. The Point of Information is in order only after a delegate has yielded to questions or during a Suspension of the Rules for the purpose of a Q&A session. It may not interrupt a speaker and has no position in the order of precedence. Delegates rising to a Point of Information during a Yield to Questions or a Suspension of the Rules do not say "Point of Information" as with other points in the rules.

## Manipulating the rules

The rules are a discrete system of procedures implemented for the purposes of managing debate. Students with a particular acumen for the rules can manipulate them to their benefit as an advantage over student participants with less proficiency. Manipulation of the rules takes skill and is only advisable for students with the necessary understanding of the logic behind them and the specific details governing each rule. Teams that have been a part of the MAL program for a long time have had the benefit of "rules wonk(s)" to develop strategies for their teams to play with the Rules of Procedure. The term "rules wonk(s)" is a playful label used to define a delegate that uses employment and manipulation of the rules as the primary strategy for moving their state's policy forward.

Specific details on how to manipulate the rules are strategies and tactics of specific teams, so cannot be included in this text. A few tips can, however, be provided for the students and advisors interested in developing their own rules strategy:

1. A rules manipulation cannot break the rules, omit rules, or in any other way contradict the Rules of Procedure in this text or in the official Handbook of the MAL program.
2. Be prepared to justify the manipulation and its interpretation of the rules to a council chair, other delegates, or the National Council representative(s).
3. Anyone at the conference, including faculty advisors, chairs, and secretariat can promote a change in structure or interpretation of the rules, so consider involving others in the planned manipulation.

## Summary

Proper understanding and use of the rules provide delegates with an advantage over those delegates who do not understand them. Demonstration of rules proficiency is often the first tip-off to other delegates that you are a prepared and skilled delegate. It also demonstrates confidence in committee, which is a further sign of your capability. Too often, students and faculty advisors underestimate how often rules proficiency is used as a meter to gauge which delegates are or are not worth working with.

Understanding the rules and proper usage of motions is the first and simplest step to establishing rules proficiency. The next step – admittedly a harder one – involves utilizing the rules to create advantages for you in committee. There is no simple way to teach this skill. It is best learned through experience, which can only be gained in practice or at conference. Now that you have read all the rules and descriptions of their use, the best next step is to start thinking about how every rule in the list can be used to create an opportunity for the motioner. Working on this in a group is a good way to share ideas and to help build your team's rules style. It is also a necessary prerequisite for developing your team's strategies for manipulating the rules.

# 5

# Research

## *How do you prepare to represent a specific country?*

Preparation for conference begins well before the conference weekend. Students should be well versed in their country's history, policy, and current geopolitical situation (in addition to having a thorough understanding of the Rules of Procedure) prior to attending a conference. The National Council on U.S.-Arab Relations (NCUSAR) recommends the following timeline for preparation and research for conference:

- 1–3 months prior: research your country's policy positions and begin studying parliamentary procedure;
- 1 month prior: write position papers to solidify policy objectives and hold mock debates to practice procedure.

Students who do not prepare before the start of conference find themselves in a perpetual state of trying to catch up. They spend most of conference researching on the fly and never really have an opportunity to participate. This does not, however, mean that on-the-fly research does not happen at conference. The best delegates have materials and tools with them or on their electronic devices to allow on-location spur of the moment research as the committee moves in various directions within the topic. This chapter provides the willing student with all the necessary information to prepare before conference and then take advantage of that preparation while at conference.

### How to research your country

Students should start with the *CIA World Factbook* or other similar database that provides a formulaic overview of a state in various topical and policy areas. It is a great source of data, basic information, and facts. It is recommended to find two such country studies just to provide different perspectives on the state you will represent. While this is a great starting place, it is inadequate to conclude research with this step. Although most country databases include a brief history, you should find something more detailed to establish your knowledge of the background of the state.

It is not necessary to read a lengthy historical account of the country you will represent. There are many edited volumes on countries of the Middle East where each chapter is devoted to one state. These chapters usually provide enough recent and not-so-recent history to adequately prepare a student for research focused more on your topic than just the country itself. Students should consider reading two chapter studies on the state to provide a diverse perspective and, more importantly, to ensure that bias in one of the chapters did not result in a critical fact or series of facts being omitted.

Once you have gained some basic knowledge and historical background on the country you are representing, the next best step is to catch up on and then maintain knowledge on current events. Several online news services, including news.google.com, allow you to subscribe to country-specific news updates. This is a great way to know when something has happened that you should be more aware of. Consider reading a daily or weekly publication that is on a topic or topics related to your council assignment and the region of the Middle East in general. This will provide some up-to-date details on current events pertaining to the Arab World and your council's generic agenda.

The next and final step is for you to become acquainted with your country's policy in the general area of your assigned council's topic. The best way to approach this if, for example, you are on the Environmental Affairs Council is to find your country's ministry of environmental affairs online. If you are unlucky and the agency is not online, does not exist, or is published only in a language you cannot read, then this requires a bit more researching. In that case, finding news stories, articles, and scholarly publications on your country's applicable ministry and policy will suffice. The point of this research is to give you some basic understanding of how your country approaches questions on policy in your council's topical area. That way, when you begin to tackle the agenda, you will already have a sense of the kind of positions your country is likely to take.

## How to interpret an agenda

Students should begin with the Provisional MAL Agenda and the topic guides provided by NCUSAR on their website: http://ncusar.org/modelarableague/current-participants/agenda/. Topic guides are written by the national chair of each committee and are a vetted, cited documents for use by all delegations attending conference.

When researching their topics, students should begin thinking about the order of the agenda they wish to submit at the beginning of their council's first session. Successful students will have researched each of their committee's topics from the point of view of the entire League as well as their assigned country. The NCUSAR has compiled a series of research resources, including general resources, multilateral treaties, and country-specific resources, which can be found here: http://ncusar.org/modelarableague/current-participants/research-resources.

While Wi-Fi is often available at conferences, students should assume that they will *not* have access to the internet. Students should have either paper copies or PDF copies of all resources for debate (research, Rules of Procedure, agenda, topic guides, etc.). Lack of internet is not recognized as a justifiable reason for not being in character or for being ill-prepared.

Regardless of experience with MAL, the challenge for all delegates is to remember that they are playing a role and representing a country. Research should be compiled as impartially as possible and should be from the point of view of the student's country, not from their personal beliefs. Furthermore, students should be well aware of the people(s) they represent; while each state in the League defines itself as Arab, most states have non-Arab citizens. And while most Arabs are Muslim, most Arab states have sizeable non-Muslim minorities. Students should be careful to compile research that speaks to all residents of their state.

The most successful students in any council are those who have not only researched their country's position, but also have a general understanding of subregional and regional politics and culture (in the Maghreb, Levant, Horn of Africa, Arabian peninsula, etc.). Exceptional students will complete a position paper on their committee's topics. Position papers are short papers that detail the state's general policy in the topic area and provide details on the state's specific policy preferences for a resolution on the topic. Position papers can be in multiple formats (essay, short summary, bullet points, etc.), but should include several key parts: a background on the topic, your country's involvement with the topic, a summary of your country's policy recommendations for the topic, and your country's objectives and goals for the topic. Ultimately, a position paper should be a summary of your research. Under no circumstances are they to be a vehicle for pre-written resolution language, as that is a violation of conference policies at all MAL conferences.

### How to start

While at first the research process seems intimidating to even the most seasoned delegate, there is a series of questions that can be asked to break the process up into workable parts. There are strong arguments for starting research either from the point of view of the country of from that of the topic holistically, but, either way, one must ask certain questions:

- Questions about countries: What type of government does my country have? What is my general population (citizens versus expatriates)? What are the main demographic groups for my country? What is my country's economic status (including GDP)? What is my country's relationship to other League members and regional partners? Which are my country's allies? What other regional/international organizations is my country a member of?

- Questions to answer in a position paper: How does this topic affect the League as a whole? How does it affect my country specifically? What can my country offer as a solution to the topic at hand? What are some general ways this topic can be resolved? What treaties, prior documents, or agreements already address this issue?

In some cases, students may find that their country may not have an official position on their topic. For instance, Comoros has no official position on cross-border Small Arms and Light Weapons (SALW) issues, as it shares no borders with any League member. As noted in Chapter 3, students should look at similar issues; in the case of the Comoros example, a student might look at policies regarding transnational crime, the sale of weapons into war zones, or domestic law covering the transport of weapons among the islands of Comoros for an inkling on their policy on SALW cross-border issues.

After this research is compiled, a student should begin to formulate a position paper on their committee's topics. The position paper is a discrete statement of the overall position of the state followed by particular outcomes that are of interest to the state. It provides anyone who reads the paper with a clear and simple snapshot of the general policy of the state along with a few areas of interest for potential resolutions on the topics.

## What to put in your conference binder

Whether you compile your research in a binder or digitally, no matter how you personally organize it, several core items should be present in your research folder:

- Alexandria Protocol
- The Charter of the League of Arab States
- JDEC Treaty
- Arab Charter on Human Rights
- The Official Council Rules/Policies from the *Model Arab League Handbook* published by the NCUSAR
- The NCUSAR topic guide for your committee
- The *CIA World Factbook* entry for your country

The first five items on this list are in appendices to this text (A, B, C, F, and G), so bringing this text to conference is your best bet to cover most of these. The rest of the items on this list are easily found online and can be included electronically or printed and put in an actual binder. From there, anything else you would bring is country and topic specific.

Here are some thoughts to help you prepare your binder:

*Country-specific research items:*

- A list of potentially relevant treaties, noting which ones your state signed and ratified, which your state only signed, and which your state neither signed nor ratified.
- A quick reference of facts relevant to your topics so you do not need to scroll through the *CIA World Factbook* or similar document.
- A list of one-line policy statements on subtopics of each topic, which you can use as a quick addition to a speech or the start of a clause for a resolution.
- Various maps of your country showing useful information relevant to your council's topics and a political map showing basic details of the state.

*Topic-specific research items:*

- Individual research for each topic (news articles, encyclopedia entries, relevant treaties/international documents).
- Statistical facts about your country and others that would be useful information in a debate on each topic.
- Maps that show relevant information for the topic (infrastructure, resources, assets, etc.).
- Copies of any documents passed by the League of Arab States or other international organizations on the topic, a subtopic within the topic, or a relevant different topic. These are great resources for ideas and facts in a debate.

## Summary

Conference preparation involves researching your state's policy, researching your council's agenda, finding a point of convergence between your state's policy and your council's agenda, and then preparing to represent that effectively to others. Preparation begins months before conference starts, but does not end until the last day of conference. As council sessions take place, delegates will steer the debate in directions most convenient for their state's policy and their research. Often, a council will end up in an area of policy that was impossible to anticipate so new research must be done on the spur of the moment. Delegates who take care to anticipate some possible alternative policy directions and build a conference binder that can lead to fast additional research when needed will be the most prepared for conference.

Once preparation is finished, it is highly advised to share your preparation with the rest of your delegation. If every member of your delegation has a copy of every other member's position paper and research links then your conference binder is a lot more versatile and better able to assist you when council debate moves in unexpected directions. This allows you to ask your head delegate or faculty advisor to assist you in getting information from another delegate when their research becomes more relevant in your committee than initially expected. In short, the broader and more in-depth your research, the more flexible and versatile your research binder will become for council sessions.

# 6

# Conference leadership
## *How to prepare as a chair/secretariat*

Model Arab League (MAL) provides a number of student leadership opportunities beyond participation in substantive debate. Normally, students who are interested in chairing a council or serving in a more senior position will gain experience by serving as a vice-chair or rapporteur while also serving as a delegate. After gaining some experience a student may apply for a chair position and go through an interview process to determine if there is an appropriate position available. Experienced council chairs may similarly apply for Assistant Secretary-General, Secretary-General, and Chief of Staff roles.

### Tips for effective chairing

Chairing, like being a delegate, is its own unique art that requires preparation, practice, and a strategy for success. We have previously discussed MAL debate as a set of hard-and-fast rules that must be followed. That is a helpful perspective for delegates, but successful chairs approach debate from a different angle.

The rules are meant to facilitate debate. (This bears repeating: *the rules are meant to facilitate debate.*) A chair has a huge amount of discretion in whether and when to enforce any given rule. When a delegate violates a rule, if the violation does not impact the speaking rights of others, otherwise does not impact the council, and particularly if stopping debate to address the violation would interrupt the momentum of the council's work, often the chair will ignore the violation. Similarly, if the construction of the rules makes it difficult for the council to procedurally accomplish something for which there is wide support, it is absolutely the chair's responsibility to assist the council in navigating the rules to the intended effect. This may include consulting with the parliamentarian, Secretary-General or Assistant Secretary-General, or, in rare cases, creatively suspending the rules or the meeting in order to circumvent an especially bothersome procedural restriction.

An effective chair also understands that debate will devolve into chaos without consistent rules. The vast amount of a chair's time is spent moderating debate by fairly and consistently applying the Rules of Procedure as written. The chair takes no substantive position on the issues at hand and has no interest in the outcome of the debate, only the fairness of the process that produced a decision and the ability of minority and dissenting opinions to be heard. Applying rules consistently (except when there is a clear and compelling reason to deviate) also helps bolster the confidence of council delegates because they know what to expect, further enhancing the quality of debate in the room.

Chairs should take the time to explain what is happening whenever a new or complicated procedural process is undertaken. This includes explaining the impact of a yes or no vote, and the number of votes needed to pass, prior to any unfamiliar or confusing procedural vote. Slowing down the pace of the council to explain what is happening also gives delegates time to catch up and increases the likelihood that even the most experienced delegates will have adequate time to consider the matter and vote appropriately. Explanations can be particularly helpful when making a judgment call that deviates from prior rulings or when ruling a point or motion dilatory (out of order, literally having no impact except to delay the work of the council).

### Gavel etiquette

Used properly, the gavel is an extremely powerful symbolic tool for the chair. The gavel should be visible to the council at all times, and the chair should not touch it unless he or she intends to use it (which should be very rare). Simply lifting the gavel should be enough to call attention to the chair, reduce conversation volume, and enhance decorum in the room.

Shortly before a delegate's speaking time expires, generally when ten seconds remain, the chair should lift the handle of the gavel off the table (without raising the head of the gavel) and sharply tap the handle against the table two or three times. This is a courtesy to the delegate who is speaking. While not absolutely necessary, in a council meeting that is working well this reminder will reduce the frequency with which the chair needs to rap the gavel to nearly zero. The chair should simply explain to the council that he or she intends to adopt this convention so that delegates understand what the handle taps mean.

The gavel is most commonly used to bring the room to order after a suspension of the meeting or some other disruption. The chair should stand, grip the gavel firmly, and slowly rap it three times, then announce that the delegates should come to order (or return to seats, etc.), pause to allow delegates to comply and then repeat as necessary. Used properly, the gavel should not bounce off the table (there should be no double raps), the sound should be loud and sharp, and its authority should originate in the rarity of its usage rather than by overpowering delegates' speech. A successful first-time chair will find a quiet room and practice beforehand; it will seem absolutely ridiculous but will pay dividends. "Gaveling down" a delegate who is out of order is improper usage of the gavel and is likely to make it more difficult for the chair to maintain order rather than improve the situation.

The chair should also rap the gavel when the meeting comes to order, once when the meeting adjourns, and once after announcing the result of a substantive vote. Otherwise the gavel should generally be left alone, displayed neatly in a position of prominence on the dais but untouched by the chair.

### Placard etiquette

Enforcing placard etiquette early in the conference will help delegates learn the rules quickly. Later in the conference, by the time the debate is intense enough that the placards have become invaluable, their proper usage will be second nature to everyone.

Every delegation should possess one placard and placard votes should be tallied based on the number of placards raised; hands are not an acceptable substitute, as it can be difficult to ensure that only one member of a two-person delegation is voting. Placards should be raised such that the country name is visible to the chair when voting, when rising to a point or motion, or in other situations where it is appropriate for a delegate to request the floor. We prefer placards with the country name on both sides, rather than a Rules of Procedure cheat sheet on the reverse, as it clarifies voting procedure for council staff and other delegations. Cheat sheets are helpful, but they do not belong on placards.

### Speaker timing

Council chairs use various methods to time delegate speeches. Some prefer the simplicity of a physical timer that does not perform any other function, while others use a timer application on a computer or smartphone. One widely accepted piece of advice is that the timer should always be set to count up rather than down. If the timer counts down, it will eventually stop and likely sound an alarm. The alarm will interrupt the speaker, eliminating the chair's ability to use discretion as to when to stop the speech. It is generally acceptable when a delegate's speaking time comes to an end to allow the delegate to finish a sentence rather than cutting in partway through. Of course, if a delegate abuses this courtesy then the delegate's speech should be interrupted.

Inevitably, at some point during the conference the chair will fail to start the timer, there will be a technical error with the timer mid speech, or the chair will lose track of time and the speech will go on longer than it should. In any case, the chair should tap the gavel handle and give the speaker time to finish the speech, tapping either a few seconds before the estimated end of the speech or immediately if the speaking time has already elapsed. The courtesy of the warning tap is generally understood to apply even if the delegate's speaking time is already longer than intended due to an error at the dais.

### Keeping track of speakers in moderated caucus

One important chairing tool is a list of delegations present during the current council session. Using this list, the chair should tally the number of times that each delegation raises a placard and is called on to make a speech (namely, substantive speeches made outside the purview of a written speakers list). This list helps the chair ensure that the chance to speak is distributed fairly across the council and points out delegations that speak less frequently so that they can be recognized on the occasions when their placards are raised. It is important to note that there will be times when one or several delegations will dominate an unmoderated caucus and there are times when this is desirable; the tick list gives the chair a tool to evaluate participation across multiple caucuses or topics and is not necessarily intended to bring every delegation into every conversation.

### Unmoderated caucus management

Unmoderated caucuses are a good time for council chairs to regroup and recharge, as it is the only time during a council session that the chair does not need to be listening or speaking. It is important for a chair to take that time. On the other hand, during unmoderated caucuses the chair cannot rely on the rules to facilitate debate and protect the speaking rights of those with minority views. The chair should spend some time during every unmoderated caucus listening to the conversations and helping to ensure that all are respected and all opinions are heard. If council members continue to marginalize those in the minority then unmoderated caucus time should be kept to a minimum.

### Proofreading resolutions

Any experienced delegate has inevitably found him or herself in a situation where it is impossible to support a fundamentally good resolution due to mistakes that cannot be resolved after the resolution has been introduced. The restrictions on preambulatory amendments are intended to minimize debate on portions of the resolution that do not have substantive impact, but in the absence of an experienced and involved dais it is all too easy for an inexperienced delegation to introduce a good resolution that will never gain the support of the council due to an error that cannot be corrected by amendment later on.

A chair first relies on the vice-chair when draft resolutions start to come to the dais. One person needs to work with delegates on proofreading the drafts and the other needs to continue to chair the council. Normally, it is very obvious whose skills better suit each task; if the chair is going to proof-read, the vice-chair should take the gavel and chair the council, but of course the chair maintains ultimate authority over all work of the council.

Whoever is proofreading should pay particular attention to the preamble, as it cannot be amended later. Overly long or even remotely inflammatory preambles should be strongly discouraged. Remember that a council's goal is to arrive at a degree of consensus and arguing for hours over a contentious preamble that can only be modified by withdrawing and reintroducing a draft resolution is highly detrimental to the work of the council and the goals of the MAL program. Normally, the chair should maintain substantive impartial-ity, but it is absolutely reasonable to approach that fine line when it comes to proofreading draft resolutions.

By the time a draft resolution is formally introduced for debate its format should be perfect and it should be free of any spelling, grammatical, or struc-tural issues. The authors and the chair should have a mutual understanding of the aspects of the draft resolution that will be controversial, and if the authors choose to introduce a controversial preamble there should be a compelling reason for doing so. It is the job of the chair to ensure that the authors of the draft resolution are prepared for the early reaction to the draft resolution.

### Voting procedure

When the council approves a Motion to Close Debate on a topic, the council will immediately enter formal voting procedure. Voting procedure operates as a special subset of the normal council session where rules are adhered to much more formally. Once the Motion to Close Debate has passed, the chair should explain that the council will enter into voting procedure and advise obser-vers, including faculty advisors, that they may either leave the council room or remain for the entirety of the voting procedure. This is intended to avoid distractions and minimize the influence of outside factors on the voting pro-cess. Dais staff should assist the chair in ensuring that nobody enters or leaves the room until voting is complete.

Division of the Question is the most complicated procedure that can occur during voting procedure. During Division of the Question, a delegate asks that part of the operative portion of the draft resolution be removed from the draft resolution and voted on separately. Normally, several sections are divided out (as separate divisions of the question), resulting in a series of votes on various sections of the draft resolution. Each division is voted on separ-ately, beginning with the most drastic division, and the undivided sections (those not divided out) are voted on, as a whole, last. All of the portions that pass are cobbled together and placed after the original preamble to be voted on as a single substantive document. Division of the Question for the purpose of introducing confusion (for example, by dividing every operative clause for no apparent reason) is dilatory; this rule, as with all other rules, is solely and exclusively intended to facilitate debate. Effective chairs only allow Division of the Question when there is a clear substantive reason for doing so.

## How to prepare as a chair/secretariat

Most delegates who have never chaired or been Upper Secretariat assume the students in these roles do not have to prepare prior to conference. The worst-run conferences all feature students who do not take their Secretariat positions seriously until the start of conference. Secretariat members are members of their teams and should feel and act that way. This means they should participate in their team's preparation for conference when possible in addition to doing their own preparation. It is crucial for the members of the Secretariat to take the following steps prior to the start of their conference.

### All Secretariat

- *Review the Rules of Procedure.* All Secretariat members should know the purpose and use of every rule in the Rules of Procedure. This does not mean knowing the exact vote count required or even if it takes speakers. The *Model Arab League Handbook* and this text (see Appendices O and P) have cheat sheets for quick reference. Ideally, you will know this information for regularly used motions such as Closure of Debate and Suspension of the Rules.
- *Practice chairing.* If your team has taken its participation in an MAL seriously, they will likely hold a few practice sessions to get ready. Secretariat members should chair their team's practices so they get experience practicing the art of chairing. Having a conference chair lead a practice makes the experience more authentic and is a valuable learning experience for everyone. Practicing to be a chair should include *all* steps of council chairing. Practice setting the agenda, taking a speakers list, chairing various types of debate structures, and closure of debate. If there is any rule you are unsure about, practice chairing that rule as well. Upper Secretariat chair the summit session, so they need this experience as well. Additionally, unexpected events come up at conference and an Assistant Secretary-General or the Secretary-General may have to chair a committee for a little while, so the Upper Secretariat members should be ready to do that as well.
- *Read the Charter* and, if applicable, the JDEC Treaty (See Appendices A to C) and ask your advisor or a National Council representative for help if any line of either document is confusing for you. As a member of Secretariat, students and even faculty may approach you for clarification on the role of

the League in some capacity. Understanding the League's most important governing documents will ensure you are able to respond to these questions.

- *Pronunciation.* Look up or ask someone about the proper pronunciation of each state's name and practice if you are not used to saying the names of all the states. The easiest way for a chair to undermine their credibility is to botch simple names of member states. Many students botch the pronunciation of Qatar, so pick an acceptable form of the pronunciation that you can be comfortable with and maintain consistency.

## *Lower Secretariat*

- *Conference binder.* Every council chair should have a binder with them in council sessions. Your conference binder should include the following: a copy of the full Rules of Procedure, the cheat sheets in this book (Appendices O and P), a one-half and two-thirds voting chart (Appendix Q), copies of the Charter, the JDEC Treaty, and the Alexandria Protocol (Appendices A, B, and C), the conference schedule, a copy of the topic guide for your committee, and blank paper. The National Council representatives will supply roll-call sheets and amendment forms, so these are unneeded.

- *Timer and gavel.* The NCUSAR always supplies gavels for the conference, but it is up to each conference to supply timers. Some chairs bring timers with them while others opt to use an app or a feature on their phone, while still others use an online stopwatch. It is best to assume you will not have access to stable internet, so do not plan to rely on an online stopwatch. In addition, do not rely on a wristwatch because in most cases features are very limited and it looks unprofessional.

- *Resolution editing.* Writing resolutions is an art that takes practice as well as the basic knowledge of the format. During your team's practices, it is best to take their resolutions and correct them as if it were a real council session. As chair, it is your responsibility to ensure that badly formatted resolutions are corrected before introduction and convoluted language is clarifiable by you and the resolution's sponsors.

## *Upper Secretariat*

- *Contact the Secretariat.* Conference is a horrible time to meet your secretariat. The Secretary-General should reach out to the entire secretariat and assist the rest of the secretariat in reaching out to each other. Every member of the Secretariat should know each other before the conference even if just by simple introduction and some biographical information. Sharing personal interests and even stories from MAL will help to provide perspective on your points of view as a Secretariat member. Lastly, pre-conference planning allows Secretariat members to share their motivation for applying to be secretariat, what they hope to get out of the experience, and to begin understanding the Secretary-General's plan and how it will work at conference.

- *Have a conference plan.* There is more than one way to organize an Upper and Lower Secretariat and there is more than one way to manage a conference. There is no right answer in this regard and many of the structural elements of Secretariat are personality and personal preference based. This even comes down to how a chair introduces themselves to the committee – what seems like something routine can set the entire tone of the session. Walking into the first day of conference with no plan and "winging it" is a surefire way to fail miserably as secretariat, and in doing so harm the conference experience of everyone in attendance. The conference plan should include how you wish to communicate, how and when your secretariat will meet, and how to divvy up responsibilities while at conference.

## Summary

The National Council representative(s), the conference director(s), and the Secretariat are the nuts and bolts of every conference. To provide a well-run conference, all of them must be prepared, but that is only half the battle. The best conferences feature a healthy relationship between National Council representative(s), conference director(s), and the Secretariat. Once conference starts, these individuals should come together to discuss their plans and their goals for the conference. If unprepared, the Secretariat members cannot participate in that discussion and thus cannot be a part of the overall direction of their own conference. This becomes immediately obvious to all conference participants when the National Council representative(s) are taking over the role of the Secretariat or the conference director is taking over the role of the National Council representatives.

The Secretariat plays an integral role in the success of any conference. It is imperative that students on the Secretariat take their role seriously, adequately prepare, and then spend conference working to provide the best learning experience for everyone present. As in the real League, the Secretariat and his or her staff provide the infrastructure necessary for delegations to represent their state's policy while forming a common League policy presumably for the betterment of all Arab states. In the MAL experience, the Secretariat provides the same function. By understanding your role as conference leadership, by keeping mindful of best practices and helpful tips for excelling as a Secretariat member, and by arriving at conference adequately prepared, the student Secretariat helps create an effective learning and competitive environment.

# 7

# The logistics of running a team

Running a team is a challenging but rewarding endeavor. The critical role advisors and team leaders play in the development of team members pays an incalculable return when you get to watch these students perform. To meet that goal, advisors and team leaders must structure their program correctly. There are many options for structuring a team, each option bringing its own advantages and disadvantages. To complicate matters, there is no best option across the board for a team structure. The reality is that an effective program is designed based on the interests of your students and the needs of your institution. From there, it is just a question of how you handle the structuring of the program, how you find funding so the team can travel, and then how you build your team. This chapter endeavors to provide options and best practices for each of those decisions, while also identifying some pitfalls that can be easily avoided.

## How to structure your program: club, class, hybrid options

There is no best practice on how to structure your program in terms of a class or club dynamic. There are examples across the United States of successful teams that are structured solely as either clubs or classes, as well as of hybrid structures involving both. The advantage of the club structure is that the program is more likely to grow a sense of camaraderie and team spirit among the student members. It also emboldens student membership to take ownership of the program and promote its well-being on your campus. Lastly, the status of an official student group may have policy and funding advantages depending on your college or university's policies.

The advantage of the classroom environment is that it is easier to maintain a training program, impose compliance with required reading assignments, introduce writing assignments, and practice simulation schedules when a grade is in the balance. Teams operating within a classroom-only environment are also less likely to lose students part way through preparation for unacceptable reasons. Finally, having it listed as a course offering acts as its own recruitment tool for your program.

The hybrid structure presents the most challenges, but also has the most advantages. This structure possesses all the advantages of both the aforementioned systems. As the advantages are complementary and do not overlap, this is a significant plus of the structure. The downside is that it requires the faculty advisor and student leadership to create a balance between the classroom and club environments. Poorly balancing the two elements diminishes the value of one of them and, by extension, the weight of the advantages of that half of the program. Furthermore, the program has to make complicated decisions about the treatment of students who participate only in the club or only in the class. In most cases, it will take several years of experimenting, balancing, and re-balancing, until a program has found the right mix of class and club requirements and class and club interactions. If found, this plan establishes a great structure that a program will benefit from for many years to come.

## Recruitment

One of the biggest challenges to starting a new team is recruitment. Recruiting members for a new program can seem like a daunting task, but it is less of a challenge when you think of potential sources of new members.

### Similar student organization

Many schools already have an existing Model United Nations or similar program. Students in these programs are already predisposed toward this type of program and are a likely addition to your MAL team. Similarly, a debate or public-speaking team tends to have students open to the idea of an MAL program with its competitive public speaking. Next, consider discipline-based student organizations already established at your institution. For example, a political science club, an international relations council, or similar program will have students who are topically interested in this type of program. Your school's office for student activities can provide any faculty member with a list of student organizations to scan for other potential groups.

In addition, consider the possibility of any ethnic, cultural, or language-based student groups at your school. An MAL program may appeal to students in an Arab student association, an Africa club, or a club for students practicing the Arabic language. The overall goal in approaching these and other student organizations is twofold: first, to tailor the advertising of your program to a group of students you are already aware of having interests in the region or to a debate program or other area of interest overlap with an MAL program; and, second, to capitalize on social networks already present in the organization to entice other students to join in order to participate with their friends or associates.

### Course credit option

For programs that have no classroom environment, faculty and student leadership of an MAL program can approach faculty members who teach courses in International Relations, Comparative Politics, Middle East Studies, or other similar areas of topical overlap and ask them to offer participation in MAL as an extra-credit opportunity in their course. Alternatively, if your institution's policy allows for one-credit courses, this can be used to create a credit-earning opportunity without having a full Model Arab League course. If the program decided to have a course element, then the instructor of record should consider university-wide requirements that may be met by the course. This provides free advertising of your program by making it a solution to graduation requirements beyond just course credit or major requirements for a smaller pool of students. Lastly, if a course does not exist and a faculty member does not wish for it to exist, the use of directed studies to provide credit can be an effective reward for student participation and, therefore, an effective tool for student recruitment.

### Student rosters

Most academic departments maintain some form of contact list for their enrolled majors and minors. Reaching out to students through department infrastructure is a great way to spread the word about an MAL program and its meeting schedule. They are also an effective way to encourage word-of-mouth recruitment. Similarly, classes with a relevant topical focus are a captive audience to present an MAL program to with the permission of the instructor of record. Sending student members of your program to these classes to speak for as little as five to ten minutes is an effective method of seeking members.

Another roster to look into is the admissions roster. Many admissions programs have lists of students by interests declared on their applications for admissions. Any major or student organization noted above are potential categories on these interest declarations and can be an effective way to build a mailing list to potential freshman members of your program.

## How to find funding

If getting students involved is not the biggest challenge to any program – especially a new program – then finding funding is the biggest headache. There is no set paradigm for funding an MAL program and every school seems to do this differently. What is important is to be aware of as many potential funding sources as possible and to explore all of them. Some universities have funding for Model UN-like programs already established in their student activities or departmental funds. Some schools have no official policy and one has to be advocated for to establish funding for a program. Still other programs are housed at schools that lack funding opportunities entirely and simply cannot support a program of this type. In the end, advisors and student leaders will have to figure out for themselves the funding realities and policies at their institutions without much guidance from this text or any other source. Once the funding situation is established, there are some options for programs that have either no funding or are underfunded.

### Solutions for underfunded or unfunded programs

Programs that lack enough money to handle its costs will have to find a solution to cover the shortfall. This can be approached logically in one of two ways: by reducing costs or increasing funds. To reduce the costs of a program consider a few of the following cost-saving options for a budget shortfall.

### Alternative travel arrangements

The most convenient means of travel is usually not the least expensive. Adjusting travel plans based on cost will make up part of a budget shortfall. If possible, driving to a conference will save the most money and can help drastically reduce the costs of attending. College/university vans make this easier, but leaning on members of the program to provide vehicles has been a solution for some teams. In worst-case scenarios, students have shared the burden of costs for gas to lessen the cost of driving even more.

Additionally, the conference hotel is not always the least expensive option for housing at a conference. While most conference hotels have a "conference rate" for participants, that rate may not be the lowest in close proximity to the conference location. Checking with your institution's administration can also let you know if the school has a deal with a specific hotel chain for a standard rate. Athletic programs often have these agreements and they are usually available to any travel for university business. The downside to alternative housing is that your team is not staying with all the other teams. This takes away some of the camaraderie among delegations that is best fostered during off-conference hours.

### Supplemental funding

Most teams get their primary funding from one or two sources: a budget from the department they are connected to or fees paid by student participants. As a supplement, advisors and student leaders can approach other, similar, funding sources for small funds to bolster the cost. Many relevant academic depart-ments can afford a few hundred dollars toward this kind of endeavor if they have one or two majors in the program. If the program is funded primarily on the back of academic departments, approaching the student activities or simi-lar office may result in a similar minor degree of funding.

Since research is a key aspect of MAL preparation, exploring your institu-tion's equivalent of the deans and provost office for undergraduate research funds may also be a potential avenue of funding for the program. Often, college or uni-versity libraries have similar research programs and may be interested in donat-ing funds. It is important to think creatively and "pitch" your MAL program as meeting the mission of your institution or of an office within your institution.

*External funding*

If all options on campus are tapped and not supplying the necessary funds, consider looking for funding off-campus. For schools in smaller communities where there are few academic institutions, local businesses and government agencies can sometimes provide some assistance. Chain restaurants often have fundraiser programs, often called "percentage nights," where they will revenue share for a single night where you host an event at their establishment. If you are in a major city where there are many academic institutions, you may find that some businesses and agencies are being hit multiple times for various types of program from several different academic institutions. In that case, the hunt for external funding can take longer.

First, continue to shop around. Look for a business that has a mission similar to or compatible with the mission and goals of an MAL team. Second, remember that options like the aforementioned chain restaurant are often at minimal cost to the company, so they are likely to say "yes" if they have that type of setup to any group that walks through their door. Last, speak with your institution's equivalent of external affairs, gifts, or government relations offices. Partnering with these offices is a great way to try to find a benefac-tor for your team. A benefactor is an individual or corporation that agrees to sponsor a program at the university for several years. There are many steps to walk through at most universities for this kind of sponsorship, but it can be a long-term solution if it works.

Finally, connect with your school's alumni office. For older programs, alumni of the program are a great financial resource. Even just five alumni donating $25 to your program is enough to pay gas to drive one carload of students to a conference. For newer programs, reaching out to alumni of the academic department can be a way to start this kind of financial support for a program. Effective alumni offices will be able to target potentially interested alumni with information about your program and an ask for support.

*Advocating your program to university officials*

A key factor in establishing and maintaining funding for an MAL program is advocating the value of the program to your college/university. An academic institution is more likely to fund a program that meets the institution's mission, promotes the value or level of success of the institution, or makes the institution look good. A crucial part of this, which is covered later in this chapter, involves placing an appropriate context on a team's performance and framing that outcome as demonstrating how the program has achieved its goals. Another key aspect is promoting the team's existence, its performance, and its successes to key individuals at the college/university.

At least once a semester, the faculty advisor and the student leadership should send a letter listing achievements, programs, and other accomplishments to the institution's equivalent of the provost, the dean that the program is governed under (both the dean of the college of the faculty advisor and the dean or vice-president under which student activities are housed), the applicable department/program heads, and your institution's public/media relations office. Once a year, or in the event of an accomplishment framable as significant, a separate letter should be sent to the institution's president.

Students should be encouraged to list their MAL participation and accomplishments in their resumes and in any applications to university-sponsored scholarships, programs, and opportunities. The more the student members of an MAL program promote the program as having value in their lives and their futures, the more this adds to the air of value of the program among relevant offices at the academic institution.

## Effective team policies

A critical aspect of running a successful MAL program is developing effective policies for management of the program. Regardless of structure, every program needs to have a few basic policies with which to govern. Having these policies provides clarity to the membership, understanding of best practices and performance measures necessary to be a participant, and legitimizes the authority of the faculty advisor and student leaders. Depending on the structure of the program, different polices are advisable for the management of an MAL team. Best practices recommend the following:

*For all programs, regardless of structure:*

- guidelines for conduct/behavior while at conference;
- a rubric for assessment of delegate performance;
- a process for selecting members for your team.

*For programs structured as a class or a hybrid class-club:*
• a course syllabus (discussed in Chapter 9).

*For programs structured as a club or a hybrid class-club:*
• the organization governing document (typically, a constitution);
• the organization bylaws governing various rules and policies.

The remainder of this section provides samples and guidance on creating the documents necessary for all programs. Chapter 9 will cover best practices for a syllabus. As student organization governing documents and bylaws are usually covered by policies at each academic institution, they are omitted from this section.

### Code of conduct

All members of an MAL program are representatives of their academic institutions as well as of themselves and their programs. Therefore, their behavior, their performance, and their personal decisions are all positive or negative reflections on all of the above. Without an established code of conduct, students may feel less accountable to prudent behavior and meaningful participation at the conference. Most academic institutions already have a code of conduct for their students which is in force at all times, including while on location at a conference. It is important to note that not all institutions have these, not all institutions' codes have provisions that cover unique issues and environments that may come up on location, and not all students are even aware these codes are relevant while on location. Therefore, it is a best practice for an MAL team to develop a code and enforce it on their participants.

It is also helpful to adopt a procedure where the rules are presented to members of the program and they are then required to sign that they have read them. This avoids future headaches related to consistency of presentation or claims they have never seen them.

### Sample <<Your Team>> Code of Conduct

<<Your Institution>> provides hotel rooms for the benefit of all students affiliated with <<Your Team>> (hereafter referred to as We). For safety and liability reasons, delegates must return to and sleep in the rooms to which they are assigned by the program.

We will represent <<Your Institution>> by respecting the dignity of all other delegates [<<Your Team>> and otherwise] both in and out of committee.

As representatives of <<Your Institution>>, we are expected to exemplify good behavior and to maintain our positive reputation while traveling.

We will abide by the reasonable requests of the head delegate and faculty advisor and will follow these rules, the applicable parts of the <<Your Institution>> Code of Conduct, and other rules/expectations set down by the faculty advisor and head delegate.

We will be accompanied by at least one other <<Your Institution>> student or advisor, noting the following exceptions: students may leave the group for a reason pre-approved by <<Your team>>.

We will not irresponsibly consume alcohol before, in transit to, or during any conference event. We will not show any signs of having been drinking while attending any conference event, where drinking is not the primary function. We will not at any time use or possess illegal substances while at conference.

We will always abide by curfews and meeting times as set by the head delegate and faculty advisor, noting that:

1) hotel curfew is defined as being inside the premises or at an outside facility of the hotel, and
2) room curfew is defined as being in your assigned hotel room.

We will always appear in proper conference attire for all committee sessions and understand that failure to bring proper attire to conference may result in being asked to leave or shop for proper attire.

The <<Your Institution>> hotel rooms are intended for the use of all members of the team for their comfort, rest, and relaxation. Our hotel rooms are not intended for any other purpose or use. We agree to respect the dignity of all delegates and to abide by <<Your Institution>> policies on sexual harassment.

We will be observant of other <<Your Institution>> delegates and shall take such steps to be proactive, supportive, and helpful should any member of the team be in need.

We will not damage or deface the hotel or other properties connected to the conference.

We will be a delegation of well-prepared delegates who add to debate and who are always in committee during session.

### Final Provisions of <<Your Team>> Code of Conduct

*Consequences*

1) It is the duty of all members to keep the team's leadership (head delegate, faculty advisor and e-board) informed of situations while on conference.
2) It is the duty of the head delegate, faculty advisor and e-board to execute consequences for infractions of this Code of Conduct.

3) If a delegate's behavior is judged to be inappropriate, the following may apply:

(a) immediate removal from conference;

(b) travel to away conferences or participation in other club activities may not be permitted;

(c) a negative impact on the delegate's grade if taking the course for credit;

(d) the situation may be reported to the appropriate University authority.

*Appeal*

If a delegate wishes to appeal, please reference <<Your Team's Policies>>

*Interpretation*

1) Interpretation of this Code shall rest with the team's leadership and the Advisor.

2) Final consideration of sanctions for breach of the Code shall rest with the team's leadership and/or Advisor.

3) The <<Your Team>> Council Code of Conduct applies to students from the moment students depart the campus and is in force until the team returns to the campus.

I, _____ [Print name], hereby acknowledge that I have read and agree to the above.

Signature Line: _____

Date: _____

## Running practices

### Designing a practice topic and guide

A practice topic should be selected that is easy to research, preferably having key aspects in common knowledge, so that the topic is not itself an inhibitor to practice. Often, the best practice topics are based on topics from that year's MAL Provisional Agenda, as many committees have overlapping topics. The purpose of holding practices is to have student participants be more comfortable with the dynamics of committee upon arrival at a conference. Many students and faculty feel practice should involve complex topics rooted in serious issues in the Middle East. This is counterintuitive, as it distracts from the purpose of the practice: to practice. The more complex a topic for practice, the more detailed the guide needs to be. Simple topics require nothing more than a description of paragraph or two to focus preparation and the start of discussion. More complicated practice topics should have a guide based on the sample found in Appendix N. The guide should be shorter because it will be for one topic and that topic should not have a lot of subtopics or side discussions. The more focused, the better.

### Assigning your team to countries

Once you have a topic, the best next step is to identify the countries *most* relevant to the debate and assign one to each student in your program who either has a lot of experience or is very confident when speaking in public. Partnering them with someone who has very little experience is a great way to mentor, if you have enough students in your program to do that. If not, create a list of "allied" countries on the topic and assign each newer or less-confident participant to those. It is important to tell the more experienced members which is their allied state, so they understand their role is to practice and to mentor that state at the same time. Finally, assign a country to yourself if you are not chairing.

### Role of the faculty advisor or head delegate in practice

The role of the faculty advisor in practice is to debate, chair, and observe. You should have some debating experience and some chairing experience, otherwise it will be harder for you to mentor your students when they have questions about participating. During practices, you should always be involved in some capacity, but you should also be observing and taking notes if necessary. The job of the advisor during practices is to promote growth on the team. That is only possible if you are able to provide constructive criticism based on your observations of the debate.

### Providing feedback

At the end of every practice, you should provide feedback on the debate. Your more experienced students can assist with this, but they will need feedback as well, so leave time for that. As a best practice, consider providing feedback publically in front of the entire program. Everyone in the room should witness a student's successes and failures mid-practice, so they can all learn from the feedback on another student regarding what was done well and what was done poorly. Make sure to use this time as an opportunity to encourage newer students with positive feedback on their growth over the past few practices and be extra sure to deflate any egos growing in the room. These egos tend to cause many headaches for an advisor at conference and usually end up embarrassing the team at some point.

Use feedback sessions to re-teach the Rules of Procedure, resolution writing, and best practices for debate participation. When an error is made, it can facilitate instruction on how to have done better or what to avoid. As part of an assessment of student performance, invite self-assessment and peer assessment to provide other perspectives and remove a adversarial atmosphere where the advisor or team leader is simply being critical of everyone's performance. Furthermore, use positive feedback opportunities as a place to provide context from readings. Students often perform strategies and political interaction discussed in the readings without realizing it. Pointing out how "delegate X's statement is a great example of what Morganthau was talking about" is a clever way to re-teach valuable ideas in the readings in a less boring format or setting.

### Rubric for assessment of delegate performance

Since effective performance as a delegate involves many different skills and levels of involvement over the course of a simulation or a series of simulations, it is helpful to provide your students with a rubric for assessment. In Table 7.1 below is a copy of the rubric used by the Northeastern University (NU) team. The NU delegation uses it not just to evaluate its team, but also as a rubric for selecting travel members of its program. Most MAL teams that are getting started or relatively small will never need a rubric this detailed for selection purposes, as they will travel the vast majority of their program. For larger teams, a process will be necessary for selecting students to participate in a conference that will not accommodate their entire membership.

The rubric is provided in its entirety to help teams of all sizes. Smaller teams should consider which parts of the rubric are less helpful for their purposes and omit them. The included rubric provides four levels of performance for each category and a description of the type of performance that is indicative at that level. It is important to assess delegates with a level-based system so they can see the relative strengths and weaknesses of each of their skills. Students given a clear and weighted assessment will be best able to identify the areas that will have the greatest return on their performance and the investment of time necessary to improve.

## Placing context on winning, losing, and the outcome of conference

Every student attending conference should have a goal for his or her performance. Attaining that goal is the definition of success in an MAL conference. Having the single goal of winning an award is a dangerous idea because awards are not always given to the best student in the room. At the end of conference, prior to returning home if at all possible (the trip back is often the perfect time for this), every team should debrief as a group and discuss what went right and what went wrong. Having a tradition for debriefing is a nice way to build

TABLE 7.1: Rubric for assessing your delegates

| Category | 4 | 3 | 2 | 1 |
|---|---|---|---|---|
| Use of facts/statistics | Every major point was well supported with several relevant facts, statistics, and/or examples. | Every major point was adequately supported with relevant facts, statistics, and/or examples. | Every major point was supported with facts, statistics, and/or examples, but the relevance of some was questionable. | Every major point was not supported. |
| Quality of information and preparation | Information clearly related to the main topic. It included several supporting details and/or examples. Preparation efforts were obvious. | Information clearly related to the main topic. It provided 1–2 supporting details and/or examples. Preparation efforts were usually obvious. | Information clearly related to the main topic. No details and/or examples were given. Preparation efforts were sometimes obvious. | Information had little or nothing to do with the main topic. Preparation efforts were not obvious. |
| Presentation style | Consistently used gestures, eye contact, tone of voice, and a level of enthusiasm in a way that kept the attention of the audience. | Usually used gestures, eye contact, tone of voice, and a level of enthusiasm in a way that kept the attention of the audience. | Sometimes used gestures, eye contact, tone of voice, and a level of enthusiasm in a way that kept the attention of the audience. | Often had a presentation style that did not keep the attention of the audience. |
| Organization | All arguments were clearly tied to an idea (premise) and organized in a tight, logical fashion. | Most arguments were clearly tied to an idea (premise) and organized in a tight, logical fashion. | All arguments were clearly tied to an idea (premise) but the organization was sometimes not clear or logical. | Arguments were not clearly tied to an idea (premise). |
| Problem solving | Actively looked for and suggested solutions to problems. | Refined solutions suggested by others. | Did not suggest or refine solutions, but was willing to try out solutions suggested by others. | Did not try to solve problems or help others solve problems. Let others do the work. |
| Focus on the task | Consistently stayed focused on the task and what needed to be done. Very self-directed. | Focused on the task and what needed to be done most of the time. Other group members could count on this person. | Focused on the task and what needed to be done some of the time. Other group members had sometimes to nag, prod, and remind to keep this person on task. | Rarely focused on the task and what needed to be done. Let others do the work. |

TABLE 7.1: *(cont.)*

| Category | 4 | 3 | 2 | 1 |
|---|---|---|---|---|
| **Contributions and committee leadership** | Routinely provided useful ideas when participating in the group. A leader who contributed a lot of effort. | Usually provided useful ideas when participating in the group. A strong group member who tried hard. | Sometimes provided useful ideas when participating in the group. A satisfactory group member who did what was required. | Rarely provided useful ideas when participating in the group. May have refused to participate. |
| **Working with others** | Almost always listened to, shared with, and supported the efforts of others. Tried to keep people working well together. | Usually listened to, shared, with, and supported the efforts of others. Did not cause "waves" in the group. | Often listened to, shared with, and supported the efforts of others, but sometimes was not a good team member. | Rarely listened to, shared with, and supported the efforts of others. Often was not a good team player. |
| **Attendance (does not include excused absenses)** | Always attended meetings. | Usually attended meetings. | Sometimes attended meetings. | Rarely attended meetings. |
| **Rules and Procedures** | Demonstrated an in-depth knowledge of the Rules and Procedures. Regularly helped others understand those rules. | Usually demonstrated an in-depth knowledge of the Rules and Procedures. Usually helped others understand those rules. | Sometimes demonstrated an understanding of the Rules and Procedures. Sometimes helped others understand those rules. | Rarely demonstrated an understanding of the Rules and Procedures. |

Note: The supplied rubric was created by Noreen Leahy and adopted by Northeastern University's MAL team as a guideline for assessing and selecting travel members of their program. (Some of the text has been edited slightly for this book.)

team spirit, tell stories about conference, and provide valuable feedback on performance.

Feedback should be tailored to each student and be based on your understanding of what the student's goal was for that particular conference. Students who win awards as part of their goal should be congratulated, but do not allow the award to substitute for positive feedback or necessary negative feedback. The award, while nice, should be irrelevant to your assessment of their performance.

Lastly, it is important to note that placing context on the outcome of conference is necessary at your institution as well as among your students. Every post-conference cleanup should include an email or letter to all relevant offices at your institution to inform them of your team's performance. The letter is pretty simple if your team won multiple awards and a little more strategic if your team did not. Remember that the participation of your institution brought something of value to the conference and that therefore the conference brought something of value to the institution. Explaining to chairs, deans, and others what value was brought to conference, and what value was brought back to campus, helps administrators understand what their investment in your program bought. Sharing those details in a carefully designed letter will bring all sorts of benefits over time.

## Summary

Running a team is a challenging but rewarding experience that requires establishing team policies, guiding a team, raising money, and managing training. In short, it requires advisors or team leaders to wear many different hats. This chapter has provided some general practices for structuring your team, leading it, and helping it to achieve its goals. These are all planning and structural elements to a program that are primarily pre-conference and pre-travel. The next chapter focuses on the role of the advisor, or student leader, while at conference.

It is important to remember that while at conference you have many resources for advice and support. Some of the best advice for funding, assessment, and so on comes from your own faculty peers at conference. Make sure to get to know your faculty peers at the meetings and outside of debate, as their institutional memory is a very valuable resource for everyone.

# 8

# The role of the faculty advisor at conference

While it may seem as though most of the work on the faculty advisor occurs before attending conference, some of your most important mentoring occurs once the conference has begun. Students will grow exponentially in their speaking, writing, and researching skills in the 48–72 hours of a conference weekend, and your continued support of them throughout the weekend will help them to navigate this (at times) stressful experience. The process of that growth also involves making good and bad decisions. Understanding which decisions are which and how to move forward from bad decisions is a critical role of the advisor mid conference.

## Observing your team

Faculty advisors should move from council room to council room observing their students *for the entirety of the conference*. Students notice if you have not been in their room and many interpret your lack of presence as lack of caring. There are many strategies for observing your students: some faculty advisors will sit in a council session for 30–45 minutes at a time, while other advisors are much more mobile. Some advisors bring assistants with them who will observe as second sets of eyes in councils while the advisor is sitting in one elsewhere or tending to other responsibilities at the conference. In any case, you should observe each of your students in formal, moderated, and unmoderated debate. Unless absolutely necessary, faculty advisors should simply witness their students in action. Interrupting students in any way can cause them to lose their flow and can be detrimental to their performance.

The best faculty advisors will check in with each of their students during the course of each day at conference with positive and constructive feedback. While this sort of feedback can come from the head delegate, a faculty advisor who is most directly involved with their team is most easily able to advocate for their team should any problems or concerns arise.

## Providing advice and expertise

While your top priority will always be your own team, upon arrival at a conference a faculty advisor's role shifts to one of being a conference advisor. Any student may approach you with questions and your role as mentor includes them as well. Many times, faculty members may be brought in as experts in their field for particular scenarios in councils, especially in the Arab Court of Justice (ACJ) or in the Joint Cabinet Crisis (JCC). For instance, at any time, the ACJ may request from the National Council on U.S.-Arab Relations (NCUSAR) an "expert witness" on a particular topic or segment of law. Faculty advisors are often chosen to be these witnesses, as each of the program's advisors come to the conference with their own unique expertise.

In advising your own team, remember that you are your team's expert on the League, on your state, and on participation at conference. Your students, as well as your head delegate, should all feel comfortable in coming to you for guidance and you should be available to provide that guidance. The consistently successful Model Arab League (MAL) teams at Nationals and most Regionals every year have the most active advisors who observe sessions, speak with their delegates, and provide assistance when asked.

Faculty advisors are also integral to suggesting and implementing new programs and the expansion of current councils for the conference. While MAL is generally a student-led conference, the advice given by faculty advisors is integral to the institutional memory of the program itself. A successful faculty advisor recognizes their role in the continued success of this program and as such will advise all those who need assistance regardless of affiliation.

## Advocating on behalf of your school and students

From small issues regarding air conditioning to larger issues such as problems with chairing, the faculty advisor is a major part of the advocating process for teams (including the head delegate). In many cases, students do not feel comfortable approaching other delegates (or other faculty advisors) with concerns, so it is the responsibility of the faculty advisor to serve as that liaison.

In addition to inter-delegate issues, faculty advisors also serve as the main advocate for their teams to the NCUSAR. As the official (namely, legal) representative of your institution and its participants at the conference, you have the authority to advocate on behalf of your team and institution. Faculty advisors, therefore, also have the responsibility of advocating for the best learning opportunity possible for their students. At each regional and national conference, there will be daily meetings of the faculty advisors, where advisors can feel free to bring up any concerns they may have to the NCUSAR and the Secretariat. While advisors should encourage students to be their own advocates in professional diplomatic ways, advisors are the last line of defense for students.

## Maintaining your team's reputation at conferences

The age range of the students attending MAL collegiate conferences is 18–22. For many, it is their first time traveling to the city hosting the conference (this is especially true for NUMAL) and, for most, alcohol is a newly recognized form of recreation. While most students make it through four years of the program without committing an egregious faux pas, there are always a special few that ruin it for everyone. Proper planning before conference (including writing a Travel Code of Conduct, reminding students of their college/university's alcohol/drug/Title IX policies, etc.) can mitigate some of these problems, but it will not eliminate the risk entirely. Once something goes wrong at a conference, faculty advisors and head delegates must swiftly respond to the situation to ensure the safety of all their participants and to preserve the reputations of their schools.

A marked negative swing in a team's reputation can have cascading consequences for a team, sometimes for years to come. Student participants tell stories from year to year and a team's reputation can be impacted by storytelling for years simply because of one incident. Depending on the severity of the situation and the likelihood of details of the incident getting back to your campus, this could result in a loss of funding or travel privileges. In some circumstances, the incident has been inappropriate or severe enough that a team was not invited back to a conference they previously enjoyed attending. The easiest way to worsen the situation, in these latter cases, is to be a faculty advisor who does not appreciate the severity of the incident.

Most individuals reading this chapter are going to assume the issues at hand here are excessive consumption of alcohol, illicit consumption, or various forms of physical or sexual harassment. While all of these can happen at conference, the more common and equally damaging incidents are the ones that are often ignored by faculty. Severe lapses in diplomatic behavior, rude or cruel treatment of other participants, promotion of racist or sexist ideas, and similar "in-committee" transgressions are far more common and far more damaging to a team's reputation because they happen in front of everyone.

Reminding your students early and often prior to a conference that their behavior affects not only themselves but their entire team goes a long way to curbing some of these problems before they can arise. Conducting practices that demonstrate proper tone and behavior at all times can help to create a culture of positive behavior for your team. Most of all, being an involved and active advisor can help mitigate these behaviors, as they are less likely to occur when faculty advisors are in committee.

## Summary

The role of the advisor at conference is simple: provide your student and your institution with effective support and representation. Too many advisors see conference as an opportunity to spend time in the host city on their university's dime, but that shortchanges the program. Faculty must observe their team in order to provide the best feedback possible, assist their students when needed, and protect the reputation of their institution and program. The best faculty advisors see their role at conference as providing this level of support at all times during council sessions. The worst faculty advisors see their role at conference as checking in once a day and are otherwise unavailable and show a general degree of disinterest in their students.

This chapter has provided some guidance on the best way for faculty advisors and team leaders to provide support for their students and their programs. Each advisor, however, needs to find a style and tone that fits their personality and grow into their role as advisor. New advisors should find mentors among the more experienced advisors who can provide advice, guidance, institutional memory, and even assist when needed. The most involved advisors tend to be supportive of other faculty peers, so reaching out to them early in a conference is a good first step to learning how to be an effective advisor.

# 9

# Model Arab League as a course

Chapter 7 showed that Model Arab League (MAL) can be offered as a course for credit out of multiple departments. Most commonly, a Political Science or International Relations department will offer the course, but a Middle East Studies, Arabic/Modern Language, Religious Studies, or History department can also offer it with success. This chapter poses solutions applicable to offering the course in a Political Science, International Relations, or Middle East Studies perspective, but the nuts and bolts of the course described in the forthcoming pages can be easily modified into a course appropriate for many other departments. The most important thing to remember is that an MAL course is a framework for exploring greater understanding of the Middle East through practical application of learning in an experiential educational framework.

## Establishing learning objectives

The primary challenge to offering MAL as a course is establishing learning objectives for the course. An effectively designed MAL course will serve two purposes: a hands-on learning environment that prepares students for participation in an MAL and a vehicle for instruction on the League of Arab States, regional politics, international law, and the nexus point of these topics. Whether your course focuses on the first or second purpose is contingent on the reason your school participates in an MAL conference, but balancing both is key to a successful course no matter the emphasis.

Courses that fail to incorporate a focus on being a delegate tend to fail in two ways. First, they do not adequately prepare a delegate to participate, which can impact on the learning experience by keeping the student from being comfortable enough to participate from the start of the conference. Students who are slower to adapt to the structure of a committee may not participate till halfway through the conference or possibly not at all. The primary mode of learning in a Model Simulation course is through practical application of knowledge in an experiential learning exercise. Failure to prepare a student for this learning scenario questions the purpose of the program as anything other than a lecture course on Middle East foreign relations. This relates to the second point of failure, which is the loss of all the student growth aspects of the MAL program.

As noted in the very beginning of this text, among the benefits of an MAL program are leadership development, public speaking, interpersonal relations, and a richer understanding of the Arab World through adopting the identity and interests of a League state. Most of these benefits are lost if the student is not encouraged and prepared to participate in a meaningful enough manner to obtain these learning objectives of the program.

## Learning assessment and grading

Many faculty advisors find it difficult to wrap their heads around the idea of grading an MAL class. Grading the course is actually very easy so long as you keep the following three absolutely critical factors in mind.

### Never grade based on awards or other forms of recognition at conference

Grading based on awards is cruel to student participants. As noted in Chapter 3 in the section discussing the awards, there are many factors not related to student performance or learning that could result in a student receiving a grade (better or worse) than the student deserves. Grading based on awards also places unfair stress on a student and has no purpose other than to ruin the learning experience for said delegate. Lastly, students whose academic progression is contingent on an award can often become unnecessarily aggressive and increasingly disrespectful the closer to the end of the conference they get if they feel their performance has not guaranteed that award, or if someone else in the room is excelling past them and threatening their grade potential.

### Never use one measure to grade every student

A best practice for grading performance is to assess the performance of each student in your program and then provide him or her with a benchmark they should meet for improvement. This allows the program to be a dynamic learning experience for all students regardless of their level of experience. It also means that the educational experience is not too low level and banal for a returning member of your program or too challenging for a new member. This grading paradigm does mean a bit more work for the faculty advisor, but comes with the benefit of better knowing the members of the team.

In order to provide a dynamic performance assessment paradigm, the faculty advisor must know each member of his team's experience in MAL and their level of performance. They must then be able to identify growth in learning through being an effective delegate. Later in this chapter, we will discuss tips for effective grading; for now, it is sufficient to note that faculty advisors who wish to use this method of grading must familiarize themselves with being a delegate while also assisting their students to become better delegates.

### Never grade solely based on accuracy of policy in debate

Students often find themselves in challenging positions where their state's policy on any given topic is either non-existent or completely incompatible with participation in debate. Every committee will have at least one topic where many states have no formal policy or interest in the topic (or, in even more indelicate situations, with an extremely unpopular formal policy) and which requires students to improvise in order to effectively participate. Remember that the order of the agenda is set by a simple majority of the committee; many states may have voted against the selection of the first topic. If a student finds themselves in a committee where their state would be marginalized due to topic relevancy, advisors and students must ask themselves if the preference is to be policy accurate and passively involved or to exaggerate the policy interest of a state to become actively involved. This is a tough balance and a generally unfair one to base a grade on.

The best practices of teams with highly competitive and highly respected programs have been to err on the side of becoming actively involved so long as the delegate is not violating the policy of the state. A delegate should never be encouraged to reverse state policy in order to participate, but a delegate should be encouraged to find areas of flexibility in state policy to allow them to be actively involved. Many ambassadors often find space between official state policy and state interests in order to negotiate with governments to which they are representatives. Advisors should be aware of this reality when grading and balance policy accuracy, state interest, and active participation as though they are all equally important. The worst delegates in conference are students who will do anything to participate, including directly violating state policy, and students who almost never participate on the pretense that their government has no relevant formal policy or influence.

Faculty advisors who wish their MAL program to be a rigorous vehicle for learning about politics and policy in the Middle East should assess that knowledge in both a non-debate situation and a debate situation. A non-debate situation, such as a position paper or a policy analysis paper, is an effective means to assess knowledge on politics and the region, because it is not affected by the dynamic of a committee experience. A debate situation allows for some assessment of policy, but only so far as it is understood that policy in a committee is a dynamic experience that changes based on the circumstances of negotiation. To that end, recall that students are often required to respond in character to a delegate who is ridiculously out of character, making policy accuracy harder in what had suddenly become the realm of fantasy.

## Tips for grading

Keeping these principles in mind, grading an MAL course becomes an effective assessment of a student's growth in an MAL experience, as well as assessing students' gained understanding of the Arab World, Middle East politics, and so on. As most faculty advisors are already familiar with the assessment of student papers, exams, and more, this section will bypass this discussion and focus solely on the assessment of performance in a conference-like experience. By "conference-like," this text implies assessment at an actual conference, at a simulation hosted on your campus by members of your team, a micro-conference experience in which two or more teams come together for a debate/practice, or in a series of shorter debate sessions that occur during class/club meetings.

Many faculty advisors find assessing performance difficult due to a lack of experience in MAL debate. Currently, only a handful of faculty advisors in the program were delegates on an MAL program during their high-school or college years, so lack of debate experience among faculty advisors is a common problem. This is another reason faculty should debate with their teams. During practices, faculty should be active participants and represent a country themselves. For grading purposes, this has two key benefits. First, by debating with your team, you learn how to be a better delegate, as do they. Over time, your experience with MAL committees will be greater than your entire team, allowing you to develop key insights in debate that can then be taught to your team. It also helps an advisor to gain an appreciation for some of the challenges of being in committee, to establish a strategy for success, and to acquire a measure for grading their students. Second, being in the debate means the faculty advisor is able to be in the midst of negotiations at all times and can gain a better sense of a student's performance, accuracy, and level of participation. Particularly experienced faculty shape debate as representatives in committee, allowing advisors to create learning opportunities in the simulation, challenge a particular student to gain a better understanding of their growth in the program, and help steer the debate back on track if the practice has lost its steam or gone in a direction that is less helpful for learning about the politics of the region or the MAL process.

Finally, for less-experienced faculty advisors, faculty advisors who themselves are uncomfortable with public speaking, or faculty advisors who are unwilling or unable to participate with their teams, consider involving one or two senior members of your program into the performance assessment process. In circumstances where the advisor is not able to effectively assess MAL debate performance, students with the requisite experience and skill can easily facilitate assessment of the use of rules, resolution writing, public speaking, and other conference aspects of the course's learning objectives.

## How to teach parliamentary procedure

Without question, the most boring (for everyone in the room) lecture in an MAL class will be instruction in the Rules of Procedure. Learning the rules can also be intimidating as the language is technical, legalistic, and complex. The easiest way to tackle this challenge is to teach the rules in a hands-on method instead of in a lecture environment. Consider having students in your program familiar with the rules demonstrate the Rules of Procedure in a scripted simulation or in a demonstration simulation. A scripted simulation is where you write a script of a council session and have your students walk through the session by reading off each motion.[1] You or one of your students can play the role of the chair in a scripted simulation learning experience. A demonstration simulation is where you have your experienced students sit in the front of a classroom and do a mini simulation with a chair. The topic can be serious or silly, as the only important aspect of the simulation is demonstrating each rule of procedure. If you are lucky to have a roughly equal number of new and experienced students, you can partner each inexperienced student with one of the experienced ones and have them be a bit more involved in the demonstration.

Whether you go the way of the demonstration or the scripted method, it is best to be realistic about how much your students can absorb in one session and use only the most important and most commonly used rules of procedure in the learning exercise until the students are comfortable with those rules. From that point on, add new rules each class/meeting and expand your students' ability to use the rules in a very methodical way. Below are suggestions of rules to introduce first, then second, and then once your students are more comfortable with the majority of the rules. Also note that the below does not include rules relevant to resolutions. It is a best practice to introduce rules relevant to resolutions at the same time as you teach how to write a resolution.

*List of rules to include in the first step of teaching parliamentary procedure:*

- Motion to Limit Debate
- Suspension of the Rules for the purpose of a Moderated Caucus
- Suspension of the Meeting
- Closure of Debate

---

[1] There is a scripted council session in Appendix J.

- Point of Order
- Point of Parliamentary Inquiry
- Point of Personal Privilege
- Yield to Another Country
- Yield to the Chair
- Yield to Points of Information

*List of rules to include in the second step of teaching parliamentary procedure:*

- Motion to Adjourn the Meeting
- Motion to Amend the Speaking Time
- Motion to Close the Speakers List
- Motion to Re-Open the Speakers List
- Motion to Expand Debate
- Right of Reply
- Motion to Suspend the Rules
- Q&A Session
- Round Robin
- Popcorn Debate
- Straw Poll
- Motion to Temporarily Revoke Delegate Rights

*List of rules that are rarely used and are not straightforward; these are best left for a student to learn in practice or at conference:*

- Motion to Appeal the Decision of the Chair
- Motion to Change a Topic's Assignment
- Motion to Change the Order of the Agenda
- Motion to Hear Speakers' Rights
- Motion to Read the Resolution
- Motion to Remove an Officer
- Motion to Set the Order of the Agenda
- Point of Reconsideration

*List of advanced rules that should be tackled only after students are comfortable with the rest of the Rules of Procedure:*

- Motion to Reconsider
- Motion to Divide the Question

## How to teach resolution writing

The best method of teaching resolution writing is to simply do it once the basic structure of the resolution has been introduced. It is important to emphasize that a resolution is nothing more than a really long sentence with two distinct parts separated by a "Be it hereby resolved" line. (See the resolution writing section in Chapter 3 for details.) Once the basic idea and structure is clear, I recommend providing a well-written sample (see page XXX for one) to your students for them to copy the format until they are comfortable with it.

Have your students sit in small groups – or individually – and draft resolutions on the same topic as a learning exercise. Once they finish, have them emailed to you and then put one or two of them up on a screen. Walk through each line of the resolution, commenting on structure/format, choice of words, and presentation of ideas. Ignore the actual policy in the document, as that is not the point of this exercise. It is important to correct every mistake visually so that students see what they can do better. In addition, it is important to identify language that, regardless of the policy, would make it very hard to pass a document. For example, a preambulatory clause that condemns "the Zionist entity" is death for a resolution because every member that has relations of any kind with Israel must, due to policy accuracy, vote against the document.

Once you have gone over a few resolutions, the best thing to do is to practice the Rules of Procedure regarding resolutions, debating a resolution, and amending a resolution. This is accomplished by having the resolutions you have just corrected introduced in a practice debate and simply walking through all of the procedures. It is, at this time, important to remember the point of this practice: to learn about the rules governing resolutions. No one should be caught up with the topic or the policy on the topic. For that reason, writing resolutions on silly or hypothetical topics is sometimes easier than conducting this learning process with a serious topic.

When introducing rules regarding resolutions, consider the level of difficulty of these rules, as we did for the Rules of Procedure in the previous section.

*List of rules to include in the first step of teaching parliamentary procedures relevant to resolutions:*

- Motion to Introduce a Draft Resolution
- Motion to Introduce Amendments
- Closure of Debate

*List of rules to include in the second step of teaching parliamentary procedures relevant to resolutions:*

- Motion to Adopt by Consent
- Motion to Vote by Roll-Call

*List of advanced rules relevant to resolutions that should be tackled only after students are comfortable with the rest of the Rules of Procedure:*

- Motion to Divide the Question

**Suggested readings**

Other than this textbook, there are no resources designed specifically for an MAL course. As such, faculty must be creative with reading requirements that will assist students in their knowledge of the international relations of the Middle East and with their performance as delegates in committee. It is worth noting that a required reading list does not have to be attached to a course and that some teams have such lists for their student groups and require completion of the reading list by all participants and not just those doing MAL for credit. Faculty should select reading assignments in the following three categories as a best practice for providing a well-rounded reading list for their course. These categories, along with some examples, are:

*Readings on the politics and foreign relations of the Middle East and the Arab World*
These readings should be scholarly or academic works that provide historically and politically accurate information about the League of Arab States, the Arab states themselves, and the politics of the Middle East. Faculty should consider readings that incorporate the relations of Arab states to Iran, Israel, Turkey, and the North African states, as these relations are often entire topics or important facets of topics.

Fawcett, Louis. 2013. *International Relations of the Middle East*, 3rd edition. Oxford: Oxford University Press.
Long, David, Mark Gasiorowski, and Bernard Reich. 2013. *The Government and Politics of the Middle East and North Africa*, 7th edition. Boulder, CO: Westview Press.

*Readings on international cooperation, international law, international regimes, and diplomacy*
These readings should be scholarly or academic works that explain political realities in international relations, possibly including the basics of realist thought, international law, or the structure of international regimes. A basic background on diplomacy is a helpful addition to any reading list, as it is at the heart of the MAL program.

Abbot, Kenneth, and Jack Snidal. 1998. "Why States Act through Formal International Organizations." *Journal of Conflict Resolution* 42.1 (February), p.3.
Axelrod, Robert. 2006. "How to Promote Cooperation." In *Evolution of Creation*. New York: Basic Books.
Morganthau, Hans. 2005. "Chapter 24: Diplomacy." In *Politics Among Nations: The Struggle for Power and Peace*. New York: McGraw-Hill Education.
Morganthau, Hans. 2005. "Chapter 25: The Future of Diplomacy." In *Politics Among Nations: The Struggle for Power and Peace*. New York: McGraw-Hill Education.

*Readings on negotiation and bargaining*

These readings should be scholarly or academic works that discuss strategies, tactics, and facets of negotiation and bargaining among states in the world. Faculty should not be concerned with finding resources that focus on the Arab World in this context for the simple reason that this part of the reading list is on best practices and strategies regardless of region or subregion.

Brams, Steven. 2003. "Superpower Crisis Bargaining and the Theory of Moves" and "Epilogue." In Steve Brahms (ed.), *Negotiation Games: Applying Game Theory to Bargaining and Arbitration.* London: Routledge.

Schelling, Thomas. 1981. "An Essay on Bargaining." In *The Strategy of Conflict.* Cambridge, MA: Harvard University Press.

Zagare, Frank. 2011. "La Guerre Européenne." In *Games of July: Explaining the Great War.* Ann Arbor: University of Michigan Press.

Below is a sample syllabus that provides learning objectives, grading, reading, and a schedule for practicing that can help a first-time MAL instructor shape an effective learning environment. Faculty and team leaders who are facilitating a program without a course may want to consider using a syllabus to show participating students the objective of their participation in the program and a sense of how preparation will take place from start until conference. In that case, it would be advised to consider how reading assignments can be deployed without grades to enforce compliance and the section on grading would need to be omitted, as it would have no purpose.

## Sample syllabus

### Course Number: Model Arab League

Professor:

Email:

Office Location:

Office Hours:

#### *Objective:*

The purpose of this course is twofold. First, it is to familiarize the student with the League of Arab States, its governing bodies, and its role in the International Community and in Arab Affairs. Second, is to prepare the student to participate in a diplomatic simulation of the politics of the Arab World at two to four conference simulations during the semester. Preparation involves the student learning about countries they will represent during the conference, learning about and synthesizing that country's policy on specific topics, and learning how to be the most effective delegate in a room with students representing 22+ Arab states.

**Required readings:**
- Reading Packet available for purchase in the bookstore.
- Your head delegate(s) may provide you with information/readings each week.
(These are in addition to reading assignments on the syllabus and are mandatory.)

## Readings

1. Morganthau, Hans. 2005. "Chapter 24: Diplomacy." In *Politics Among Nations: The Struggle for Power and Peace.* New York: McGraw-Hill Education.
2. Morganthau, Hans. 2005. "Chapter 25: The Future of Diplomacy." In *Politics Among Nations: The Struggle for Power and Peace.* New York: McGraw-Hill Education.
3. Axelrod, Robert. 2006. "How to Promote Cooperation." In *Evolution of Creation.* New York: Basic Books.
4. Keohane, Robert. 2005. "Cooperation and International Regimes." In *After Hegemony.* Princeton, NJ: Princeton University Press.
5. Schelling, Thomas. 1981. "An Essay on Bargaining." In *The Strategy of Conflict.* Cambridge, MA: Harvard University Press.
6. Mintz, Alex, and Karl De Rouen. 2010. "International Domestic, and Cultural Factors Influencing Foreign Policy Decision Making." In Alex Mintz and Karl De Rouen, *Understanding Foreign Policy Decision Making.* Cambridge: Cambridge University Press.

**Grading:**
Travel conferences (if applicable) and on-campus simulation*: 50%
Class simulation performance**: 20%
Class participation and attendance***: 20%
Rules of Procedure and League documents quiz: 10%
*All students are also required to attend the on-campus simulation. Those students selected for travel are required to fulfill all requirements of partici-pation in their assigned conference.*
** *All students are required to participate in the weekly simulation during class sessions.*
*** *Active participation includes demonstrating that readings, research, and other expected preparation is done by the student.*

*Conference participation:*
In order to earn full credit for conference participation, students will be expected to:

i. attend ALL head delegate sessions prior to the conference,

ii. attend ALL sessions of the conference,
iii. actively participate and contribute to the debate,
iv. adhere to university and IRC policies while at conference, and
v. hand in all paperwork required by the conference, professor, or the head delegate.

### *Attendance and participation policies:*

- Attendance at weekly class sessions is mandatory.
- Participation is defined as regular and meaningful contribution to class discussions and debates.
- Attendance at all conference sessions is required. Attendance at all conference events is required unless the professor approves a request for absence.
- Attendance at all other meetings, practices, and similar events is expected. Any necessary absence should be discussed with the professor and head delegate in advance.

### Academic Honesty/Integrity and Conference Etiquette

<<Your Institution's Academic Dishonesty Statement should go here >> For this course, a significant portion of your work will be representing the ideas/positions of others. You will also be working toward goals as a team. As such, it is understood that a significant portion of your work will involve synthesizing the best ideas/goals of your team and of your assigned government at conference. Plagiarism of any kind outside of the formal position of your state will not be tolerated at any time and may result in an F for any part of or the entire course.

During the course, information on conference rules, the College's Code of Student Conduct, and other matters pertaining to your actions at conference will be discussed. You are expected to hold to all of these. As the team's advisor, I hold the sole discretion to dismiss any member of the team from the conference. A dismissal from the conference may result in the lowering of your grade, or an F. Lastly, significant behavioral matters that would result in breach of the College's Code of Student Conduct will be handled according to the Constitution of International Relations Council and the policies of the Office of Student Conduct and Conflict Resolution.

### *Class and Conference Schedule:*
### Week 1

- Course/Program Introduction
- Rules of Procedure
- Icebreaker Simulation I

### Week 2

- Resolution Writing Rules and Tips
- Information Session I: LIST YOUR TOPIC HERE
- Morganthau I and II Readings

### Week 3

- Topic I Debate Session I

### Week 4

- Topic I Debate Session II

### Week 5

- Topic I Debate Session III

### Week 6

- Information Session II: LIST YOUR TOPIC HERE
- Koehane Readings

### Week 7

- Topic II Debate Session I

### Week 8

- Topic II Debate Session II

### Week 9

**Spring Break: No Classes**

### Week 10

- Topic II Debate Session III

### Week 11

- Information Session III: LIST YOUR TOPIC HERE
- Schelling, Mintz and De Rouen Readings

### Week 12

- Topic III Debate Session I

### Week 13

- Topic III Debate Session II

### Week 14

- Topic III Debate Session III

### Week 15/Finals Week

- Course Wrap-up
- End of Year Celebration

## Summary

Offering Model Arab League as a course at first sounds daunting, but it is a rather simple process once perspective is placed on the types of learning endeavors necessary for an effective course. The only real challenge is becoming accustomed to the different learning outcomes, measures of assessment, and course facilitation necessary for delivering an experiential education-based course.

Faculty who choose to offer an MAL course are often intimidated by their own lack of knowledge on how to be an effective delegate, chair a council, or draft a resolution. As all of these aspects are practice-oriented learning, it cannot be over-emphasized that the faculty are facilitators of this learning experience and not the sole experts. Engaging students into the teaching and mentoring is more beneficial than attempting to self-teach an MAL learning experience. Accepting that you are a part of the learning side of the course as well as the instructional side will not only assist you in teaching the course but will help build camaraderie on your team by involving you in the learning and participatory aspects of the MAL experience.

# Appendices section 1

## Important treaties

### Appendix A: Alexandria Protocol[1]

*The Alexandria Protocol; October 7, 1944*

The undersigned, chiefs and members of Arab delegations at the Preliminary Committee of the General Arab Conference, viz:

*The President of Preliminary Committee*

H.E. Mustafa al-Nahhas Pasha, Egyptian Prime Minister and Minister of Foreign Affairs; head of the Egyptian delegation;

*Syrian Delegation*

H.E. Sa'dallah al-Jabiri, Syrian Prime Minister and head of the Syrian delegation;
H.E. Jamil Mardam Bey, Minister of Foreign Affairs;
H E. Dr. Nagib al-Armanazi, Secretary General of the Presidency of the Syrian Republic;
H.E. M. Sabri al-'Asali, deputy of Damascus;

*Trans-Jordanian Delegation*

H.E. Tawliq Abu al-Huda Pasha, Trans-Jordanian Prime Minister and Minister of Foreign Affairs, head of the Trans-Jordanian delegation;
H.E Sulayman al-Sukkar Bey, Financial Secretary of the Ministry of Foreign Affairs;

---

[1] This text is taken from US Department of State 1947. Some typographical errors found in the original have been corrected.

*Iraqi Delegation*

H.E. Hamdi al-Bahjaji, Iraqi Prime Minister and head of the Iraqi delegation;
H.E. Arshad al-'Umari, Minister of Foreign Affairs;
H.E. Nuri al-Sa'id, former Iraqi Prime Minister;
H. E. Tahein al-'Askari, Iraqi Minister Plenipotentiary in Egypt;

*Lebanese Delegation*

H.E. Riyad al-Sulh Bey, Lebanese Prime Minister and head of the Lebanese
    delegation;
H.E. Salim Taqla Bey, Minister of Foreign Affairs;
H.E. Musa Mubarak, Chief of the Presidential Cabinet;

*Egyptian Delegation*

H.E. Nagib al-Hilali Pasha, Minister of Education;
H.E. Muhammad Sabri Aub-'Alam Pasha, Minister of Justice;
H.E. Muhammad Salah-al-din Bey, Under Secretary of State of the Ministry
    of Foreign Affairs,

Anxious to strengthen and consolidate the ties which bind all Arab countries
and to direct them toward the welfare of the Arab world, to improve its conditions, insure its future, and realize its hopes and aspirations,

And in response to Arab public opinion in countries,

Have met at Alexandria from Shawwal 8, 1363 (September 25, 1944) to
Shawwal 20, 1363 (October 7, 1944) in the form a Preliminary Committee of
the General Arab Conference, and have agreed as follows:

## 1. League of Arab States

A League will be formed of the independent Arab States which consent to join
the League. It will have a council which will be known as the "Council of the
League of Arab States" in which all participating states will be represented on
an equal footing.

The object of the League will be to control the execution of the agreements which the above states will conclude; to hold periodic meetings which
will strengthen the relations between those states; to coordinate their political
plans so as to insure their cooperation, and protect their independence and
sovereignty against every aggression by suitable means; and to supervise in a
general way the affairs and interests of the Arab countries.

The decisions of the Council will be binding on those who have accepted
them except in cases where a disagreement arises between two member states
of the League in which the two parties shall refer their dispute to the Council

for solution. In this case the decision of the Council of the League will be binding.

In no case will resort to force to settle a dispute between any two member states of the League be allowed. But every state shall be free to conclude with any other member state of the League, or other powers, special agreements which do not contradict the text or the present dispositions.

In no case will the adoption of a foreign policy which may be prejudicial to the policy of the League or an individual member state be allowed.

The Council will intervene in every dispute which may lead to war between a member state of the League and any other member state or power, so as to reconcile them.

A subcommittee will be formed of the members of the Preliminary Committee to prepare a draft of the statutes of the Council of the League and to examine the political questions which may be the object of agreement among Arab States.

## 2. Cooperation in Economic, Cultural, Social, and Other Matters

A. The Arab States represented on the Preliminary Committee shall closely cooperate in the following matters:
   1 Economic and financial matters, i.e., commercial exchange, customs, currency, agriculture, and industry.
   2 Communications, i.e., railways, roads, aviation, negation, posts and telegraphs.
   3 Cultural matters.
   4 Questions of nationality, passports, visas, execution of Judgments, extradition of criminals, etc.
   5 Social questions.
   6 Questions of public health.
B. A subcommittee of experts for each of the above subjects will be formed in which the states which have participated in the Preliminary Committee will be represented. This subcommittee will prepare draft regulations for cooperation in the above matters, describing the extent and means of that collaboration.
C. A committee for coordination and editing will be formed whose object will be to control the work of the other subcommittees, to coordinate that part of the work which is accomplished, and to prepare drafts of agreement which will be submitted to the various governments.
D. Then all the subcommittees have accomplished their work. The Preliminary Committee will meet to examine the work of the subcommittees as a preliminary step toward the holding of the General Arab Conference.

### 3. Consolidation of These Ties in the Future

While expressing its satisfaction at such a happy step, the Committee hopes that Arab States will be able in the future to consolidate that step by other steps, especially if post-war world events should result in institutions which will bind various Powers more closely together.

### 4. Special Resolution Concerning Lebanon

The Arab States represented on the Preliminary Committee emphasize their respect of the independence and sovereignty of Lebanon in its present frontiers, which the governments of the above States have already recognized in consequence of Lebanon's adoption of an independent policy, which the Government of that country announced in its program of October 7, 1943, unanimously approved by the Lebanese Chamber of Deputies.

### 5. Special Resolution Concerning Palestine

A. The Committee is of the opinion that Palestine constitutes an important part of the Arab World and that the rights of the Arabs in Palestine cannot be touched without prejudice to peace and stability in the Arab World.

The Committee also is of the opinion that the pledges binding the British Government and providing for the cessation of Jewish immigration, the preservation of Arab lands, and the achievement of independence for Palestine are permanent Arab rights whose prompt implementation would constitute a step toward the desired goal and toward the stabilization of peace and security.

The Committee declares its support of the cause of the Arabs of Palestine and its willingness to work for the achievement of their legitimate aims and the safeguarding of their just rights.

The Committee also declares that it is second to none in regretting the woes which have been inflicted upon the Jews of Europe by European dictatorial states. But the question of these Jews should not be confused with Zionism, for there can be no greater injustice and aggression than solving the problem of the Jews of Europe by another injustice, i.e., by inflicting injustice on the Arabs of Palestine of various religions and denominations.

B. The special proposal concerning the participation of the Arab Governments and peoples in the "Arab National Fund" to safeguard the lands of the Arabs of Palestine shall be referred to the committee of financial and economic affairs to examine it from all its angles and to submit the result of that examination to the Preliminary Committee in its next meeting.

In faith of which this protocol has been signed at Faruq I University at Alexandria on Saturday, Shawwal 20, 1363 (October 7, 1944).

Translation of the official communiqué of the Pan-Arab Preliminary Conference made by the American Delegation, Cairo; and collated with the Arabic text published in *Al-Ahram* (Cairo), Oct. 8, 1944, p. 3.

## Appendix B: Charter of the League of Arab States[2]

*Article I*

The League of Arab States is composed of the independent Arab states which have signed this Charter.

Any independent Arab state has the right to become a member of the League. If it desires to do so, it shall submit a request which will be deposited with the Permanent Secretariat General and submitted to the Council at the first meeting held after submission of the request.

*Article II*

The League has as its purpose the strengthening of the relations between the member-states, the coordination of their policies in order to achieve co-operation between them and to safeguard their independence and sovereignty; and a general concern with the affairs and interests of the Arab countries. It has also as its purpose the close co-operation of the member-states, with due regard to the organisation and circumstances of each state, on the following matters:

A.   Economic and financial affairs, including commercial relations, customs, currency and questions of agriculture and industry.
B.   Communications; this includes railroads, roads, aviation, navigation, telegraphs and posts.
C.   Cultural affairs.
D.   Nationality, passports, visas, execution of judgments and extradition of criminals.
E.   Social affairs.
F.   Health affairs.

*Article III*

The League shall possess a Council composed of the representatives of the member-states of the League; each state shall have a single vote, irrespective of the number of its representatives.

It shall be the task of the Council to achieve the realisation of the objectives of the League and to supervise the execution of agreements which the member-states have concluded on the questions enumerated in the preceding Article, or on any other questions.

It likewise shall be the Council's task to decide upon the means by which the League is to co-operate with the international bodies to be created in the

---

[2]   The official name of this document in the 1940s was "Pact of the League of Arab States." This text is taken from US Department of State 1957a. Some typographical errors found in the original have been corrected.

future in order to guarantee security and peace and regulate economic and social relations.

## Article IV

For each of the questions listed in Article II there shall be set up a special committee in which the member-states of the League shall be represented. These committees shall be charged with the task of laying down the principles and extent of co-operation. Such principles shall be formulated as draft agreements to be presented to the Council for examination preparatory to their submission to the aforesaid states.

Representatives of the other Arab countries may take part in the work of the aforesaid committees. The Council shall determine the conditions under which these representatives may be permitted to participate and the rules governing such representation.

## Article V

Any resort to force in order to resolve disputes between two or more member-states of the League is prohibited. If there should arise among them a difference which does not concern a state's independence, sovereignty, or territorial integrity, and if the parties to the dispute have recourse to the Council for the settlement of this difference, the decision of the Council shall then be enforceable and obligatory.

In such case, the states between whom the difference has arisen shall not participate in the deliberations and decisions of the Council.

The Council shall mediate in all differences which threaten to lead to war between two member-states, or a member-state and a third state, with a view to bringing about their reconciliation.

Decisions of arbitration and mediation shall be taken by majority vote.

## Article VI

In case of aggression or threat of aggression by one state against a member-state, the state which has been attacked or threatened with aggression may demand the immediate convocation of the Council.

The Council shall by unanimous decision determine the measures necessary to repulse the aggression. If the aggressor is a member-state, his vote shall not be counted in determining unanimity.

If, as a result of the attack, the government of the state attacked finds itself unable to communicate with the Council, the state's representative in the Council shall request the convocation of the Council for the purpose indicated in the foregoing paragraph. In the event that this representative is unable to communicate with the Council, any member-state of the League shall have the right to request the convocation of the Council.

*Article VII*

Unanimous decisions of the Council shall be binding upon all member-states of the League; majority decisions shall be binding only upon those states which have accepted them.

In either case the decisions of the Council shall be enforced in each member-state according to its respective laws.

*Article VIII*

Each member-state shall respect the systems of government established in the other member-states and regard them as exclusive concerns of those states. Each shall pledge to abstain from any action calculated to change established systems of government.

*Article IX*

States of the League which desire to establish closer co-operation and stronger bonds than are provided for by this Charter may conclude agreements to that end.

Treaties and agreements already concluded or to be concluded in the future between a member-state and another state shall not be binding or restrictive upon other members.

*Article X*

The permanent seat of the League of Arab States is established in Cairo. The Council may, however, assemble at any other place it may designate.

*Article XI*

The Council of the League shall convene in ordinary session twice a year, in March and in September. It shall convene in extraordinary session upon the request of two member-states of the League whenever the need arises.

*Article XII*

The League shall have a permanent Secretariat-General which shall consist of a Secretary-General, Assistant Secretaries and an appropriate number of officials.

The Council of the League shall appoint the Secretary-General by a major-ity of two thirds of the states of the League. The Secretary-General, with the approval of the Council, shall appoint the Assistant Secretaries and the principal officials of the League.

The Council of the League shall establish an administrative regulation for the functions of the Secretariat-General and matters relating to the staff.

The Secretary-General shall have the rank of Ambassador and the Assistant Secretaries that of Ministers Plenipotentiary.

The first Secretary-General of the League is named in an Annex to this Charter.

## Article XIII

The Secretary-General shall prepare the draft of the budget of the League and shall submit it to the Council for approval before the beginning of each fiscal year.

The Council shall fix the share of the expenses to be borne by each state of the League. This may be reconsidered if necessary.

## Article XIV

The members of the Council of the League as well as the members of the committees and the officials who are to be designated in the administrative regulation shall enjoy diplomatic privileges and immunity when engaged in the exercise of their functions.

The buildings occupied by the organs of the League shall be inviolable.

## Article XV

The first meeting of the Council shall be convened at the invitation of the head of the Egyptian Government. Thereafter it shall be convened at the invitation of the Secretary-General.

The representatives of the member-states of the League shall alternately assume the presidency of the Council at each of its ordinary sessions.

## Article XVI

Except in cases specifically indicated in this Charter, a majority vote of the Council shall be sufficient to make enforceable decisions on the following matters:

A. Matters relating to personnel.
B. Adoption of the budget of the League.
C. Establishment of the administrative regulations for the Council, the committees and the Secretariat-General.
D. Decisions to adjourn the sessions.

*Article XVII*

Each member-state of the League shall deposit with the Secretariat-General one copy of treaty or agreement concluded or to be concluded in the future between itself and another member-state of the League or a third state.

*Article XVIII*

If a member-state contemplates withdrawal from the League, it shall inform the Council of its intention one year before such withdrawal is to go into effect.

The Council of the League may consider any state which fails to fulfill its obligations under the Charter as separated from the League, this to go into effect upon a unanimous decision of the states, not counting the state concerned.

*Article XIX*

This Charter may be amended with the consent of two thirds of the states belonging to the League, especially in order to make firmer and stronger the ties between the member-states, to create an Arab Tribunal of Arbitration, and to regulate the relations of the League with any international bodies to be created in the future to guarantee security and peace.

Final action on the amendment cannot be taken prior Final action on an amend... hich the motion to the session following the session in which the motion was initiated. [sic]

If a state does not accept such an amendment it may withdraw at such time as the amendment goes into effect, without being bound by the provisions of the preceding Article.

*Article XX*

This Charter and its annexes shall be ratified according to the basic laws in force among the High Contracting parties.

The instruments of ratification shall be deposited with the Secretariat-General of the Council and the Charter shall become operative as regards each ratifying state fifteen days after the Secretary-General has received the instruments of ratification from four states.

This Charter has been drawn up in Cairo in the Arabic language on this 8th day of Rabi' II, thirteen hundred and sixty four H. (March 22, 1945), in one copy which shall be deposited in the safe keeping of the Secretariat-General.

An identical copy shall be delivered to each state of the League.

## (1) Annex Regarding Palestine

Since the termination of the last great war the rule of the Ottoman Empire over the Arab countries, among them Palestine, which had become detached from that Empire, has come to an end. She has come to be autonomous, not subordinate to any other state.

The Treaty of Lausanne proclaimed that her future was to be settled by the parties concerned.

However, even though she was as yet unable to control her own affairs, the Covenant of the League (of Nations) in 1919 made provision for a regime based upon recognition of her independence.

Her international existence and independence in the legal sense cannot, therefore, be questioned, any more than could the independence of the other Arab countries.

Although the outward manifestations of this independence have remained obscured for reasons beyond her control, this should not be allowed to interfere with her participation in the work of the Council of the League.

The states signatory to the Pact of the Arab League are therefore of the opinion that, considering the special circumstances of Palestine and until that country can effectively exercise its independence, the Council of the League should take charge of the selection of an Arab representative from Palestine to take part in its work.

## (2) Annex Regarding Cooperation with Countries Which Are Not Members of the Council of the League

Whereas the member-states of the League will have to deal in the Council as well as in the committees with matters which will benefit and affect the Arab world at large;

And whereas the Council has to take into account the aspirations of the Arab countries which are not members of the Council and has to work toward their realization;

Now, therefore, it particularly behooves the states signatory to the Pact of the Arab League to enjoin the Council of the League, when considering the admission of those countries to participation in the committees referred to in the Pact, that it should spare no effort to learn their needs and understand their aspirations and hopes; and that it should work thenceforth for their best interests and the safeguarding of their future with all the political means at its disposal.

## (3) Annex Regarding the Appointment of a Secretary-General of the League

The states signatory to this Pact have agreed to appoint His Excellency Abdul-Rahman 'Azzam Bey, to be Secretary-General of the League of Arab States.

This appointment is made for two years. The Council of the League shall hereafter determine the new regulations for the Secretary-General.

## Appendix C: Joint Defense and Economic Cooperation Treaty (JDEC)[3]

*Treaty of Joint Defense and Economic Cooperation Between the States of the Arab League, June 17, 1950*

The Governments of:

THE HASHIMITE KINGDOM OF JORDAN
THE SYRIAN REPUBLIC
THE KINGDOM OF IRAQ
THE KINGDOM OF SAUDI ARABIA
THE LEBANESE REPUBLIC
THE KINGDOM OF EGYPT
THE MOTAWAKILITE KINGDOM OF YEMEN

In view of the desire of the above-mentioned Governments to consolidate relations between the States of the Arab League; to maintain their independence and their mutual heritage; in accordance with the desire of their peoples, to cooperate for the realization of mutual defense and the maintenance of security and peace according to the principles of both the Arab League Pact and the United Nations Charter, together with the aims of the said Pacts; and to consolidate stability and security and provide means of welfare and development in the countries.

The following government delegates of …, having been duly accredited and fully authorized by their respective governments, approve the following:

*Article 1*

The Contracting States, in an effort to maintain and stabilize peace and security, hereby confirm their desire to settle their international disputes by peaceful means, whether such disputes concern relations among themselves or with other Powers.

*Article 2*

The Contracting States consider any [act of] armed aggression made against any one or more of them or their armed forces, to be directed against them all. Therefore, in accordance with the right of self-defense, individually and collectively, they undertake to go without delay to the aid of the State or States

---

[3] This text is taken from US Department of State 1957b. Some typographical errors found in the original have been corrected.

against which such an act of aggression is made, and immediately to take, individually and collectively, all steps available, including the use of armed force, to repel the aggression and restore security and peace. In conformity with Article 6 of the Arab League Pact and Article 51 of the United Nations Charter, the Arab League Council and U.N. Security Council shall be notified of such act of aggression and the means and procedure taken to check it.

*Article 3*

At the invitation of any one of the signatories of this Treaty the Contracting States shall hold consultations whenever there are reasonable grounds for the belief that the territorial integrity, independence, or security of any one of the parties is threatened. In the event of the threat of war or the existence of an international emergency, the Contracting States shall immediately proceed to unify their plans and defensive measures, as the situation may demand.

*Article 4*

The Contracting States, desiring to implement fully the above obligations and effectively carry them out, shall cooperate in consolidating and coordinating their armed forces, and shall participate according to their resources and needs in preparing individual and collective means of defense to repulse the said armed aggression.

*Article 5*

A Permanent Military Commission composed of representatives of the General Staffs of the armies of the Contracting States shall be formed to draw up plans of joint defense and their implementation. The duties of the Permanent Military Commission which are set forth in an Annex attached to this Treaty, include the drafting of necessary reports on the method of cooperation and participation mentioned in Article 4. The Permanent Military Commission shall submit to the Joint Defense Council, provided hereunder in Article 6, reports dealing with questions within its province.

*Article 6*

A Joint Defense Council under the supervision of the Arab League Council shall be formed to deal with all matters concerning the implementation of the provisions of Articles 2, 3, 4, and 5 of this Treaty. It shall be assisted in the performance of its task by the Permanent Military Commission referred to in Article 5. The Joint Defense Council shall consist of the Foreign Ministers and the Defense Ministers of the Contracting States or their representatives. Decisions taken by a two-thirds majority shall be binding on all the Contracting States.

*Article 7*

The Contracting States, in order to fulfill the aims of this Treaty, and to bring about security and prosperity in the Arab countries, and in an effort to raise the standard of living in them, undertake to cooperate in the development of their economies and the exploitation of their natural resources; to facilitate the exchange of their respective agricultural and industrial products; and generally to organize and coordinate their economic activities and to conclude the necessary inter-Arab agreements to realize such aims.

*Article 8*

An Economic Council consisting of the Ministers in charge of economic affairs, or their representatives if necessary, shall be formed by the Contracting States to submit recommendations for the realization of all such aims as are set forth in the previous article. The Council may, in the performance of its duties, seek the cooperation of the Committee for Financial and Economic Affairs referred to in Article 4 of the Arab League Pact.

*Article 9*

The Annex to this Treaty shall be considered an integral and indivisible part of it.

*Article 10*

The Contracting States undertake to conclude no international agreements which may be contradictory to the provisions of this Treaty, nor to act, in their international relations, in a way which may be contrary to the aims of this Treaty.

*Article 11*

No provision of this Treaty shall in any way affect, or is intended to affect, any of the rights or obligations devolving upon the Contracting States from the United Nations Charter or the responsibilities borne by the United Nations Security Council for the maintenance of international peace and security.

*Article 12*

After a lapse of 10 years from the date of the ratification of this Treaty, any one of the Contracting States may withdraw from it, providing 12 months' notice is previously given to the Secretariat-General of the Arab League. The Secretariat-General of the League shall inform the other Contracting States of such notice.

*Article 13*

This Treaty shall be ratified by each Contracting State according to the constitutional procedure of its own government. The Treaty shall come into force for the ratifying States 15 days after the receipt by the Secretariat-General of the instruments of ratification from at least four States.

This Treaty is drafted in Arabic in Cairo on April 13, 1950. One signed copy shall be deposited with the Secretariat-General of the Arab League; equally authentic copies shall be transmitted to each of the Contracting States.

*Military Annex*

1. The Permanent Military Commission provided for in Article 5 of the Joint Defense and Economic Cooperation Treaty between the States of the Arab League, shall undertake the following:
   (a) in cooperation with the Joint Defense Council, to prepare plans to deal with all anticipated dangers or armed aggression that may be launched against one or more of the Contracting States or their armed forces, such plans to be based on the principles determined by the Joint Defense Council;
   (b) to submit proposals for the organization of the forces of the Contracting States, stipulating the minimum force for each in accordance with military exigencies and the potentialities of each State;
   (c) to submit proposals for increasing the effectiveness of the forces of the Contracting States in so far as their equipment, organization, and training are concerned; so that they may keep pace with modern military methods and development; and for the unification and coordination of all such forces;
   (d) to submit proposals for the exploitation of natural, agricultural, industrial, and other resources of all Contracting States in favor of the inter-Arab military effort and joint defense;
   (e) to organize the exchange of training missions between the Contracting States for the preparation of plans, participation in military exercises and maneuvers and the study of their results, recommendations for the improvement of methods to ensure close cooperation in the field, and for the general improvement of the forces of all the Contracting States;
   (f) to prepare the necessary data on the resources and military potentialities of each of the Contracting States and the part to be played by the forces of each in the joint military effort;
   (g) to discuss the facilities and various contributions which each of the Contracting States, in conformity with the provisions of this Treaty,

might be asked to provide, during a state of war, on behalf of the armies of such other Contracting States as might be operating on its territory.

2. The Permanent Military Commission may form temporizer or permanent subcommittees from among its own members to deal with any of the matters falling within its jurisdiction. It may also seek the advice of any experts whose views on certain questions are deemed necessary.

3. The Permanent Military Commission shall submit detailed reports on the results of its activities and studies to the Joint Defense Council provided for in Article 6 of this Treaty, as well as an annual report giving full particulars of its work and studies during the year.

4. The Permanent Military Commission shall establish its headquarters in Cairo but may hold meetings in any other place the Commission may specify. The Commission shall elect its Chairman for two years; he may be reelected. Candidates for the Chairmanship shall hold at least the rank of a high commanding officer. Each member of the Commission must have as his original nationality that of the Contracting State he represents.

5. In the event of war, the supreme command of the joint forces shall be entrusted to the Contracting State possessing the largest military force taking actual part in field operations, unless, by unanimous agreement, the Commander-in-Chief is selected otherwise. The Commander-in-Chief shall be assisted in directing military operations by a Joint Staff.

(1) League of Arab States Treaty Series. Agreements and Conventions Concluded between Member States Within the Framework of the Arab League, p. 10. Instruments of ratification deposited by Syria, Oct. 31, 1951, by Egypt, Rev. 22, 1951; by Jordan, Mar. 31, 1952, by Iraq, Aug. 7, 1952, by Saudi Arabia, Aug. 19, 1952; by Lebanon, Dee. 24, 1952; and by Yemen, Oct. 11, 1953; entered into force Aug. 22, 1952.

## Appendix D: Sykes–Picot Agreement

It is accordingly understood between the French and British Governments:

*One*

That France and Great Britain are prepared to recognize and protect an independent Arab states [sic] or a confederation of Arab states (a) and (b) marked on the annexed map,[4] under the suzerainty of an Arab chief.

That in area (a) France, and in area (b) Great Britain, shall have priority of right of enterprise and local loans. That in area (a) France, and in area

---

[4] The map has not been included here due to copyright restrictions.

(b) Great Britain, shall alone supply advisers or foreign functionaries at the request of the Arab state or confederation of Arab states.

*Two*

That in the blue area France, and in the red area Great Britain, shall be allowed to establish such direct or indirect administration or control as they desire and as they may think fit to arrange with the Arab state or confederation of Arab states.

*Three*

That in the brown area there shall be established an international administration, the form of which is to be decided upon after consultation with Russia, and subsequently in consultation with the other allies, and the representatives of the sheriff of Mecca.

*Four*

That Great Britain be accorded (1) the ports of Haifa and Acre, (2) guarantee of a given supply of water from the Tigris and Euphrates in area (a) for area (b). His Majesty's Government, on their part, undertake that they will at no time enter into negotiations for the cession of Cyprus to any third power without the previous consent of the French Government.

*Five*

That Alexandretta shall be a free port as regards the trade of the British empire, and that there shall be no discrimination in port charges or facilities as regards British shipping and British goods; that there shall be freedom of transit for British goods through Alexandretta and by railway through the blue area, or area (b), or area (a); and there shall be no discrimination, direct or indirect, against British goods on any railway or against British goods or ships at any port serving the areas mentioned.

That Haifa shall be a free port as regards the trade of France, her dominions and protectorates, and there shall be no discrimination in port charges or facilities as regards French shipping and French goods.

There shall be freedom of transit for French goods through Haifa and by the British railway through the brown area, whether those goods are intended for or originate in the blue area, area (a), or area (b), and there shall be no discrimination, direct or indirect, against French goods on any railway, or against French goods or ships at any port serving the areas mentioned.

*Six*

That in area (a) the Baghdad railway shall not be extended southwards beyond Mosul, and in area (b) northwards beyond Samarra, until a railway connecting

Baghdad and Aleppo via the Euphrates valley has been completed, and then only with the concurrence of the two governments.

*Seven*

That Great Britain has the right to build, administer, and be sole owner of a railway connecting Haifa with area (b), and shall have a perpetual right to transport troops along such a line at all times.

It is to be understood by both governments that this railway is to facilitate the connection of Baghdad with Haifa by rail, and it is further understood that, if the engineering difficulties and expense entailed by keeping this connecting line in the brown area only make the project unfeasible, that the French Government shall be prepared to consider that the line in question may also traverse the polygon Banias-Keis Marib-Salkhad Tell Otsda-Mesmie before reaching area (b).

*Eight*

For a period of twenty years the existing Turkish customs tariff shall remain in force throughout the whole of the blue and red areas, as well as in areas (a) and (b), and no increase in the rates of duty or conversions from ad valorem to specific rates shall be made except by agreement between the two powers.

There shall be no interior customs barriers between any of the above mentioned areas. The customs duties leviable on goods destined for the interior shall be collected at the port of entry and handed over to the administration of the area of destination.

*Nine*

It shall be agreed that the French Government will at no time enter into any negotiations for the cession of their rights and will not cede such rights in the blue area to any third power, except the Arab state or confederation of Arab states, without the previous agreement of His Majesty's Government, who, on their part, will give a similar undertaking to the French Government regarding the red area.

*Ten*

The British and French Governments, as the protectors of the Arab state, shall agree that they will not themselves acquire and will not consent to a third power acquiring territorial possessions in the Arabian peninsula, nor consent to a third power installing a naval base either on the east coast, or on the islands, of the Red Sea. This, however, shall not prevent such adjustment of the Aden frontier as may be necessary in consequence of recent Turkish aggression.

*Eleven*

The negotiations with the Arabs as to the boundaries of the Arab states shall be continued through the same channel as heretofore on behalf of the two powers.

*Twelve*

It is agreed that measures to control the importation of arms into the Arab territories will be considered by the two governments.

I have further the honour to state that, in order to make the agreement complete, His Majesty's Government are proposing to the Russian Government to exchange notes analogous to those exchanged by the latter and your Excellency's Government on the 26th April last.

Copies of these notes will be communicated to your Excellency as soon as exchanged. I would also venture to remind your Excellency that the conclusion of the present agreement raises, for practical consideration, the question of claims of Italy to a share in any partition or rearrangement of Turkey in Asia, as formulated in Article 9 of the agreement of the 26th April, 1915, between Italy and the Allies.

His Majesty's Government further consider that the Japanese Government should be informed of the arrangements now concluded.

## Appendix E: Montevideo Convention on the Rights and Duties of States[5]

The Governments represented in the Seventh International Conference of American States:

Wishing to conclude a Convention on Rights and Duties of States, have appointed the following Plenipotentiaries:

[List of plenipotentiaries omitted]

Who, after having exhibited their Full Powers, which were found to be in good and due order, have agreed upon the following:

*Article 1*

The state as a person of international law should possess the following qualifications:

a.    a permanent population;
b.    a defined territory;
c.    government; and
d.    capacity to enter into relations with the other states.

---

[5] The text of this treaty was provided by the Organization of American States treaty system.

*Article 2*

The federal state shall constitute a sole person in the eyes of international law.

*Article 3*

The political existence of the state is independent of recognition by the other states. Even before recognition the state has the right to defend its integrity and independence, to provide for its conservation and prosperity, and consequently to organize itself as it sees fit, to legislate upon its interests, administer its services, and to define the jurisdiction and competence of its courts. The exercise of these rights has no other limitation than the exercise of the rights of other states according to international law.

*Article 4*

States are juridically equal, enjoy the same rights, and have equal capacity in their exercise. The rights of each one do not depend upon the power which it possesses to assure its exercise, but upon the simple fact of its existence as a person under international law.

*Article 5*

The fundamental rights of states are not susceptible of being affected in any manner whatsoever.

*Article 6*

The recognition of a state merely signifies that the state which recognizes it accepts the personality of the other with all the rights and duties determined by international law. Recognition is unconditional and irrevocable.

*Article 7*

The recognition of a state may be express or tacit. The latter results from any act which implies the intention of recognizing the new state.

*Article 8*

No state has the right to intervene in the internal or external affairs of another.

*Article 9*

The jurisdiction of states within the limits of national territory applies to all the inhabitants. Nationals and foreigners are under the same protection of the law and the national authorities and the foreigners may not claim rights other or more extensive than those of the nationals.

*Article 10*

The primary interest of states is the conservation of peace. Differences of any nature which arise between them should be settled by recognized pacific methods.

*Article 11*

The contracting states definitely establish as the rule of their conduct the precise obligation not to recognize territorial acquisitions or special advantages which have been obtained by force whether this consists in the employment of arms, in threatening diplomatic representations, or in any other effective coercive measure. The territory of a state is inviolable and may not be the object of military occupation nor of other measures of force imposed by another state directly or indirectly or for any motive whatever even temporarily.

*Article 12*

The present Convention shall not affect obligations previously entered into by the High Contracting Parties by virtue of international agreements.

*Article 13*

The present Convention shall be ratified by the High Contracting Parties in conformity with their respective constitutional procedures. The Minister of Foreign Affairs of the Republic of Uruguay shall transmit authentic certified copies to the governments for the aforementioned purpose of ratification. The instrument of ratification shall be deposited in the archives of the Pan American Union in Washington, which shall notify the signatory governments of said deposit. Such notification shall be considered as an exchange of ratifications.

*Article 14*

The present Convention will enter into force between the High Contracting Parties in the order in which they deposit their respective ratifications.

*Article 15*

The present Convention shall remain in force indefinitely but may be denounced by means of one year's notice given to the Pan American Union, which shall transmit it to the other signatory governments. After the expiration of this period the Convention shall cease in its effects as regards the party which denounces but shall remain in effect for the remaining High Contracting Parties.

*Article 16*

The present Convention shall be open for the adherence and accession of the States which are not signatories. The corresponding instruments shall be deposited in the archives of the Pan American Union which shall communicate them to the other High Contracting Parties.

In witness whereof, the following Plenipotentiaries have signed this Convention in Spanish, English, Portuguese and French and hereunto affix their respective seals in the city of Montevideo, Republic of Uruguay, this 26th day of December, 1933.

## Appendix F: Arab Charter on Human Rights[6]

The Governments of the member states of the League of Arab States

*Preamble*

Given the Arab nation's belief in human dignity since God honoured it by making the Arab World the cradle of religions and the birthplace of civilizations which confirmed its right to a life of dignity based on freedom, justice and peace,

Pursuant to the eternal principles of brotherhood and equality among all human beings which were firmly established by the Islamic Shari'a and the other divinely-revealed religions,

Being proud of the humanitarian values and principles which it firmly established in the course of its long history and which played a major role in disseminating centres of learning between the East and the West, thereby making it an international focal point for seekers of knowledge, culture and wisdom,

Conscious of the fact that the entire Arab World has always worked together to preserve its faith, believing in its unity, struggling to protect its freedom, defending the right of nations to self-determination and to safeguard their resources, believing in the rule of law and that every individual's enjoyment of freedom, justice and equality of opportunity is the yardstick by which the merits of any society are gauged,

---

[6] "Council of the League of Arab States, Arab Charter on Human Rights, September 15, 1994," available at the University of Minnesota Human Rights Library: www1.umn. edu/humanrts/instree/arabcharter.html. Also found at: http://arableague-us.org/wp/ student-resources/research/important-documents/.

Rejecting racism and zionism, which constitute a violation of human rights and pose a threat to world peace,

Acknowledging the close interrelationship between human rights and world peace,

Reaffirming the principles of the Charter of the United Nations and the Universal Declaration of Human Rights, as well as the provisions of the United Nations International Covenants on Civil and Political Rights and Economic, Social and Cultural Rights and the Cairo Declaration on Human Rights in Islam,

In confirmation of all the above, have agreed as follows:

*Part I*

*Article 1*

(a)  All peoples have the right of self-determination and control over their natural wealth and resources and, accordingly, have the right to freely determine the form of their political structure and to freely pursue their economic, social and cultural development.

(b)  Racism, zionism, occupation and foreign domination pose a challenge to human dignity and constitute a fundamental obstacle to the realization of the basic rights of peoples. There is a need to condemn and endeavour to eliminate all such practices.

*Part II*

*Article 2*

Each State Party to the present Charter undertakes to ensure to all individuals within its territory and subject to its Jurisdiction the right to enjoy all the rights and freedoms recognized herein, without any distinction on grounds of race, colour, sex, language, religion, political opinion, national or social origin, property, birth or other status and without any discrimination between men and women.

*Article 3*

(a)  No restriction upon or derogation from any of the fundamental human rights recognized or existing in any State Party to the present Charter in virtue of law, conventions or custom shall be admitted on the pretext that the present Charter does not recognize such rights or that it recognizes them to a lesser extent.

(b)  No State Party to the present Charter shall derogate from the fundamental freedoms recognized herein and which are enjoyed by the nationals of another State that shows less respect for those freedoms.

*Article 4*

(a) No restrictions shall be placed on the rights and freedoms recognized in the present Charter except where such is provided by law and deemed necessary to protect the national security and economy, public order, health or morals or the rights and freedoms of others.

(b) In time of public emergency which threatens the life of the nation, the States Parties may take measures derogating from their obligations under the present Charter to the extent strictly required by the exigencies of the situation.

(c) Such measures or derogations shall under no circumstances affect or apply to the rights and special guarantees concerning the prohibition of torture and degrading treatment, return to one's country, political asylum, trial, the inadmissibility of retrial for the same act, and the legal status of crime and punishment.

*Article 5*

Every individual has the right to life, liberty and security of person. These rights shall be protected by law.

*Article 6*

There shall be no crime or punishment except as provided by law and there shall be no punishment in respect of an act preceding the promulgation of that provision. The accused shall benefit from subsequent legislation if it is in his favour.

*Article 7*

The accused shall be presumed innocent until proved guilty at a lawful trial in which he has enjoyed the guarantees necessary for his defence.

*Article 8*

Everyone has the right to liberty and security of person and no one shall be arrested, held in custody or detained without a legal warrant and without being brought promptly before a judge.

*Article 9*

All persons are equal before the law and everyone within the territory of the State has a guaranteed right to legal remedy.

*Article 10*

The death penalty may be imposed only for the most serious crimes and anyone sentenced to death shall have the right to seek pardon or commutation of the sentence.

*Article 11*

The death penalty shall under no circumstances be imposed for a political offence.

*Article 12*

The death penalty shall not be inflicted on a person under 18 years of age, on a pregnant woman prior to her delivery or on a nursing mother within two years from the date on which she gave birth.

*Article 13*

(a) The States parties shall protect every person in their territory from being subjected to physical or mental torture or cruel, inhuman or degrading treatment. They shall take effective measures to prevent such acts and shall regard the practice thereof, or participation therein, as a punishable offence.
(b) No medical or scientific experimentation shall be carried out on any person without his free consent.

*Article 14*

No one shall be imprisoned on the ground of his proven inability to meet a debt or fulfil any civil obligation.

*Article 15*

Persons sentenced to a penalty of deprivation of liberty shall be treated with humanity.

*Article 16*

No one shall be tried twice for the same offence.

Anyone against whom such proceedings are brought shall have the right to challenge their legality and to demand his release.

Anyone who is the victim of unlawful arrest or detention shall be entitled to compensation.

*Article 17*

Privacy shall be inviolable and any infringement thereof shall constitute an offence. This privacy includes private family affairs, the inviolability of the home and the confidentiality of correspondence and other private means of communication.

*Article 18*

Everyone shall have the inherent right to recognition as a person before the law.

*Article 19*

The people are the source of authority and every citizen of full legal age shall have the right of political participation, which he shall exercise in accordance with the law.

*Article 20*

Every individual residing within the territory of a State shall have the right to liberty of movement and freedom to choose his place of residence in any part of the said territory, within the limits of the law.

*Article 21*

No citizen shall be arbitrarily or unlawfully prevented from leaving any Arab country, including his own, nor prohibited from residing, or compelled to reside, in any part of his country.

*Article 22*

No citizen shall be expelled from his country or prevented from returning thereto.

*Article 23*

Every citizen shall have the right to seek political asylum in other countries in order to escape persecution. This right shall not be enjoyed by persons facing prosecution for an offence under the ordinary law. Political refugees shall not be extraditable.

*Article 24*

No citizen shall be arbitrarily deprived of his original nationality, nor shall his right to acquire another nationality be denied without a legally valid reason.

*Article 25*

Every citizen has a guaranteed right to own private property. No citizen shall under any circumstances be divested of all or any part of his property in an arbitrary or unlawful manner.

*Article 26*

Everyone has a guaranteed right to freedom of belief, thought and opinion.

*Article 27*

Adherents of every religion have the right to practise their religious observances and to manifest their views through expression, practice or teaching, without prejudice to the rights of others. No restrictions shall be imposed on the exercise of freedom of belief, thought and opinion except as provided by law.

## Article 28

All citizens have the right to freedom of peaceful assembly and association. No restrictions shall be placed on the exercise of this right unless so required by the exigencies of national security, public safety or the need to protect the rights and freedoms of others.

## Article 29

The State guarantees the right to form trade unions and the right to strike within the limits laid down by law.

## Article 30

The State guarantees every citizen's right to work in order to secure for himself a standard of living that meets the basic requirements of life. The State also guarantees every citizen's right to comprehensive social security.

## Article 31

Free choice of work is guaranteed and forced labour is prohibited. Compelling a person to perform work under the terms of a court judgement shall not be deemed to constitute forced labour.

## Article 32

The State shall ensure that its citizens enjoy equality of opportunity in regard to work, as well as a fair wage and equal remuneration for work of equal value.

## Article 33

Every citizen shall have the right of access to public office in his country.

## Article 34

The eradication of illiteracy is a binding obligation and every citizen has a right to education. Primary education, at the very least, shall be compulsory and free and both secondary and university education shall be made easily accessible to all.

## Article 35

Citizens have a right to live in an intellectual and cultural environment in which Arab nationalism is a source of pride, in which human rights are sanctified and in which racial, religious and other forms of discrimination are rejected and international cooperation and the cause of world peace are supported.

*Article 36*

Everyone has the right to participate in cultural life, as well as the right to enjoy literary and artistic works and to be given opportunities to develop his artistic, intellectual and creative talents.

*Article 37*

Minorities shall not be deprived of their right to enjoy their culture or to follow the teachings of their religions.

*Article 38*

(a) The family is the basic unit of society, whose protection it shall enjoy.
(b) The State undertakes to provide outstanding care and special protection for the family, mothers, children and the aged.

*Article 39*

Young persons have the right to be afforded the most ample opportunities for physical and mental development.

*Part III*

*Article 40*

(a) The States members of the League's Council which are parties to the Charter shall elect a Committee of Experts on Human Rights by secret ballot.
(b) The Committee shall consist of seven members nominated by the member States Parties to the Charter. The initial elections to the Committee shall be held six months after the Charter's entry into force. The Committee shall not include more than one person from the same State.
(c) The Secretary-General shall request the member States to submit their candidates two months before the scheduled date of the elections.
(d) The candidates, who must be highly experienced and competent in the Committee's field of work, shall serve in their personal capacity with full impartiality and integrity.
(e) The Committee's members shall be elected for a three-year term which, in the case of three of them, shall be renewable for one further term, their names being selected by lot. The principle of rotation shall be observed as far as possible.
(f) The Committee shall elect its chairman and shall draw up its rules of procedure specifying its method of operation.

(g) Meetings of the Committee shall be convened by the Secretary-General at the Headquarters of the League's Secretariat. With the Secretary-General's approval, the Committee may also meet in another Arab country if the exigencies of its work so require.

*Article 41*

1. The States Parties shall submit reports to the Committee of Experts on Human Rights in the following manner:
   (a) An initial report one year after the date of the Charter's entry into force.
   (b) Periodic reports every three years.
   (c) Reports containing the replies of States to the Committee's questions.
2. The Committee shall consider the reports submitted by the member States Parties to the Charter in accordance with the provisions of paragraph 1 of this article.
3. The Committee shall submit a report, together with the views and comments of the States, to the Standing Committee on Human Rights at the Arab League.

*Part IV*

*Article 42*

(a) The Secretary-General of the League of Arab States shall submit the present Charter, after its approval by the Council of the League, to the member States for signature and ratification or accession.
(b) The present Charter shall enter into effect two months after the date of deposit of the seventh instrument of ratification or accession with the Secretariat of the League of Arab States.

*Article 43*

Following its entry into force, the present Charter shall become binding on each State two months after the date of the deposit of its instrument of ratification or accession with the Secretariat. The Secretary-General shall notify the member States of the deposit of each instrument of ratification or accession.

# Appendices section 2

# Official policies of the Model Arab League program

### Appendix G: NCUSAR policies and regulations governing all Model Arab League programs

The following are official policies of the National Council on U.S.-Arab Relations (NCUSAR) for all Model Arab League (MAL) programs. They are provided in this appendix for the convenience of participants. These policies are official as of 2015. In the event of inconsistencies, the reproduction of policies on the NCUSAR website should take precedence while at an official MAL conference.

*** 

*Personal behavior*

The Model Arab League is a formal diplomatic simulation. All participants are expected to maintain the highest levels of decorum and professionalism during all conference-related events and activities. The National Council maintains the authority to eject violators of the behavior and professional conduct policies established herein.

The use of alcohol or illegal drugs at any official MAL event or activity is unacceptable. Conference attendees found in violation of this policy will be reported to their advisor or home institution, and ejected from the program without further warning. Smoking is permitted only in designated areas. Illegal activity may be reported to local police.

The use of crude, offensive, derogatory, or abusive language will not be tolerated, whether within or without the context of delegate role-playing. The repercussions for such language will be at the discretion of the National Council representative(s), including expulsion from the program. In the case of physical violence of any kind, local police will be contacted.

*Dress code*

While in session, all conference attendees must dress in professional attire appropriate for formal diplomatic discussions. For men, a dress shirt, tie, slacks, and jacket are appropriate. For women, dresses, suits, or slacks and blouses are acceptable. Revealing or immodest clothing, at the discretion of the National Council representative(s), is not acceptable. Under no circumstances should jeans, t-shirts, tennis shoes, athletic wear, baseball caps, or shorts be worn during Plenary Session, Council Sessions, or Summit Session without the express permission of the conference organizers. Traditional dress from the region is also prohibited.

Dress code violations may result in temporary expulsion from a session, removal as an officer, or, if the problem persists, permanent expulsion from the conference. Under most circumstances, changing into appropriate attire grants a return to participation.

*In-character role-playing*

When participating in a MAL conference, delegates role-play as diplomats from their assigned country. It is vital to the success of the program and the quality of participants' learning and leadership development experience that all delegates represent their countries as accurately as possible. Delegates should think in terms of their assigned countries' best interests and policy objectives, and thus avoid arguments based on personal beliefs and background. This is in order to maintain the highest levels of academic integrity at the conference, as well as to enhance the central learning objectives of the exercise.

If a delegate feels that one of his or her fellow delegates is not performing within these guidelines, and that the situation is interfering with the proper functioning of the proceedings, the delegate should speak with a National Council representative. Alternatively, delegates may bring concerns to the attention of the Council Chair or his or her own Faculty Advisor, who should then inform the National Council representative. The National Council representative will address these concerns with the affected student's Faculty Advisor. It is the responsibility of Faculty Advisors to ensure their students are playing their character accurately. Under no circumstances should a delegate accuse another delegate of inaccurate role-playing during formal proceedings, which would constitute a technical break in character on the part of the accuser.

The MAL functions first and foremost as a learning experience, and participants should always feel encouraged to contribute to the proceedings where possible. Delegates should not be afraid to ask questions of their Faculty Advisors, Chairs, and/or fellow delegates outside of formal debate. The best way to improve skills is through active participation.

*Pre-written resolutions*

In the spirit of diplomacy and accuracy of role-playing, pre-written resolutions are prohibited. A pre-written resolution is defined as a complete working paper written by a single country delegation prior to the start of a conference which has been designed to pass in a Council vote without debate or revision.

A key goal of the MAL program is to develop strong leadership skills among its participants, including working collaboratively, making compromises, and negotiating to protect national interests. None of this is possible if the work of writing resolutions is done by individuals outside of the Council environment. Further, resolutions written by only one country will inherently not reflect the will of the body, but rather a single delegation, and thus break the cardinal rule of in-character role-playing described above.

Before attending a Model, all delegates are strongly encouraged to write position papers. A position paper is a short summary of a country's position on the Agenda topics, usually in paragraph format. The paper should mention the issue at hand, and lay out the country's opinions and policy objectives along with the delegate's proposed solutions. Keeping in mind the prohibition on pre-written resolutions and maintaining the spirit of debate, delegates are nonetheless invited to include sample clauses for potential resolutions. This might include language that reflects the interests of one country or enumerates a specific policy suggestion, but does not comprise a fully formed resolution.

*Registration and country assignments*

All teams should register using an easy online form found on the National Council's website. The form requires some basic contact information and team details, and includes country assignment preferences. In order to register for an upcoming conference a team must be up to date on its payments for previous conferences.

Teams will not be allowed to represent the same country in a four year period, barring ancillary circumstances. If a school wishes to represent multiple countries in the same year, the assigned countries will, ideally, be geographically, socio-economically, and ideologically varied. Some conferences have additional restrictions. Check with the National Council to find out more about the country assignment process at your conference.

*Crisis simulation*

Many Model Arab League conferences feature crisis simulations. The content and process of these scenarios vary widely. Crisis situations are intended to confront students with immediate challenges in order to simulate real-world diplomatic and geopolitical emergency situations, enhance the delegate experience, and enable delegates to develop problem-solving skills while under extreme pressure and time constraints.

## Appendix H: Model Arab League Rules and Procedures

### Decorum

Parliamentary procedure dictates a level of professionalism and mutual respect between all participants, called decorum. Maintaining decorum is one of the critical skills gained through participation – learning to navigate potentially tense situations in a professional and courteous manner like any diplomat must. In a general sense, decorum constitutes avoiding disruptive behavior and maintaining respect for all delegates and officers. During formal debate, delegates must adopt the following standards of decorum:

1. *Never speak until recognized by the presiding officer, and stand to address the body;*
2. *Address the presiding officer respectfully as "Honorable Chair", etc.;*
3. *Do not exceed the allotted speaking time after the Chair bangs the gavel;*
4. *Do not direct speeches at individual delegates, but rather to the whole Council;*
5. *Avoid using personal pronouns by referring to fellow delegates as "the delegate from _____" or "the previous speaker" and referring to your own delegation in the 3rd person; and,*
6. *Pass notes to communicate rather than talking aloud and refrain from moving about the room while another delegate is giving a speech;*
7. *Be punctual.*

Disciplinary actions ... may be taken against delegates who do not treat their colleagues with civility and respect at all times.[7]

### Quorum

In order to ensure majority rule, Councils must maintain quorum to complete any *substantive* business. Quorum equals 1/2 of all initially-present countries. If the number of countries present in the room drops below quorum, for example if countries are working outside the council room, debate continues as usual although no substantive vote may be held. Procedural votes may be held, adjusting the majority to the number of present countries.

---

[7]  Listed in NCUSAR 2014: 29–30.

## Conference Authority

In addition to those powers specified elsewhere, the presiding officer shall:

1. *Interpret the rules of the Handbook where necessary;*
2. *Declare the opening and closing of all sessions;*
3. *Direct the discussion during the proceedings;*
4. *Accord the right to speak;*
5. *Set an initial speaking time and ensure all have equal opportunities to speak;*
6. *Put business items to a vote and announce decisions;*
7. *Have complete control of the proceedings and ensure the observance of parliamentary procedure; and*
8. *Entertain motions or suggest certain actions intended to increase the productivity of the body at his or her discretion, particularly for bodies of less experienced delegates.*

In all matters, including disputation of the rules of procedure and other parliamentary procedure matters, the order of authority is as follows:

1. *National Council representative(s)*
2. *Local Coordinator*
3. *MAL Rules of Procedure (Handbook)*
4. *Members of the Secretariat*

## Motions for Plenary, Council, and Summit Sessions

*Plenary Sessions*

Procedural Points: Order; Personal Privilege; Parliamentary Inquiry

*Regular Motions*

i.   Suspend the Meeting
ii.  Appeal the Decision of the Chair
iii. Amend the Speaking Time
iv.  Add, Delete, or Amend a Topic
v.   Change a Topic's Assignment
vi.  Adopt the Agenda

*Council Sessions*

Procedural Points: Order; Personal Privilege; Parliamentary Inquiry

*Regular Motions*

i.   Adjourn the Meeting
ii.  Suspend the Meeting

iii.  Suspend the Rules
iv.  Remove an Officer
v.  Close Debate
vi.  Close/Re-Open the Speakers List
vii.  Appeal the Decision of the Chair
viii. Temporarily Revoke Delegate Rights *(Chair only)*
ix.  Introduce a Right of Reply
x.  Set the Order of the Agenda
xi.  Change the Order of the Agenda
xii.  Introduce a Draft Resolution/Amendment
xiii. Limit Debate
xiv. Expand Debate
xv.  Amend the Speaking Time

*Voting Motions*

xvi.  Reconsider the Vote
xvii.  Divide the Question
xviii. Roll-Call Vote
xix.  Adopt by Consent

*Summit Sessions*

Procedural Points: Order; Personal Privilege; Parliamentary Inquiry

*Regular Motions*

i.  Adjourn the Meeting
ii.  Remove an Officer
iii.  Appeal Decision of the Secretary General

*Voting Motions*

iv.  Read the Resolution
v.  Hear Speakers' Rights
vi.  Reconsider the Vote
vii.  Roll-Call Vote
viii. Adopt by Consent

### Official Rules of Procedure

1. Motion to <u>Add, Delete, or Amend a Topic</u> allows delegates to change the language of the Agenda topics, add new topics, or delete existing topics. After the motion is stated and seconded, the changes must be submitted to

the Chair in writing to be read aloud. If any changes are passed, they must be reported to the Secretary General immediately. The motion requires a second, is debatable with two speakers for and two speakers against and requires a simple majority to pass.

2. Motion to <u>Adjourn the Meeting</u> concludes a Council or Summit until the following year. Councils may not adjourn before the scheduled end of Council Sessions. Councils that finish their Agenda early must immediately inform the Secretariat, who will provide instructions. Requires a second and a simple majority to pass.

3. Motion to <u>Adopt by Consent</u> is a time-saving measure which may be used if the vote is expected to be unanimous. This is the only motion that requires neither seconds, procedural speeches, nor a procedural vote. If this motion is made, the Chair will bang the gavel and say "Without Objection" three times. Any delegate who wishes to vote "No" should state loudly "Object," in which case the Chair will conduct a vote. Abstentions should not be grounds for objections. If no delegate objects, the item is automatically passed. Objections are considered procedural, thus Observers may object.

4. Motion to <u>Adopt the Agenda</u> accepts the current language of the Agenda topics. If no changes are proposed, this motion is made immediately. After this motion passes, no substantive changes may be made to the Agenda for the remainder of the conference. The passage of this motion marks the end of the Plenary Session. The motion requires a second and simple majority to pass.

5. Motion to <u>Amend the Speaking Time</u> changes the length of time each speaker is allowed during formal debate. The motion requires a second and a simple majority to pass.

6. Motion to <u>Appeal the Decision of the Chair</u> overrides a decision the Chair has made, most often dealing with procedural matters left to the Chair's discretion. However, this motion does not allow the Council to break any stated rule expressly stated in [the official rules as noted in the MAL Handbook]. The motion requires a second, is debatable with two speakers for and two speakers against and requires a supermajority to pass.

7. Motion to <u>Change a Topic's Assignment</u> allows a Council to remove a topic from its Agenda and send it to another Council for consideration. If passed, the Secretary General must be informed immediately. The Secretary General will then inform the Council to which the topic is being sent, and that Council may accept or reject the topic by a majority vote, as the last topic on its Agenda. The motion requires a second, is debatable with two speakers for and two speakers against and requires a simple majority to pass.

8. Motion to <u>Change the Order of the Agenda</u> changes the order in which Agenda topics are to be considered. [It is in order] at any point after

a Motion to Set the Order of the Agenda passes. The motion requires a second, is debatable with two speakers for and two speakers against and requires a supermajority to pass.

9. Motion to <u>Close Debate</u> permanently ends debate on a topic, draft resolution, or unfriendly amendment, and initiates voting procedure on that item as well as any subsidiary items. Debate may not be closed on items broader in scope than the item being discussed currently. For example, if debate is limited to a resolution, a Motion to Close Debate on a topic is not in order. If passed, a Motion to Close Debate also initiates substantive votes on all subsidiary items. Closure of debate is permanent, so the speakers list for that item may be discarded, as well as any speakers lists for subsidiary items voted upon. The motion requires a second, is debatable with two speakers for and two speakers against and requires a supermajority to pass.

10. Motion to <u>Close the Speakers List</u> ends discussion on an item after allowing the current speakers list to expire, after which voting procedure is initiated in the same manner as a closure of debate. Mimics exactly a Motion to Close Debate, with the exception that it allows countries already on the speakers list to speak before moving directly into a vote. No new speakers may be added. This motion is out of order if made during the initial establishment of a speakers list. The motion requires a second and a simple majority to pass.

11. Motion to <u>Divide the Question</u> allows the Council to vote on pieces of a draft resolution separately. The delegate making this motion must specify which pieces are to be voted upon separately, each piece being at least one full clause. The nature of this motion makes it a somewhat confusing voting process. The Chair will first conduct a procedural vote on whether to divide the question; a "yes" vote being in favor of voting on sections of the resolution separately as specified by the Motion; a "no" vote signifies the delegate would like to proceed with a single vote on the entire resolution. If this procedural vote passes, the Chair will then conduct a substantive vote on each section of the resolution as specified in the motion. The Chair will then conduct a final substantive vote on the whole resolution as it stands after the previous votes. The motion requires a second, is debatable with two speakers for and two speakers against and requires a simple majority to pass.

12. Motion to <u>Expand Debate</u> broadens the scope of the debate to a more general business item, returning to the previous speakers list. No *substantive* vote is taken; if passed, this motion essentially tables the item being discussed. The speakers list is not deleted, but is saved so the Council can go back and debate that item in the future. The motion requires a second, is debatable with two speakers for and two speakers against and requires a simple majority to pass.

13. Motion to <u>Hear Speakers' Rights</u> compels the Secretary General to hear substantive speeches – two speakers in favor of the draft resolution and two speakers opposed. Speakers are chosen in the same manner as procedural speeches, though these speeches may be substantive in nature. Speaking time is set at 30 seconds. The motion requires multiple seconds.

14. Motion to <u>Introduce an Amendment</u> brings an amendment to the floor for discussion. Amendments must have Sponsors totaling at least 1/8 of the countries present, with a minimum of two. Amendments may only modify operative clauses. The Chair must approve all amendments, verifying the correct number of Sponsors, ensuring the amendment makes sense, and assigning it a designation. This motion requires only a second to pass. The Chair will immediately verify if the amendment is friendly or unfriendly; friendly amendments are automatically accepted; unfriendly amendments remain on the floor to be debated and must be voted upon.

15. Motion to <u>Introduce a Draft Resolution</u> brings a working paper before the Council to be discussed, amended, and eventually voted upon. It is important to be active, as competition to introduce and limit debate to a particular resolution can be high. Draft resolutions must comply with standard formatting rules, and have Sponsors and Signatories totaling at least 1/4 of the countries present (minimum three). The Chair must approve all amendments, verifying the correct number of Sponsors, ensuring the amendment makes sense, and assigning it a designation. Multiple resolutions may be introduced at the same time by phrasing the motion "*moves to introduce all draft language before the Chair.*" All these items may be discussed until debate is limited to just one. The motion requires a second.

    a. Sponsors are the primary authors of a draft resolution, listed at the top of the document. After a draft resolution is introduced, Sponsors may remove themselves by sending a written request to the Chair. Only one Sponsor is necessary to keep a draft resolution on the floor. No new Sponsors may be added after introduction unless all other Sponsors have withdrawn. If all Sponsors withdraw, the Chair will ask if any other country wishes to assume sponsorship. All those wishing to do so may become Sponsors at that time. If no one wishes to become a Sponsor at that time, the draft resolution fails by default and is taken off the floor permanently.

    b. Signatories are countries that agree generally with a draft resolution, or find it valuable enough to debate, but are not primary authors. Signatories are not required in order to keep a draft resolution on the floor, and may request to be removed by written request to the Chair. They are listed at the bottom of the document.

16. Motion to <u>Introduce a Right of Reply</u> responds to extraordinary language clearly insulting to personal or national dignity or to correct information presented in committee by another delegation that inaccurately presents facts about or the policy of their state. This motion requires no second, but must be accepted by the Chair. Should the Chair accept this motion, the delegate making the motion may compose a written Reply for the Chair to read. The Chair reviews the Reply at his or her earliest convenience and, if deeming it appropriate, reads the Reply to the Council. The Chair may choose not to read the Reply. The decision of the Chair on a Right of Reply is not subject to appeal. There is no Right of Reply to a Reply. Right of Reply can only be accorded in response to a formal speech, and may be granted only to a delegate directly mentioned in the offending speech.

17. Motion to <u>Limit Debate</u> narrows the scope of debate to a more specific business item. This motion sets aside the current speakers list (but does not delete it), and opens a new speakers list with a narrower scope. Debate may again be limited several times, creating "threads" of debate linking ever more specific items connected at the top by the General Speakers List. The motion requires a second and simple majority to pass.

18. Motion to <u>Read the Resolution</u> compels the Secretary General to read the operative clauses to the body. This motion may be used to confirm that the language of a resolution is correct, to compel all delegations to thoroughly consider a document, or to give a spare moment before the vote. The motion requires multiple seconds to pass.

19. Motion to <u>Reconsider the Vote</u> takes a re-vote on a substantive or procedural matter immediately after the initial vote concludes. It may only be made immediately following the initial vote and is used only if a country wishes to change its vote. The motion requires a second, is debatable with two speakers for and two speakers against and requires a simple majority to pass. If the motion passes, the chair will immediately accept any precedential motions to the motion that was reconsidered. If none are made, the Chair immediately re-takes the vote.

20. Motion to <u>Remove an Officer</u> removes a negligent officer, replacing with a subordinate or by election. If this motion is invoked, the Council immediately recesses and notifies the Secretariat and the National Council representative(s). The Secretary General under the supervision of the National Council representative will hear this motion. The motion requires a second, is debatable with two speakers for and two speakers against and requires a supermajority to pass.

21. Motion to <u>Re-Open the Speakers List</u> nullifies a Motion to Close the Speakers List. This motion is in order between the passage of a Motion to Close the Speakers List and before the speakers list is exhausted. The motion requires a second and a simple majority to pass.

22. Motion to <u>Vote by Roll-Call</u> allows each country to vote individually. The Chair will begin at a random place on the roster, and following alphabetical order ask each country how they vote. Voting by roll-call allows countries to vote "Yes," "No," "Abstain," "Pass," or "No with Rights." Delegates who vote "Pass" will be called upon again after the roster has been exhausted, at which time they must vote "Yes," "No," or "Abstain." Delegates who vote "No with Rights" will be given 30 seconds to explain their vote after the result is announced by the Chair. The Chair will call any delegate using "No with Rights" for any other reason, including rehashing previous arguments, out of order. If the substantive vote fails, "No with Rights" will not be recognized. The motion requires multiple seconds to pass.

23. Motion to <u>Set the Order of the Agenda</u> must be passed before the Council can move on to discussing the topics. This motion allows the Council to prioritize the topics it wishes to discuss. In many cases, the motion will keep the original order of the Agenda (1-2-3-4). Topics retain the number originally listed on the Agenda, a detail particularly important to the Chair for giving draft resolution designations. Changes to the Agenda order must be reported to the Secretariat. The motion requires a second and a simple majority to pass.

24. Motion to <u>Suspend the Meeting</u> allows the Council to recess for scheduled breaks in the conference schedule or enter an unmoderated caucus. A time limit must be specified for unmoderated caucuses, with a maximum of 10 minutes, with a possible extension of 5 additional minutes. The motion requires a second and a simple majority to pass.

25. Motion to <u>Suspend the Rules</u> allows the Council to engage in a variety of informal actions and debate styles, which should be specified when making the motion. Proposed action or debate style must be specified in the motion, as well as a time limit when applicable. The most common reason to suspend the rules is for a moderated caucus. Other useful ways to utilize a suspension of the rules include straw-poll votes, round robin, popcorn style, or question-and-answer sessions. No new motions may be made during a suspension of the rules. The motion requires a second and a supermajority to pass.

    a. <u>Moderated Caucus</u> [is a debate style] during which the Chair calls on delegates as they raise their placards – there is no speakers list. No delegate may speak twice consecutively, and the caucus may be terminated for lack of speakers. Motions to suspend the rules for a moderated caucus must delineate speaking time limit, the overall length of the caucus, and a stated purpose. The Chair may allow a delegate who proposed the motion to speak first or last.

    b. <u>Straw-Poll Votes</u> allow the Council a way to quickly take the temperature of the room on anything: a piece of draft language, the willingness of the committee to move on from a topic, etc. All countries are asked to vote yes, no, or abstain, but are not required to participate. The motioner must state the question to be voted on when making the motion. No time limit is required as the council returns to formal debate upon conclusion of the poll.

c. <u>Round Robin</u> debates provide all states in the room an opportunity to speak on a specific topic. Motions to suspend the rules for a round robin must have a speaking time limit and a stated purpose. The first speaker in the round robin is the state that made the motion and then countries speak in order clockwise around the room (or similar for another table arrangement) until every country has been heard once. Countries may choose not to speak.

d. <u>Popcorn Style</u> is used to facilitate a quick discussion between delegates that is directed primarily by the delegates themselves. A delegate wishing to enter into popcorn debate must propose a length of time and a topic. A proposed speaking time limit is optional. If the motion passes, the Chair asks the delegate who made the motion to name the first speaker. They may name any delegation in the room including themselves. From there, each speaker names the next speaker until time has elapsed.

e. <u>Question-and-Answer [Q&A] Session</u> allows the Council to hold a question-and-answer period with an individual or individuals that can provide needed information, clarification, or explanation that will benefit the work of the Council. The motion must include a length of time and name the respondents for the session. The respondents can be any delegate, an expert witness, or another guest to the Council. Once begun, the Chair calls on countries wishing to ask a question and questions are posed to the Chair. The Chair asks the respondents if they accept the question prior to their responding. The Chair keeps time for the Q&A session by timing only the responses to questions but not the questions. Follow-up questions are at the discretion of the Chair.

26. Motion to <u>Temporarily Revoke Delegate Rights</u> may be used in the case of a delegate, after multiple warnings, continuing to engage in behavior that is unacceptable and disruptive to the debate process. This motion may only be initiated at the discretion of the Chair, and must include a time limit (maximum 20 minutes). If his or her rights are revoked, a delegate must stay in the Council room until time expires and rights returned, and maintains the right to vote on substantive matters. The motion requires a second, is debatable with two speakers for and two speakers against and requires a supermajority to pass.

27. <u>Procedural Points</u>. There are three important tools delegates may use at any time, called points. Delegates raise their placards and call out a point.

The Chair will recognize the delegate, who will then provide rationale for raising the point.

a.  A <u>Point of Order</u> should be called if parliamentary procedure is used improperly, either by a delegate or the Chair. This point may interrupt a speaker if necessary; the Chair will not count this time against the interrupted speaker's time. This point should not be used for any purpose other than a breach in the rules of parliamentary procedure. After hearing the rationale, the Chair immediately states whether the rules were indeed breached. If the Chair is uncertain, the Parliamentarian may be tasked with checking the Handbook. The ultimate authority in any dispute over the rules is the National Council representative(s).

b.  A <u>Point of Personal Privilege</u> is used to bring the Chair's attention to physical distractions that impair the delegate's ability to participate in the proceedings. This point may interrupt a speaker. Examples include uncomfortable room temperature, noise inside or outside the Council room, the volume of a speaker, an obstructed view of the proceedings, etc. If it is within the power of the Chair, he or she will alleviate the distraction and move forward.

c.  A <u>Point of Parliamentary Inquiry</u> may be called if any delegate needs an explanation of the current proceedings, or would like to ask a question pertaining specifically to parliamentary procedure. This point may interrupt a speaker. This point is never used to ask a substantive question or to ask a question directly to another delegate. This is an extremely helpful tool for delegates new to parliamentary procedure.

d.  A <u>Point of Reconsideration</u> is used for the purpose of informing the Chair that the state rising to the point wishes to change their vote. The Chair will record the change and announce if it alters the outcome of the vote. In a case where the Chair is uncertain as to how the state voted previously or to the new final outcome, the Chair may opt to take the vote a second time for the sake of accuracy. This point is in order only immediately after an outcome of the vote is announced and rights, if applicable, are entertained. The motion is out of order if the committee moved on to other business. This point may not interrupt a speaker.

e.  A <u>Point of Information</u> is in order after a speaker has yielded to points of information or during a Suspension of the Rules for the purpose of a Question-and-Answer Session. It may not interrupt a speaker and has no position in the order of precedence. Delegates rising to a point of information do not say "Point of Information" as with other points in the rules.

28. <u>Yields</u>. If there is any time remaining at the end of a formal speech, the delegate must yield that time. There are three appropriate yields: Yield to the Chair, Yield to Points of Information, and Yield to Another Delegate.

a. <u>Yield to the Chair</u> simply means that the remaining time is discarded and the Chair may recognize the next speaker.
b. <u>Yield to Points of Information</u> means that other delegates may ask the speaker questions for the remainder of his or her speaking time. Delegates wishing to ask questions raise their placards, wait for recognition from the Chair, and ask a question not directed at the individual speaker. Only the speaker's answers count against the speaking time, not questions. The older less formal language of "Yield to Questions" is an acceptable alternative statement by a delegate yielding to points of information.
c. <u>Yield to Another Country</u> means the remaining time is transferred to another delegate. A specific country must be named; the specified country may accept or reject the yielded time. Yielded time may not be re-yielded.

## Appendix I: Statute of the Arab Court of Justice

*Article 1*

The Arab Court of Justice, established by the League of Arab States as its principal judicial organ, shall be constituted and shall function in accordance with the provisions of the present Statute and Rules and the Model Arab League Handbook.

*Article 2*

The Court shall be composed of a body of independent judges, elected or appointed from among persons of high moral character.

*Article 3*

Section 3.01 The Court shall consist of ten member states, except in cases where time constraints shall demand that fewer cases be heard. In those cases, the number of states represented will be determined on an individual basis.

Section 3.02 Membership on the Court shall rotate among the members of the League of Arab States on an annual basis, such that states scheduled to appear before the Court will always be represented on the Court.

Section 3.03 Each member state shall be permitted up to two seats on the Bench, except while a country is being represented in the case currently being heard by the court. Such members shall recuse themselves for the duration of the proceedings of the case in question.

(a) Each seat on the Bench shall be represented in formal procedure by a Justice of the Court. Justices of the Court must be present for the entirety of all proceedings of the Court;

(b) The declaration to be made by every Member of the Court shall be as follows: "I solemnly declare that I will perform my duties and exercise my powers as judge honorably, faithfully, impartially, and conscientiously."

*Article 4*

Section 4.01 The Chief Justice of the Court shall represent a member state of the League of Arab States, but need not represent a member state of the Court.

Section 4.02 The Chief Justice shall have no voting rights on substantive matters, but may vote in procedural matters to break a tie.

*Article 5*

Section 5.01 An Assistant Chief Justice of the Court shall be elected from among the justices. The Assistant Chief Justice shall retain all rights of access afforded to the Chief Justice.

Section 5.02 When the Chief Justice is not present the Assistant Chief Justice shall act as a representative for the Chief Justice and shall have all rights and privileges afforded to the Chief Justice.

*Article 6*

Section 6.01 The Chief Justice, the Secretariat, and other leadership of the League of Arab States together shall appoint a Bailiff of the Court. The Bailiff shall perform duties as indicated in this Statute and otherwise assist the Chief Justice as needed.

Section 6.02 Before taking up his/her duties, the Bailiff of the Court shall make the following declaration at a meeting of the Court: "I solemnly declare that I will perform the duties incumbent upon me as Bailiff of the Arab Court of Justice in all loyalty, discretion and good conscience, and that I will faithfully observe all provisions of the Statute and Rules of the Court."

*Article 7*

Members of the Court shall be bound, unless prevented from attending by illness or other serious reasons duly explained to the Chief Justice of the Court, to hold themselves permanently at the disposal of the Court while the Court is in session.

*Article 8*

Section 8.01 Justices are expected to recuse themselves from any proceeding in which their impartiality might be reasonably questioned.

Section 8.02 If, for some other special reason, a member of the Court considers that he/she should not take part in the decision of a particular case, the member shall so inform the Chief Justice of the Court.

Section 8.03 If the Chief Justice of the Court considers that for some special reason one of the members of the Court should not sit in a particular case, the Chief Justice shall give the member notice accordingly.

Section 8.04 If in any such case the member of the Court and the Chief Justice disagree, the matter shall be settled by a majority decision of the Court. Should such a decision cause controversy, the matter will be addressed by the Secretary General or National Council representative.

Section 8.05 In no case shall a member of the Court sit in a case where his/her country is a party.

*Article 9*

Section 9.01 The full court shall sit except when it is expressly provided otherwise in the present Statute.

Section 9.02 A quorum of nine judges – including the Chief Justice – shall suffice to constitute the Court. In cases where a fewer number of Justices sit, the quorum shall remain proportional thereto.

*Article 10*

Section 10.01 The jurisdiction of the Court comprises all cases which the parties refer to it and all matters specially provided for in the Charter of the League of Arab States or in treaties and conventions in force.

Section 10.02 The states party to the present Statute may at any time declare that they recognize as compulsory ipso facto and without special agreement, in relation to any other state accepting the same obligation, the jurisdiction of the Court in all legal disputes concerning:

a. the interpretation of a treaty;
b. any question of international law;
c. the existence of any fact which, if established, would constitute a breach of an international obligation;
d. the nature or extent of the reparation to be made for the breach of an international obligation.

Section 10.03 The declarations referred to above may be made unconditionally or on condition of reciprocity on the part of several or certain states, or for a certain time.

Section 10.04 Such declarations shall be deposited with the Secretary-General of the Arab League, who shall transmit copies thereof to the parties to the Statute and to the Court.

Section 10.05 In the event of a dispute as to whether the Court has jurisdiction, the matter shall be settled by the decision of the Court, guided by the provisions of this Article.

*Article 11*

Shall there be several parties in the same interest, they shall be reckoned as one party only and shall be represented by the member state listed on the Docket of the Court. Any doubt upon this point shall be settled by a majority decision of the Court.

*Article 12*

Only states may be parties in cases before the Court. The League of Arab States may be party to a case, as either plaintiff or defendant. It may also bring cases or have cases brought against it for which it is the only interested party. In either case, the League shall appoint a willing member state to represent its interests before the court.

*Article 13*

The Court, subject to and in conformity with its Rules, may request of public international organizations information relevant to cases before it, and shall receive such information presented by such organizations on their own initiative.

*Article 14*

In the event of a dispute as to the Court's jurisdiction, the matter shall be settled by a majority decision of the Court.

*Article 15*

Section 15.01 The Court, whose function is to decide in accordance with international law such disputes as are submitted to it, shall apply:
(a) International conventions, whether general or particular, establishing rules expressly recognized by the contesting states;
(b) International custom, as evidence of a general practice accepted as law;
(c) The general principles of law recognized by Arab nations;
(d) Subject to the provisions of Article 21, judicial decisions and the teachings of the most highly qualified publicists of the various Arab nations, as subsidiary means for the determination of rules of law.
Section 15.02 This provision shall not prejudice the power of the Court to decide a case ex aequo et bono (according to the commonly accepted standards of what constitutes appropriate behavior), if the parties agree thereto.

*Article 16*

The Court shall have the power to indicate, if it determines that circumstances so require, any provisional measures which ought to be taken to preserve the respective rights of either party. Pending the final decision, notice of the measures suggested shall forthwith be given to the parties and to the Joint Defense Council.

*Article 17*

Section 17.01 The parties being heard shall be represented by agents.
Section 17.02 The agents may have the assistance of counsel or advocates before the Court.

*Article 18*

Section 18.01 The procedure of the Court shall consist of two parts: written and oral.
Section 18.02 The written portion shall consist of the communication to the Court of memorials, counter-memorials and, if necessary, replies and rejoinders; also all papers and documents in support:
(a) The Court may authorize or direct that there shall be a Reply by the applicant and a Rejoinder by the respondent if the parties are so agreed, or if the Court decides, proprio motu (of its own volition) or at the request of one of the parties, that these pleadings are necessary;
(b) A Memorial shall contain:
   1) A statement of the relevant facts,
   2) A statement of relevant law;
(c) A Counter-Memorial shall contain:
   1) An admission or denial of the facts stated in the Memorial,
   2) Any additional facts, if necessary,
   3) Observations concerning the statement of relevant law in the Memorial,
   4) A statement of law in answer thereto;
(d) The Reply and Rejoinder, whenever authorized by the Court, shall not merely repeat the parties' contentions, but shall be directed to bringing out the issues that still divide them;
(e) Every pleading shall set out the party's submissions at the relevant stage of the case, distinctly from the arguments presented, or shall confirm the submissions previously made;
(f) There shall be annexed to every pleading copies of any relevant documents cited in support of the contentions in the pleading;
(g) A list of all documents annexed to a pleading shall be furnished at the time the pleading is filed;

(h) These communications shall be made through the Chief Justice, in the order and within the time fixed by therein;

(i) A copy of every document produced and all evidence introduced by each party shall be communicated to the other party within a reasonable period of time;

(j) After the closure of the written proceedings, no further documents may be submitted to the Court by either party except with the consent of both parties:

   (i) In the absence of consent, the Chief Justice Court, after hearing the parties, may, if he or she considers the document necessary, authorize its distribution,

   (ii) If a new document is produced under Section 18.02(j), the other party shall have an opportunity of commenting upon it and of submitting documents in support of its comments,

   (iii) The Chief Justice shall, if he or she believes the introduction of a new document would unfairly prejudice the proceedings, exclude any document introduced under Section 18.02(j) that does not have the consent of both parties,

   (iv) If the Court or the Parties object to the decision to exclude under Section 18.02(j)(iii) they may appeal to the Secretary General who shall issue a final ruling on the matter not subject to further appeal.

Section 18.03 The Court's Docket shall be determined by the Chief Justice.

Section 18.04 The oral proceedings shall consist of the hearing by the Court of witnesses, experts, agents, counsel, and advocates:

(a) The Plaintiff shall present its case first, and shall be allotted twenty minutes to do so;

(b) The Court shall question the Plaintiff on the merits of its case for twenty minutes;

(c) The Defendant shall then present its case and respond to the questions of the Court in the same manner and within the same time allotments as the Plaintiff;

(d) If deemed prudent by the Court, and time allows, the Court may enter into a question period between the Plaintiff and the Defendant. The Court shall have discretion as to the length of time, but both sides must be granted equal time to ask and to respond to questions. The Chief Justice may bring such period to an end if it becomes unproductive for the proceedings of the Court;

(e) The Plaintiff, followed by the Defendant, shall make a five minute closing remark.

(f) Should the Plaintiff find the Defendant's closing remark grossly offensive or inaccurate, it may rise to a Right of Reply, which may be granted at the discretion of the Court and shall not exceed one minute;

(g) The time restrictions imposed by Section 18.04 may be extended at any time at the discretion of the Court;

(h) No reference may be made during the oral proceedings to the contents of any document which has not been produced in accordance with Section 18.02, unless this document is part of a publication readily available to all parties at the time the reference is made, or if the document is part of accepted public knowledge:

    (i)   In case of dispute as to the admissibility of a document under any of the criteria laid out in Section 18.04(h), the Chief Justice shall rule as to whether a document may be introduced,

    (ii)  If the Court or either of the Parties object to the ruling of the Chief Justice under Section 18.04(h)(i) then they may appeal to the Secretary General who shall issue a final decision on the matter;

(i) Without prejudice to the provisions of the Statute concerning the production of documents, each party shall communicate to the Chief Justice and the other party, in sufficient time before the opening of the oral proceedings, information regarding any evidence which it intends to produce or which it intends to request the Court to obtain;

(j) The Court may, if necessary, arrange for the attendance of a witness or expert to give evidence in the proceedings:

    (i)   Every witness shall make the following declaration before giving any evidence: "I solemnly declare upon my honor and conscience that I will speak the truth, the whole truth, and nothing but the truth,"

    (ii)  Every expert shall make the following declaration before giving any evidence: "I solemnly declare upon my honor and conscience that I will speak the truth, the whole truth, and nothing but the truth and that my statement will be in accordance with my sincere belief."

Section 18.05 The hearing shall be presided over by the Chief Justice.

Section 18.06 The hearing in Court shall be public:

(a) All parties executing or observing the functions of the Court must display official credentials issued by the Secretariat of the League of Arab States at all times. The Bailiff of the Court may deny entry to any party not displaying proper credentials;

(b) The Bailiff of the Court may, propiro motu (of its own volition) or at the discretion of the Court or Chief Justice, temporarily or permanently dismiss members of the press from the hearing.

Section 18.07 The Court may, at any time, call upon the agents to produce any document or to supply any explanations. Formal note shall be taken of any refusal.

Section 18.08 During the hearing any relevant questions are to be put to the witnesses and experts under the conditions laid down in Section 18.04.Section 18.09 When, subject to the control of the Court, the parties have completed their presentation of the case, the Chief Justice shall declare the hearing closed. The Court shall withdraw for sixty minutes to consider judgment and write opinions:

(a) The Chief Justice and Justices will participate in deliberations;
(b) The deliberations of the Court shall take place in private and remain secret until they are read at a special session of the Court in conjunction with the Summit Session of the League of Arab States:
    (i)   No representative of the states party to the case being deliberated may observe any part of the deliberations for any reason,
    (ii)  No representative of the press may observe the deliberations,
    (iii) Individuals wishing to gain access to the deliberations of the Court must submit a written request to be submitted to the National Council representative. Only upon the acceptance of that request, will credentials for access to the Court be granted. Credentials are revoked upon departure from the court. All individuals wishing further access must resubmit their request in order to gain access. The Secretary General, Assistant Secretary Generals, and National Council staff are the only individuals allowed unrestricted access to the Court,
    (iv) The Bailiff of the Court is responsible for granting and denying access to deliberations subject to Section 17.09(b)(i) and Section 17.09(b)(ii). The Bailiff will keep records of all parties that have had access to the Court by retaining signed and dated copies of requests for access. Requests for access will include the precise range of time parties had access to the Court,
    (v)  All parties executing or observing the deliberations of the Court must display official credentials issued by the Secretariat of the League of Arab States at all times. All parties receiving credentials have, in displaying credentials, accepted the rules of the Court and are therefore bound to them. The Bailiff of the Court shall deny entry to any party not displaying proper credentials;
(c) When the deliberations of the Court result in a draft judgment with apparent support of several Justices, the Chief Justice shall call a vote;
(d) Justices will vote by indicating their favor or opposition to the Chief Justice;
(e) If the draft judgment receives a majority of the votes, the Chief Justice will assign a Justice to write the judgment without announcing the vote. The Chief Justice will, in cases where the vote of the justices was not unanimous, also assign a Justice to write the dissenting opinion and may allow for concurring opinions;
(f) If the draft judgment fails to receive a majority of the votes, the Chief Justice will instruct the Justices to continue deliberations;

(g) Each judgment and dissenting opinion shall state and explain the reasons on which it is based;

(h) Each judgment or dissenting opinion shall contain an abstract of 200 words or less on the first page;

(i) Judgments shall be submitted to the Chief Justice for review and processing;

(j) Justices shall not reveal the nature of their deliberations to any individual not present for the deliberation. Such information will be revealed at the reading of the Court's judgments and dissenting opinions at the special session of the Court in conjunction with the Summit Session of the League of Arab States;

(k) Deliberations may be extended by one and only one full session, as defined in Section 18.09, at the discretion of the Chief Justice;

(l) Decisions of the Court shall remain secret until officially announced at a session of the Court held for this purpose and occurring alongside a Summit Session of the League of Arab States:

(i) At the request of the Secretary General of the League of Arab States, the Chief Justice may lift this restriction for any individual case where failure to immediately disclose the decision would be detrimental to the work of any organ of the League of Arab States.

*Article 19*

The Chief Justice or the Court, at its discretion, may declare any person in breach of any of the Statute and Rules to be in contempt of court. If the person in contempt is a Justice or Clerk of Court, the Chief Justice may remove their speaking privileges for a period of time, not to exceed two full case sessions unless approved by the Secretariat and National Council; if the person is an observer, the Chief Justice may remove that person from the Court until further notice.

*Article 20*

Whenever one of the parties does not appear before the Court, or fails to defend its case, the other party may call upon the Court to decide in favor of its claim. The Court must, before doing so, satisfy itself, not only that it has jurisdiction, but also that the claim is well founded in fact and law. The Chief Justice may determine whether those requirements are met, and either reschedule the proceedings or remove the case from the Court docket.

*Article 21*

The decision of the Court has no binding force except between the parties and in respect of that particular case.

*Article 22*

The judgment of the Court is final and without appeal. In the event of a dispute as to the meaning or scope of the judgment, the Court shall explain it upon the request of any party.

*Article 23*

Section 23.01 Should a state consider that it has an interest of a legal nature which may be affected by the decision in the case, it may submit a request to the Court to be permitted to intervene. It shall be for the Court to decide upon this request.

Section 23.02 Whenever the construction of a convention to which states other than those concerned in the case are parties is in question, the Chief Justice shall notify all states forthwith. Every state so notified has the right to intervene in the proceedings; but if it uses this right, the construction given by the judgment will be equally binding upon it.

*Article 24*

Section 24.01 Should any body of the League of Arab States request an advisory opinion on a point of law, the Court may provide such an opinion. Requests must be presented to and approved by the Secretariat, after which the Court has the right to either hear the request or reject it.

Section 24.02 Questions upon which the advisory opinion of the Court is asked shall be laid before the Court by means of a written request containing an exact statement of the question upon which an opinion is required, and accompanied by all documents likely to throw light upon the question.

Section 24.03 The Court shall deliver its advisory opinions in open court, notice having been given to the Secretary General and to the representatives of the League of Arab States and of other international organizations immediately concerned.

Section 24.04 In the exercise of its advisory functions the Court shall further be guided by the provisions of the present Statute which apply in contentious cases to the extent to which it recognizes them to be applicable.

*Article 25*

If at any time a party to a case feels that these rules have been violated, any member of the Court or advocate to the Court may submit a written or oral objection. The objection shall be ruled upon by the Chief Justice.

*Article 26*

The parties to a case may jointly propose particular modifications or additions to the rules contained herein, which may be applied by the Court if the Court considers them appropriate in the circumstances of the case and they are in accordance with the Model Arab League handbook.

# Appendices section 3

## Sample session and documents

### Appendix J: Scripted council session

This scripted interpretation of the Rules of Procedure provides a practical explanation of, and a guide for, the way in which the Rules are applied in committee sessions. Illustrations of both the basic flow of the committee and of the proper procedure for certain motions found in the Rules are provided.

*OPENING THE SESSION*

1.0 The first committee session of each Model begins with all of the delegates formally introducing themselves.

1.1 The Chair conducts elections for the Committee Officers (Vice-Chair, Rapporteur, and Parliamentarian) as he or she sees fit.

1.2 Once the election of the Committee Officers has been completed, the Chair declares the committee "in order" and takes attendance. Each delegation responds "present and voting" when the name of the country it is representing is announced. The Chair circulates the Committee Roster and instructs the committee that any late-arriving delegates need to send a note to the Chair before they can receive speaking and voting privileges.

1.3 The next order of business for the committee is to open a speakers list to discuss the ordering of the agenda. A motion to set the order of the topics on the committee's agenda requires a second, is not debatable, and needs a simple majority for passage. After the order of the agenda has been set, the committee may then proceed to debate the first topic.

2.0 The Chair opens a speakers list on the first topic on the committee's agenda and sets the initial time limit for speeches.

2.1 To be placed on the speakers list, committee members raise their placards in order to be recognized by the Chair.

2.2 The Chair will direct his or her attention to the speakers list. A useful phrase is "Seeing no points or motions on the floor, the Chair will recognize <country name> for <time limit>. <Country name>, you have the floor."

2.3 At any time, when the floor is open, a delegate may make a motion to amend the speaker's time (Rule 16). The appropriate procedure for this motion is as follows:

– Delegate from Tunisia raises her placard.
– Chair responds, "Delegate from Tunisia, to what point do you rise?"
– Delegate from Tunisia replies, "I move to amend the speaker's time to two minutes."
– Chair answers, "Yes, delegate, that is in order. Is there a second?"
– Delegate from Iraq raises his placard.
– Chair acknowledges, "Thank you, delegate from Iraq."

––––

2.4 A delegate may yield his or her time at any point during a speech (Rule 13).

2.5 A delegate may also yield to another delegate at any time. An example would be as follows:

– Chair: "Seeing no other motions on the floor ... the delegate from Palestine is next on the speakers list and is recognized for two minutes."
– Delegate from Palestine: "Thank you, Honorable Chair. Palestine would like to ... [Delegate speaks for 1 minute 20 seconds]. Palestine would like to yield the remainder of its time to the delegate from Lebanon."
– Chair: "Delegate from Lebanon, you now have 40 seconds to address the committee."
– Delegate from Lebanon: "Thank you Honorable Chair. The people of Lebanon ... [speaks for 30 seconds]."
– Chair taps his or her gavel ten seconds before the expiration of the time to signal that the delegate's time is about to expire and should begin to conclude his or her remarks.
– Delegate from Lebanon continues to speak.
– Chair raps gavel, and says: "Delegate from Lebanon, your time has expired."
– Delegate from Lebanon: "Honorable Chair, may I have a few moments to conclude my remarks?"

– Chair: "I'm sorry, delegate, but if you wish to continue your remarks you have two choices, either have another delegate yield his or her time, or place your country on the speakers list again … Seeing no other motions on the floor, the delegate from the UAE is now recognized for two minutes."

The final way that a delegate may yield is to questions. Such a yield would allow the Chair to recognize Points of Information questioning the delegate about the contents of his or her speech.

## Appendix K: Annotated resolution

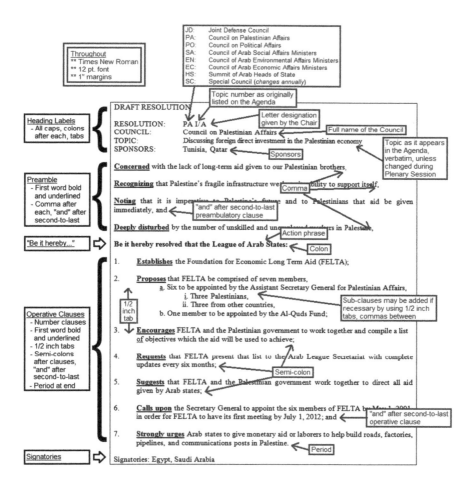

**Appendix L: Sample Memorial**

## ARAB COURT OF JUSTICE
## APPLICATION
## INSTITUTING PROCEEDINGS
filed in the Registry of the Court

on 25 February 2005

### CONTROL OF THE HALA'IB TRIANGLE
(THE REPUBLIC OF THE SUDAN v. ARAB REPUBLIC OF EGYPT)

*2005 General List No. 003*

APPLICATION OF THE REPUBLIC OF THE SUDAN

25 February 2005.

I, the undersigned, being duly authorized by The Republic of the Sudan, being the Ambassador of The Republic of the Sudan accredited by the Arab Court of Justice:

have the honor to refer to the declarations made by the The Republic of the Sudan and by The Arab Republic of Egypt respectively, accepting the jurisdiction of the Court as provided for in Articles 10, 11, 12, and 13 of the Statute and Rules of the Arab Court of Justice, and by virtue of the consent to the jurisdiction based upon those instruments and in accordance with Article 17 Section 2.0 of the Statute and Rules of the Court, make this application instituting proceedings in the name of The Republic of the Sudan against Arab Republic of Egypt on the following grounds:

*MEMORIAL OF THE REPUBLIC OF THE SUDAN*

*I. STATEMENT OF FACTS*

The Republic of the Sudan is the sovereign authority of the Hala'ib Triangle. This truth has existed both since the Sudan became independent and while it remained under the British as the Anglo-Egyptian Sudan. As the only state with the right to administer the Hala'ib, the Sudan is the lone authority to administer the law in the area as well as to oversee the use of the land and its resources. This, in accordance with international law, extends to the waters of the Red Sea off the coast of the Hala'ib. The right of the Sudanese government to total jurisdiction in the area has been severely limited due to actions taken by the Arab Republic of Egypt. Egyptian refusal to recognize Sudanese jurisdiction coupled with inane claims to sovereign control of the Hala'ib Triangle have resulted in economic and diplomatic losses for the Sudan. Egyptian policies have also resulted in a constant and unnecessary territorial dispute between our two states. This entire situation has been the result of unsubstantiated claims by the Egyptian government which completely ignore the legal precedences set forth in numerous treaties on the region.

## II. LEGAL GROUNDS ON WHICH THE CLAIM IS BASED

After the final reconquest of parts of the territory now know as the Sudan and after the end of Turkish domination of both Egypt and the Sudan, Great Britain and Egypt met to settle administrative questions in the area. In 1899, the United Kingdom and Egypt signed the Anglo-Egyptian Condominium Agreement. In this Treaty, the Republic of the Sudan was defined as all territories south of the 22nd Parallel. Egypt's Khedive would rule all lands north of the 22nd Parallel, while the United Kingdom would maintain administrative authority over the Sudan. This document is the typical basis for Egyptian claims to the Hala'ib Triangle, which lays north of the 22nd Parallel. This is, however, completely inaccurate.

The United Kingdom, which maintained sovereign authority over Egypt during this period, had final say over the agreements. Both the Egyptians and the British made several changes to the 1899 Condominium which form the basis of Sudanese control. The changes were:

1. The enclave of Suakin was given to the Sudan in July, 1899.
2. Wadi Halfa Salient was given to the Sudan by Egypt in March, 1899.
3. On July 25, 1902, the area known as the Hala'ib Triangle was "decreed" a part of the Sudan by Britain and Egypt [represented by Egypt's Minister of the Interior]. The territory was then formally annexed to the Anglo-Egyptian Sudan on November 4, 1902. The 1902 Arrete and Decree corrects administrative problems by placing the lands of the Ababda tribe, in an area south of the 22nd Parallel under Egyptian control and placing the lands of the Beja tribe, north of the 22nd Parallel, under Sudanese control.
4. On June 16, 1907, the placement of the lands of the Ababda tribe [south of the 22nd Parallel] under Egyptian jurisdiction was rescinded upon the request of the Egyptian Intelligence Service.

Of the changes to the Condominium of 1899, all but the fourth are valid still today. According to Article 5 of the Treaty, Egypt was not given the authority to make any law or decree that applied to the Sudan or Sudanese territories. Such authority was vested only in the British government. The original 1899 Condominium and the first three changes to it were attempts at re-structuring administrative control of territories into a more feasible structure and, as a result of this, were done by the British and the Egyptian Minister of the Interior. The fourth change, a request of the Intelligence Service which was granted by the Egyptian government is not clearly established as having had British involvement. Maps of the area during this period support this argument as they indicate the first three changes to Egyptian/Anglo-Egyptian Sudan borders but do not indicate the fourth and final change.

To summarize, for these purposes, the 1899 Condominium establishes the 22nd Parallel as the administrative boundary between Egypt and the Anglo-Egyptian Sudan. This agreement was then changed, by an Arrete and Decree promulgated in 1902, which clearly defines the areas currently known as the Hala'ib Triangle to the Anglo-Egyptian Sudan. No other treaty or agreement altered the boundaries between Egypt and the Sudan. Article V of the Condominium restricts Egyptian actions with reference to the Sudan and therefore nullifies any other attempted change to the borders that the Egyptian government would attempt to institute. Two other treaties, the Sykes–Picot Treaty and the Treaty of Lausanne, will now be referenced to further solidify Sudanese claims to the Hala'ib Triangle.

The Sykes–Picot Treaty of 1916 established demarcations of control of colonial powers, particularly between the French and the British, thus resulting in even more diplomatic agreements on borders of colonial jurisdiction that would eventually become the basis for the borders of the Sovereign States of Africa. This treaty has often been quoted as having altered the boundaries of the Anglo-Egyptian Sudan. This is true but ultimately misleading as it has no impact on the Northern Boundary of the Sudan. The Sykes–Picot Treaty settled African land disputes between the French and British empires. It has no jurisdiction on domestic border changes within the British Empire. Therefore, since Egypt and the Anglo-Egyptian Sudan were still both parts of the British Empire, the treaty had no effect on the border dispute in question. Therefore, by the end of 1916 the Condominium and its amendments were all still valid demarcations of the border in question.

The Treaty of Lausanne, which was signed on July 24, 1923, settled all post World War I disputes between Turkey and several European powers, including the British Empire. The Treaty establishes and demarcates boundaries between Turkey, the British Empire, and all other sovereigns in the areas of former Ottoman control. The Treaty clearly delineates that the Hala'ib Triangle remained within the British Empire after Egyptian independence on February 28, 1922. The Treaty also indicates that it did not alter Egyptian borders with reference to territories relinquished by Turkey and that questions on the recognition of the State of Egypt would be settled by the powers in question. As the British Empire already recognized the independence of Egypt, any boundaries between that state and the Empire, as depicted in the Treaty of Lausanne, should be considered legally binding. Egypt, at this point, is now separated from the British Empire, which means any future alterations to the boundary between Egypt and the Sudan would have to be conducted bilaterally between Egypt and the British or, after Sudanese independence, between Egypt and the Sudan. No bilateral agreements, treaties, or other documents exist to indicate that Egypt was ever given control of the Hala'ib Triangle after the Treaty of Lausanne was signed.

Egyptian unilateral actions were also impossible. As a recognized independent state, Egypt was detached from the Britsh Empire and the Anglo-Egyptian Sudan. While independent, Egypt still accepted the Condominium Agreement as the source of its southern border and relations with the Sudan. With the Condominium Agreement still in force, Egypt, by Article V, was still prohibited from enacting policy on the Sudan. Thus, no Egyptian decision since the signing of the Treaty of Lausanne could cause the detachment of the Hala'ib Triangle from the rest of the Sudan. Egypt, with complete and utter disregard for international law and the sovereignty of others, treated the 22nd Parallel as the border between the two states.

As for the lands of the Ababda tribe, The Republic of the Sudan had previously and does once again indicate that it accepted rulership of this area. The Republic of the Sudan recognizes Egypt's right as a sovereign state to relinquish claims to ownership of the lands of the Ababda tribe which lay below the 22nd Parallel. While we accepted this decision of the Egyptian goverment, we do not consider any further extention of the 22nd Parallel eastward to be an appropriate boundary between our two states ... This attempt at illegally claiming territories within the Sudan is not recognized by the Sudan and should not be recognized by the international community. To do so would undermine the very basis of all international law by allowing one state to redefine the boundaries of another without its consideration, input, and consent. Egypt was well outside the bounds of its own authority by claiming control of the Beja tribal lands that constituted the Hala'ib Triangle simply because there is no evidence that either the British Empire or The Republic of the Sudan ever willfully and legally relinquished the Hala'ib Triangle to Egyptian control.

Numerous maps, treaties, and other publications of the British Empire, from before and after the signing of the Treaty of Lausanne, indicate that the British continued to draw the border between Egypt and the Anglo-Egyptian Sudan so as to incorporate the Hala'ib Triangle into their territory. This would remain true up until Sudanese independence. Since Sudanese independence, we have considered the Hala'ib Triangle an integral part of our territory and have no plans of ever relinquishing our control of it.

The Republic of the Sudan also, in its sovereign right to control of the Hala'ib Triangle, claims control of the waters off the coast of the Triangle as well. International standards of demarcation specifically establish control of coastal waterways.

## THE NATURE OF THE CLAIM

On the basis of the foregoing Memorial, and while reserving its right to supplement and or to amend this Application, and subject to the presentation to the Court of the relevant evidence and legal argument, The Republic of the Sudan requests the Court to adjudge and declare that:

1. Reasserts that all lands south of the 22nd Parallel that were either a) part of the Anglo-Egyptian Sudan, or b) not ceded by Sudanese agreement to bordering states other than Egypt, as the Sovereign territory of the Sudan.

    We believe that any basis for a decision on the Hala'ib Triangle must first begin with recognizing that the 1899 Condominium was the first legal delineation of a boundary between Egypt and the Sudan. Through international agreements and negotiations, the Sudan has officially established all other borders with its neighboring states. This would formally establish the Egyptian–Sudanese boundary up till the areas contested due to changes in the Condominium. In doing so, we ask that the Court also restate the first two changes to the Condominium, which draw the line north of Wadi Halfa [at $22°12'12''$] and also incorporate the area of Suakin, both alterations that neither the Sudan nor Egypt dispute.

2. We ask the Court to rule that the area known as the Hala'ib Triangle be reaffirmed as sovereign territory of The Republic of the Sudan.

    The Republic of the Sudan requests the Court to establish the eastern portion of the Egyptian–Sudanese border as originally established in the 1902 Arrete and Decree. This would demarcate the boundary accordingly: 776 miles to the east of the western-most point of the Sudanese–Egyptian border, the border moves "$33°10'$ east for 31 miles to Jebel Bartazuga, east northeastward 29 miles to Bir Hesmet 'Umar, north northeastward about 32 miles to Jabal al Deiga … east northeastward about 35 miles to Jabal Umm at Tuyur al Fawaqani, north northeastward about 42 miles to Jabal Niqrub al Faqqani, southeastward to Bir Meneiga about 17 miles and northeastward to Bi'r Shalatayn and the Red Sea about 36 miles." [International Boundary Study, No. 18 Sudan – Egypt (United Arab Republic) Boundary, pg. 4–5.]

3. We ask that the Court authorizes the Sudan to remove all Egyptian officials from the Hala'ib Triangle if Egypt fails to do so in three months.

    The Sudan is willing to give Egypt and Egyptian nationals living in the area, which do not wish to remain, adequate amount of time to settle their respective affairs and exit the area. We do not, however, feel that the presence of Egyptian officials is necessary for this entire process. We ask that the

Court not allow Egypt to further harm the Sudanese state by not having a strict schedule to adhere to for their complete and total relinquishment of the Hala'ib Triangle to Sudanese control.

4. We ask that the Court establish a demilitarized zone, on the Egyptian side of the border, of 10 miles from the Egyptian–Sudanese Border, along the Hala'ib Triangle, into which no Egyptian military personnel or equipment may be placed.

    The Egyptian goverment has shown a disregard for Sudanese sovereignty in the area, and even demonstrated that disregard with military actions in the Hala'ib in 1992. Once established as Sudanese territory, it would be in the best interests of peace that Egypt be forbidden to militarize the immediate area.

5. The Republic of the Sudan requests that The Arab Republic of Egypt be found in violation of treaties and agreements dating back over 100 years and therefore pay restitutions to the Sudan to make up for all losses that the Sudan incurred during the time period we were unable to access our natural resources.

    The Republic of the Sudan feels it is only appropriate that the Court order The Arab Republic of Egypt to pay to the Sudan all profits the government collected during its illegal attempts at administration of the area. We also feel that proper restitutions, including interest and inflation, be assessed to the Sudan to account for economic losses incurred due to the Sudan being blocked from tapping the resources of the Hala'ib. Third, and finally, we feel that The Arab Republic of Egypt should pay further restitutions to account for costs involved in re-establishing diplomatic ties with governments and companies that are currently unwilling to work with the Sudan in the Hala'ib until the jurisdiction of the Sudan is formally established.

6. We ask that the Court publish its finding that the Hala'ib Triangle is the territory of the Sudan and make such legal rights of the Sudan clear to all states currently holding in abeyance treaties and agreements on the access of this area.

    The Republic of the Sudan requires that the court provide legally binding documentation of the decision of the case in order to establish, for foreign investment into the region, that the Sudan was, is, and always will be the only state with the authority to administrate the Hala'ib Triangle.

    The Government of The Republic of the Sudan has designated the undersigned as its Agents for the purposes of these proceedings. All communications relating to this case should be directed to these Agents.

Respectfully submitted,

X.X.

<STUDENT NAME>                  <STUDENT NAME>

Agents of The Republic of the Sudan

Appendix M: Sample Counter-Memorial

### ARAB COURT OF JUSTICE
### THE FAILURE OF HAMAS TO ACCEPT THE 2002 ARAB PEACE INITIATIVE
(THE LEAGUE OF ARAB STATES vs. THE STATE OF PALESTINE)

2007 General List No. 1

### COUNTER-MEMORIAL
### OF THE GOVERNMENT OF THE STATE OF PALESTINE
filed in the Registry of the Court

on 9 March 2007

## I. COMMENT ON FACTS STATED IN THE MEMORIAL OF THE LEAGUE OF ARAB STATES

*Admitted facts:*

Palestine is recognized by the League of Arab States (League) as an independent sovereign state and a full member of the League.

Harakat al Muqawama al-Islamiyya (Hamas) is an independent organization of the Palestinian people formed in 1987.

According to the 1988 Hamas Charter:

- The ideology of Hamas is Islam (Articles 1, 2, 5).
- Hamas proclaims that Palestine, as an Islamic Waqf, cannot be divided by man (Article 11).
- Waging Jihad is the national and religious duty of every citizen of Palestine (Article 12).
- Hamas accepts other Islamist movements, only so long as they profess a similar ideological background (Articles 22, 25).

In 1993 the PLO and Israel signed the Declaration of Principles, which provided for an interim Palestinian government.

In 2002 the League of Arab States unanimously approved the Arab Peace Initiative, proposing a comprehensive framework for peace in the region.

In 2006, Hamas won the majority of parliamentary seats in the Palestinian election and became the ruling party in Palestine. Since that time Hamas has not sought to change the Palestinian Constitution.

*Refuted and Qualified facts:*

According to the 1988 Hamas Charter:

- "They [Hamas] is committed to the removal of the State of Israel (Articles 6, 8)."

Here Hamas states its commitment to the promotion of Islam (Articles 6, 8).

- "Therefore accepting any initiatives to achieve a peaceful resolution to the Palestinian conflict is tantamount to renouncing Islam (Article 13)."

Hamas is unable to accept any initiatives regarding "so-called peaceful solutions" in the event that Hamas is forced to renounce "any part of Palestine" since "renouncing any part of Palestine means renouncing part of the religion" (Article 13).

- "They [Hamas] denounce any intervention from the East or the West (Articles 22, 25, 26, 28)."

Hamas does not denounce all forms of intervention from the East and West, but specifically denounces those individuals and organizations who "act for the interests of Zionism" (Articles 22, 25, 26, 28).

- "They [Hamas] reject the Palestinian Liberation Organization (PLO) as a valid representation of the Palestinian people because of the PLO's desire to establish a secular government (Article 27).

Hamas does not reject the PLO, but in fact refers to the organization as "among the closest to the Hamas, for it constitutes a father, a brother, a relative, a friend." The Charter goes on to state that "we do not denigrate its role in the Arab–Israeli conflict, we cannot substitute it for the Islamic nature of Palestine by adopting secular thought." Therefore, while the Hamas cannot fully accept the PLO, its charter does not "reject" the organization as a whole (Article 27).

"During the 2002 Beirut Summit, Hamas actively worked to derail the Arab Peace Initiative and has continually sought to disrupt such peaceful measures."

- Any aggressions made by militant individuals of Hamas during this time period were a direct result of Israeli aggression toward and oppression of the Palestinian people. Therefore, Hamas did not seek to disrupt the "peaceful measures," but to defend Palestinians.

## II. ADDITIONAL FACTS

- Following the signing of the Mecca Agreement (2007), Mahmoud Abbas explained, "Hamas will not be required to recognize Israel, since, as a Palestinian movement, and even as a government, it is not authorized to conduct diplomatic negotiations, as negotiations and the signing of treaties in the name of the Palestinian people are the exclusive prerogative of the PLO and its head, Mahmoud Abbas."
- Abbas also declared that "organizations participating in the future national unity government will not be obligated to the government's position; only the ministers will be obligated to these positions."
- Azzam Al-Ahmad, head of the Fatah faction in the Legislative Council, stated that "the recognition of countries is not the affair of organizations and parties but of governments. Hamas need not declare its explicit and legal recognition of Israel, and Fatah also need not do this; no Palestinian faction needs to do it … Each faction and organization is entitled to retain its own special ideology and platform, but each must be committed to its national entity and its representatives."
- Despite its purpose of peace, Israeli Foreign Minister Tzipi Livini stated, "It's impossible for Israel to accept the Arab peace initiative in its current version."
- Hamas and Fatah signed the Mecca Agreement on February 8, 2007, displaying cooperation on the part of Hamas.

## III. OBSERVATIONS CONCERNING THE STATEMENT OF RELEVANT LAW IN THE MEMORIAL OF THE LEAGUE OF ARAB STATES

- While it is true that Article VII of the Charter of the League of Arab States reads, "Unanimous decisions of the Council shall be binding upon all member-states of the League," the fact remains that Hamas is not an Arab state, but a political faction. "Yusuf and another v European Council and another (Case T-306/01), [2006] All ER (EC) 290 Wherein the European Community found that regional organizations may 'adopt measures not only in respect of third countries but also in respect of individuals who and non-state bodies which are not necessarily linked to the governments or regimes of those countries.'"
- The Arab League member states do not abide by the laws or measures adopted within the European Community, but by the laws of international bodies to which the individual Arab League member states belong.

## IV. STATEMENT OF RELEVANT LAW

*The Charter of the Hamas (1988):*

### Article XXVII

"The PLO is among the closest to the Hamas, for it constitutes a father, a brother, a relative, a friend. Can a Muslim turn away from his father, his brother, his relative or his friend? Our homeland is one, our calamity is one, our destiny is one and our enemy is common to both of us. Under the influence of the circumstances which surrounded the founding of the PLO, and the ideological invasion which has swept the Arab world since the rout of the Crusades, and which has been reinforced by Orientalism and the Christian Mission, the PLO has adopted the idea of a Secular State, and so we think of it. Secular thought is diametrically opposed to religious thought. Thought is the basis for positions, for modes of conduct and for resolutions. Therefore, in spite of our appreciation for the PLO and its possible transformation in the future, and despite the fact that we do not denigrate its role in the Arab–Israeli conflict, we cannot substitute it for the Islamic nature of Palestine by adopting secular thought. For the Islamic nature of Palestine is part of our religion, and anyone who neglects his religion is bound to lose ... When the PLO adopts Islam as the guideline for life, then we shall become its soldiers, the fuel of its fire which will burn the enemies. And until that happens, and we pray to Allah that it will happen soon, the position of the Hamas toward the PLO is one of a son toward his father, a brother toward his brother, and a relative toward his relative who suffers the other's pain when a thorn hits him, who supports the other in the confrontation with the enemies and who wishes him divine guidance and integrity of conduct."

*2007 Mecca Agreement between Fatah and Hamas:*

"Based on the noble initiative of the Custodian of the Holy Places, King Abdallah bin Abd Al-'Aziz, king of the Saudi Arab Kingdom, and under the auspices of His Highness, a dialogue was held in the holy [city of] Mecca between the two movements Fatah and Hamas, during February 6 through 8, 2007, [in order to arrive at] a Palestinian agreement. The dialogue was crowned with success, with the help of Allah, may He be praised and exalted, and the following agreement was achieved:

a)   Palestinian blood is sacred and all means should be used and all arrangements should be made in order to prevent bloodshed. National unity is important as a basis for steadfastness on the national level, for rising up against the occupation, for actualizing the national and legitimate goals of the Palestinian people, and for adopting the language of negotiation as the only foundation for solving the political disagreements in the Palestinian arena. In this framework, we give many thanks to our brothers in Egypt and to the Egyptian security delegation in Gaza, who invested great efforts in calming the situation in the [Gaza] Strip in the recent period.

b) A final agreement was reached to establish a Palestinian national unity government in accordance with a detailed and ratified agreement between the sides, [and it was also agreed] to launch rapid action to take the constitutional steps for establishing it [i.e., the national unity government].

c) Steps forward should continue to be taken for [re-]activating the PLO, for its development, and for reform within it. [Likewise,] the activity of the preparatory committee based on the Cairo and Damascus understandings should be speeded up. The detailed steps [to be taken] in this matter are set out in detail.

d) Emphasis was placed on the principle of political partnership based on Palestinian Authority laws and based on political pluralism, in accordance with the agreement ratified between the sides. We bring the agreement to the Palestinian public, and to the peoples of the Arab Islamic nation, and to all [our] friends in the world. We are committed to the spirit and to the letter [of the agreement], so that we can now turn to attaining our national goals, to freeing ourselves from the occupation, to restoring our rights, and to tackling the main issues, which are first and foremost Jerusalem, the refugees, the Al-Aqsa Mosque, the prisoners, and dealing with the fence and the settlements."

## *The Letter of Appointment*

"To Mr. Isma'il Abd Al-Salam Haniya
"As chairman of the executive committee of the PLO and president of the Palestinian Authority, after examining the basic Law and based on my authority:

a) I appoint you to establish the next Palestinian government within the time frame set out in the Basic Law.

b) After the government is put together and presented before me, it will be presented to the Legislative Council for a vote of confidence.

c) I call upon you, as prime minister of the next government, to be committed to the interests of the Palestinian people, to defend its rights and its achievements and to develop them, and also to act to actualize its national aims as confirmed by the decisions of the Palestinian National Council conferences, by the articles of the Basic Law, by the National Accord document [a watered-down version of the 'prisoners' document'], and by the decisions of the Arab summits. On this basis, I call upon you to honor the U.N. resolutions, the decisions of Arab legitimacy, and the agreements signed by the PLO."

## *UN Resolution 194:*

11. Resolves that the refugees wishing to return to their homes and live at peace with their neighbours should be permitted to do so at the earliest practicable date, and that compensation should be paid for the property of those choosing

not to return and for loss of or damage to property which, under principles of international law or in equity, should be made good by the Governments or authorities responsible; Instructs the Conciliation Commission to facilitate the repatriation, resettlement and economic and social rehabilitation of the refugees and the payment of compensation, and to maintain close relations with the Director of the United Nations Relief for Palestine Refugees and, through him, with the appropriate organs and agencies of the United Nations.

## V. CONCLUSION

Accordingly, on the basis of the facts and arguments set forth in this Counter-Memorial, and without prejudice to the right further to amend and supplement these submissions in the future, The State of Palestine asks the Court to adjudge and declare that:

Since Hamas is an independent political party within the State of Palestine:

1. The League recognizes and accepts the rights of Hamas, as a political party, to not fully accept all of the terms stated in the Arab Peace Initiative, since Hamas' ideology is not necessarily that of the Palestinian government.
2. The League acknowledges that Hamas has meaningfully addressed the Arab Peace Initiative by signing the Mecca Agreement, since this agreement encompasses many of the terms laid out in the Arab Peace Initiative.
3. The League does not demand any payment from Hamas as Hamas has broken no law by adhering to its political party's ideology.

The Government of The State of Palestine has designated the undersigned as its Agents for the purposes of these proceedings. All communications relating to this case should be directed to these Agents.

Respectfully submitted,
X.X.
&lt;STUDENT NAME&gt;
Agents of The State of Palestine.

&lt;STUDENT NAME&gt;

## Appendix N: Sample formal topic guide

### Council of Arab Social Affairs Ministers

1. Mitigating the social and economic effects of substance abuse on family structures, public order, and national development.
2. Addressing challenges facing political activists and civil society organizations in the Arab World, including the status of minorities.

3. Guaranteeing access to basic and continuing education for all people, especially girls, women, and other vulnerable populations.
4. Assessing compliance with the Arab Charter of Human Rights and other international human rights conventions to provide safeguards against denials and violations of human rights.
5. Re-examining public health as a human right in accordance with the 2009 UNDP Human Security Report, with particular attention paid to concerns related to H1N1, HIV/AIDS, maternal health and infant mortality, substance abuse, and disabilities.

*1. Mitigating the social and economic effects of substance abuse on family structures, public order, and national development*

*What's the issue?*
Substance abuse is becoming a leading cause for the death of countless individuals in the Arab World. Experts report that substance abuse has been linked to an increase in HIV/AIDS, that women are using drugs more often than men, and that the age of drug users has been decreasing. In addition, many drug users have not been seeking treatment to become less dependent on the substances due to lack of education and access to such programs.

*Relevance to the Arab World*
Great importance is put on family structure in the Arab World and this important structure is often undermined when family members resort to drug use. One such cause for this drug use is high unemployment – in some cases, it has been shown that poor economic infrastructure makes it a more desirable environment for drug trades to take place illegally than for money to be made by legal means. In addition, failure to integrate workers who have moved from more rural environments to city environments causes people to resort to drug use since they are unable to identify with their newer, more unfamiliar forms of government.

*Questions to consider from your nation's unique perspective:*

• What are the leading causes for substance abuse in the country that I represent?
• What programs have already been put into place to stop substance abuse – what has worked and what has not?
• What is the role of NGOs in this debate?
• How does substance abuse affect the personal lives of the citizens of the country that I represent?
• How is national development suffering as a result of substance abuse in the country that I represent?
• How can countries proactively help to curb drug trafficking between borders?

*Resources to review*[8]

"Drug Use Problems in the Middle East" (a presentation created by experts from around the world).

Article: Addressing HIV and drug use in the Middle East and North Africa.

United Nations Office on Drugs and Crime (UNODC): Drug Prevention in the Middle East.

## 2. Addressing challenges facing political activists and civil society organizations in the Arab World, including the status of minorities

*What's the issue?*

As more and more Arab nations embrace a spirit of free speech, both spoken and written, many activists and organizations are speaking out against their respective governments. Governments, in turn, are reacting to these individuals and groups with unprecedented force; incarceration is not uncommon when an individual or group speaks out against a government official, and reports about these incarcerations have caught the attention of many human rights organizations worldwide.

The effects of these incarcerations have therefore hindered journalists' ability to, in their estimation, accurately report certain issues prevalent in Arab nations. In addition, minority groups often rely on the press and human rights organizations to make their concerns known to other nations and organizations in an effort to bring resolution to problems that are occurring. Arab governments, meanwhile, contend that the reporting of these issues presents a threat to the security and welfare of the citizens in the respective nations.

*What are Civil Society Organizations and political activists?*

The London School of Economics Centre for Civil Society defines Civil Society Organizations as:

> Civil society refers to the arena of uncoerced collective action around shared interests, purposes and values ... Civil societies are often populated by organisations such as registered charities, development non-governmental organisations, community groups, women's organisations, faith-based organisations, professional associations, trades unions, self-help groups, social movements, business associations, coalitions and advocacy group.

Political activists are similar to Civil Society Organizations in that they look to make a statement not as an organization but as a group of individuals.

---

[8] Note: links for resources are omitted from the sample; URL links for resources provided should be included in an official topic guide.

*Questions to consider from your nation's unique perspective:*

- How do officials treat political activists and Civil Society Organizations if they speak out against the government?
- Does a complaint against the government present a threat to the security and welfare of the nation and its citizens?
- Is it possible for activists to coexist in society without threatening the stability of that society?
- How do the internet and new forms of media and rapid information distribution (as used in blogs, forums, and RSS feeds) impact the discussion when addressing challenges facing activists?
- What role do foreign media and international NGOs play in this debate?

*Resources to review*

Definition for Civil Society Organizations (in full).
Reporters Without Borders – an organization which reports information about journalists worldwide.

*3. Guaranteeing access to basic and continuing education for all people, especially girls, women, and other vulnerable populations*

*What's the issue?*
The World Bank reported earlier this year that "the quality of education in the Arab world is falling behind other regions and needs urgent reform if it is to tackle unemployment." This serious lack of access to quality education has been the root cause of many challenges facing the Arab World, including lack of infrastructure, increasing unemployment and a continuing disparity between the lower and upper classes. In addition, the lack of education for women has created a significant disparity between males and females in society, with illiteracy rates of females double when compared with their male counterparts in many countries in the Arab World. With regard to young people, parents are often encouraging young children to go to work instead of school due to economic conditions at home.

*What is being done now?*
Many NGOs, including UNESCO (United Nations Educational, Scientific and Cultural Organization) are working within Arab nations to provide educational opportunities for all, however economic infrastructure present in Arab nations has hampered the progress of these organizations.

*Questions to consider from your nation's unique perspective:*

- How does a lack of access to education for women and children affect the economic situation in my country?
- Should women and children receive access to education?
- Is education a luxury or a right for citizens of my country?
- What role(s) do NGOs play in providing access to education for all?
- How can Arab nations work together to improve the quality of education in our respective nations?
- What can be done to reduce the cost of education for citizens of my country?

*Resources to review*

BBC article: "Arab Education Falling Behind."
Empowering Women, Developing Society: Female Education in the Middle East and North Africa.
United Nations Activities and Publications for the Advancement of Arab Women.

*4. Assessing compliance with the Arab Charter of Human Rights and other international human rights conventions to provide safeguards against denials and violations of human rights*

*What's the issue?*
The Revised Arab Charter of Human Rights and its references to the Universal Declaration of Human Rights, the International Covenants on Civil and Political Rights and Economic, Social and Cultural Rights and the Cairo Declaration on Human Rights in Islam have been great steps in recording many basic human rights owed to all citizens of the Arab World. Please find the texts of all of these Charters and Declarations below.

The issue arises with implementation. While some nations in the Arab World have embraced concepts with regard to the rights of citizens as described in these documents, the unfair treatment of citizens and instability within Arab nations have caused many to review these documents and assess governments' compliance with the demands set forth in these documents.

*Questions to consider from your nation's unique perspective:*

- What issue(s) are stopping Arab nations from complying with clauses in these documents (below)?
- What can be done to determine specific violations?

- How can Arab League countries work together to provide an environment which safeguards against denials and violations of human rights?
- What role(s) do NGOs play in the context of safeguarding against human rights violations?
- What role(s) do nations outside of the Arab League play in this debate?

*Resources to review*

Revised Charter of Human Rights (2004) text.
The Revised Arab Charter on Human Rights: A Step Forward? – a commentary on the Arab Charter of Human Rights.
United Nations: Universal Declaration of Human Rights text.
United Nations: International Covenants on Civil and Political Rights and Economic, Social and Cultural Rights text.
Cairo Declaration on Human Rights in Islam text.

*5. Re-examining public health as a human right in accordance with the 2009 UNDP Human Security Report, with particular attention paid to concerns related to H1N1, HIV/AIDS, maternal health and infant mortality, substance abuse, and disabilities*

*What's the issue?*
Significant improvements have been made with regard to public health in the Arab World but more are needed due to still increasing mortality rates and decreasing birth rates in some countries in the Arab World. The United Nations Development Programme (UNDP) describes its 2009 UNDP Human Security Report as follows:

> The report argues that human security is a prerequisite for human development, and that the widespread absence of human security in Arab countries undermines people's options. Human security refers not only to questions of survival, but also basic needs such as access to clean water and quality of life concerns.

The report is broken down into the following segments:

- Applying the concept of human security in the Arab countries;
- The environment, resource pressures and human security in the Arab countries;
- The Arab State and human security – performance and prospects;
- The personal insecurity of vulnerable groups;
- Challenges to economic security;
- Hunger, nutrition and human security;
- Approaching health through human security – a road not taken;

- Occupation, military intervention and human insecurity;
- Concluding reflections.

*The role of the UNDP*
The UNDP is an office of the United Nations which produces reports to serve as recommendations for other bodies which enact policy, such as the League of Arab States.

*Questions to consider from your nation's unique perspective:*

- How is the country that I represent already putting into action the recommendations found in the 2009 UNDP Human Security Report?
- Working with other Arab League nations, how can we use the recommendations in the report to combat viruses, maternal health, mortality rates, substance abuse and disabilities?
- What role(s) do multi-national companies, along with NGOs play in this debate?
- What are the educational requirements needed to successfully implement recommendation(s) from this report?

*Resources to review*

Article: Threats to human security impede development in the Arab countries.
UNDP Arab Human Development Report text.
UNDP website dedicated to Arab States.

# Appendices section 4

## Reference documents

### Appendix O: Rules of Procedure cheat sheet

| # | Rule | Description | Second | Speakers | Vote | Interrupt a Speaker |
|---|------|-------------|--------|----------|------|---------------------|
| 7.1 | | Points | | | | |
| 7.1.1 | Point of Personal Privilege | Bring an uncomfortable situation to the attention of the Chair | n/a | n/a | n/a | Yes |
| 7.1.2 | Point of Order | Point out an improper usage of the Rules of Procedure | n/a | n/a | n/a | Yes |
| 7.1.3 | Point of Parliamentary Inquiry | Ask a question regarding the Rules of Procedure | n/a | n/a | n/a | No |
| 7.1.4 | Point of Reconsideration | Change your vote in a procedural or substantive vote | n/a | n/a | n/a | No |
| 7.2 | | Motions in the Order of Precedence | | | | |
| 7.2.1 | Adjourn the Meeting | Conclude the meeting until the next year | 1 | n/a | 1/2 | No |
| 7.2.2 | Quorum Call | Used to determine if a voting percentage of the Committee is present | n/a | n/a | n/a | No |
| 7.2.3 | Suspension of the Meeting | Recess a Committee for a Caucus or scheduled break | 1 | n/a | 1/2 | No |
| 7.2.4 | Suspension of the Rules | Used to suspend all rules in order to enter a Moderated Caucus or to suspend a specific rule | 1 | n/a | 2/3 | No |

| # | Rule | Description | Second | Speakers | Vote | Interrupt a Speaker |
|---|------|-------------|--------|----------|------|---------------------|
| 7.2.5 | Close Debate | End debate on an amendment, draft resolution or a topic and move into voting procedures | 1 | 2+/2 | 2/3 | No |
| 7.2.5.1 | Divide the Question | Used to vote on the inclusion of groups of operative clauses into the final draft resolution once debate has been closed | 1 | 2+/2 | 1/2 | No |
| 7.2.5.2 | Roll-Call Vote | Vote by a call of names | 2+ | n/a | n/a | No |
| 7.2.6 | Postponement of Debate | Used to "table" a resolution or topic | 1 | 2+/2 | 1/2 | No |
| 7.2.7 | Resume Debate | Used to resume debate previously postponed | 1 | n/a | 1/2 | No |
| 7.2.8 | Reconsideration | Ask the Committee to reconsider a hasty action on a draft resolution | n/a | 2+/2 | 1/2 | No |
| 7.2.9 | Impeach an Officer | Remove a negligent officer | 1 | 2+/2 | 2/3 | No |
| 7.2.10 | Appeal the Chair's Decision | Send a ruling of the Chair to the Committee for reconsideration | 1 | 2+/2 | 2/3 | No |
| 7.2.11 | Limit/Expand Debate | Can be used to limit debate to certain topics or resolutions or to expand debate from a limited state | 1 | n/a | 1/2 | No |
| 7.2.12 | Introduce a Resolution | Bring a draft resolution to the floor | 4+ | n/a | n/a | No |
| 7.2.13 | Amend Speaker's Time | Change the amount of time allotted for a speaker on the speakers list | 1 | n/a | 1/2 | No |

| # | Rule | Description | Second | Speakers | Vote | Interrupt a Speaker |
|---|------|-------------|--------|----------|------|---------------------|
| 7.2.14 | Introduce an Amendment | Bring an amendment to the floor | 4+ | (2+/2–)+ | 1/2 | No |
| 7.2.15 | Change the order of the Agenda | Alter the order of consideration of agenda topics | 1 | 2+/2 | 2/3 | No |
| 7.2.16 | Set the Agenda | Determine the order agenda topics will be discussed | 1 | n/a | 1/2 | No |
| 7.3 | | Rules outside the order of precedence | | | | |
| 7.3.1 | Adopt by Consent | Immediately adopt a motion, amendment, or draft resolution without objection | n/a | n/a | n/a | No |
| 7.3.2 | Author's Rights | Allows the author of an amendment or draft resolution to read the operative clauses and then briefly speak on the document | n/a | n/a | n/a | No |
| 7.3.3 | Right of Reply | Used to respond to a statement if a delegate feels impugned or wronged. Also used to correct incorrect information stated about a delegate or delegation | n/a | n/a | n/a | No |
| 7.3.4 | Withdrawal of a Motion or Paper | Used to withdraw a motion, amendment, or draft resolution prior to closure of debate | n/a | n/a | n/a | No |
| 7.4 | | Yields | | | | |

| # | Rule | Description | Second | Speakers | Vote | Interrupt a Speaker |
|---|------|-------------|--------|----------|------|---------------------|
| 7.4.1 | Yield to Another Delegate | Gives a delegate's remaining speaking time to another delegate | n/a | n/a | n/a | No |
| 7.4.2 | Yield to Questions | Gives a delegate's remaining speaking time to address points of information from the Committee | n/a | n/a | n/a | No |
| 7.4.3 | Yield to the Chair | Gives a delegate's remaining speaking time back to the Chair | n/a | n/a | n/a | No |
| 7.4.4 | Yield to Comments | Allows for two other members of the Committee to comment on the substance of the previous delegate's speech | n/a | n/a | n/a | No |

## Appendix P: Rules of Procedure precedence cheat sheet

The order of precedence of motions is as follows:

a. Point of Order
b. Point of Personal Privilege
c. Point of Parliamentary Inquiry
d. Point of Reconsideration
e. Adjourn the Meeting
f. Suspend the Meeting
g. Suspend the Rules
h. Close Debate
i. Close Speakers List
j. Suspend Debate
k. Resume Debate
l. Impeachment of Committee Officers
m. Appeal Decision of the Chair
n. Reconsideration
o. Temporarily Revoke/Reinstate Voting and Speaking Privileges

p.  Set Order of Agenda
q.  Change Order of Agenda
r.  Introduce Draft Resolution or Amendment
s.  Read the Resolution
t.  Division of the Question
u.  Roll-Call Vote
v.  Adoption by Consent
w.  Limit Debate
x.  Amend Speaker's Time
y.  Plenary Motions

## Appendix Q: One-half and two-thirds voting chart

| Number of Countries | Simple Majority (1/2) | Supermajority (2/3) |
|---|---|---|
| 1 | 1 | 1 |
| 2 | 2 | 2 |
| 3 | 2 | 2 |
| 4 | 3 | 3 |
| 5 | 3 | 4 |
| 6 | 4 | 4 |
| 7 | 4 | 5 |
| 8 | 5 | 6 |
| 9 | 5 | 6 |
| 10 | 6 | 7 |
| 11 | 6 | 8 |
| 12 | 7 | 8 |
| 13 | 7 | 9 |
| 14 | 8 | 10 |
| 15 | 8 | 10 |
| 16 | 9 | 11 |
| 17 | 9 | 12 |
| 18 | 10 | 12 |
| 19 | 10 | 13 |
| 20 | 11 | 14 |
| 21 | 11 | 14 |
| 22 | 12 | 15 |
| 23 | 12 | 16 |
| 24 | 13 | 16 |
| 25 | 13 | 17 |
| 26 | 14 | 18 |
| 27 | 14 | 18 |
| 28 | 15 | 19 |
| 29 | 15 | 20 |
| 30 | 16 | 20 |

## Appendix R: Preamble and operative clause starting word list

*Preambulatory clause starting words*

| | | | |
|---|---|---|---|
| Acknowledging | Confident | Keeping in mind | Respecting |
| Alarmed | Conscious of | Noting | Seeking |
| Angered | Considering | Observing | Stressing |
| Appalled | Convinced of | Prompted by | Understanding |
| Aware | Disturbed by | Realizing | Valuing |
| Bearing in mind | Emphasizing | Recalling | Viewing |
| Believing | Expressing | Recognizing | |

*Operative clause starting words*

| | | | | | |
|---|---|---|---|---|---|
| Accepts | Calls for | Decreases | Expands | Opens | Requests |
| Addresses | Calls upon | Deems | Expresses | Praises | Separates |
| Adheres | Chooses | Defines | Gives | Proclaims | States |
| Advocates | Condemns | Demands | Guarantees | Proposes | Suggests |
| Affirms | Congratulates | Denies | Hopes | Provides | Supports |
| Agrees | Considers | Designates | Improves | Reaffirms | Trusts |
| Approves | Constructs | Deplores | Increases | Recognizes | Urges |
| Asks | Continues | Encourages | Insists | Recommends | Venerates |
| Asserts | Creates | Endorses | Insures | Regrets | |
| Begins | Declares | Establishes | Invites | Reminds | |

# Glossary of terms[1]

**abstention:**   A vote signifying a country wishes its vote to be removed from consideration, altering the majorities.

**adjournment:**   Close of business for the year; the conclusion of council sessions and the summit session.

**agenda:**   A list of business items, or topics, to be considered by the body. See also **provisional agenda**.

**agenda topic:**   An issue of concern to a given council as enumerated in the agenda.

**ambassador (JCC):**   The only person with the power to travel between committees without prior consent of the JCC Coordinator. In the case of an ambassador representing an international body or a country not in the crisis, they have the ability to speak on behalf of the government and to advocate for policy.

**amendment:**   A suggested alteration to the operative clauses of an introduced draft resolution.

**amendment form:**   A half-sheet standard form on which all amendments must be written in order to be introduced.

**Assistant Secretary-General:**   The second-highest student authority; responsible for assisting the Secretary-General in all duties and overseeing vice-chairs in collecting and correctly recording all passed draft resolutions.

**Assistant Secretary-General for Information:**   The student responsible for coordinating the Press Corps.

**author:**   The delegate partially or fully responsible for the writing language of a draft resolution. See also **sponsor**.

**Call to Order:**   The official start to formal proceedings and initiation of the use of parliamentary procedure.

---

[1] Terms defined in the Glossary of the official *Model Arab League Handbook* (NCUSAR 2014) have been included here for the sake of clarity. Terms not defined in the Handbook, but used in this and other materials, are defined by the authors and contributors of the text.

**chair:**   The student officer responsible for moderating council proceedings.

**chair's discretion:**   The right of the chair to rule on matters not explicitly stated in the Handbook.

**character:**   The role which delegates must play, accurately emulating real-world diplomats and advocating policies based on research rather than personal feelings.

**Chief Justice:**   The student responsible for moderating the Arab Court of Justice.

**Chief of Staff:**   The student responsible for assisting the Secretariat with all administrative duties, as needed.

**clause:**   A grammatically independent section of a draft resolution, separated by commas in the preamble or semicolons in the operatives, describing a single idea or action proposed by that draft resolution.

**Closure of Debate:**   The procedure which prompts a substantive vote on an item and its subsidiary items, and eliminates any speakers lists associated with said item(s).

**communiqué (JCC):**   A private communication between a cabinet and another party. This party could be another cabinet, a specific person, or an international body like the UN or NATO. Also sometimes called a memo.

**consent:**   The agreement of all present and voting countries to vote in the affirmative on a substantive item.

**consideration:**   The council's commitment to hear and vote upon a resolution, amendment, or motion.

**correct format:**   See **format.**

**council:**   An assembly of one or two delegates representing each present country, led by a chair, charged with addressing thematically linked concerns related to the Arab World.

**council chair:**   See **chair.**

**council session:**   The period of time specified in the conference schedule wherein councils meet and debate.

**country:**   One of the twenty-two member states of the League of Arab States or an observer state; sometimes refers to the one- or two-person delegation representing a country in a given council.

**crisis scenario:**   A situation urgently requiring action, outside the original parameters of the agenda, presented to a council to debate and address; may be factually-based or simulated.

**debatable:**   Denotes that a motion requires procedural speeches.

**debate:**   The scope of discussion, limited or expanded, embodied by the current speakers list.

**decision of the body:**   The binding result of a procedural or substantive vote.

**decorum:**   The rules dictating aspects of professionalism and mutual respect between all participants.

**delegate:** An individual participant representing a country on a given council; may or may not have a partner.

**delegation:** A group of delegates representing the same country across all councils, for example, "the Delegation of Jordan"; also, a delegate or pair of delegates representing a country on a given council, for example, "the delegation of Jordan to the Joint Defense Council."

**designation:** The shorthand name for a resolution or amendment; for resolutions, a combination of the topic's roman numeral and a letter assigned by the chair at introduction; for amendments, a number assigned by the chair at introduction.

**destructive:** An action's level of impact, for example, a five-minute caucus is less destructive than a ten-minute caucus.

**dilatory:** A measure or action intended to waste time or delay the work of the council.

**directive (JCC):** A directive is an order given by the cabinet leader to infrastructure within their government for the purpose of carrying out some action.

**discretion of the chair:** See **chair's discretion**.

**draft resolution:** A council's response to a topic, written in standard formatting, introduced to the council. See also **resolution**; **working paper**.

**elections:** The selection of the vice-chair, rapporteur, and parliamentarian from among the council's present delegates during a plenary session by majority vote.

**exhausted:** Denotes that no present delegate wishes to continue with the current debate or speakers list.

**expired:** Denotes that the pre-set time limit has been exceeded; for example, speaking time or a caucus.

**extension:** The additional time added to a caucus at the discretion of the chair.

**faculty advisor:** Any staff or faculty person responsible in full or in part for the organization of a delegation.

**failed:** Denotes that a substantive or procedural vote has not met the required number of yes votes to pass.

**floor:** The objectification of debate which may be held by a speaker, receive speeches as the embodiment of the council, or have actions proposed through it.

**flow of debate:** The system of limiting and expanding debate, and creating, maintaining, and closing speakers lists.

**formal debate:** A discussion subject to the parameters of parliamentary procedure laid out in the Handbook.

**format:** All specifications for the grammar and structure of a draft resolution are followed.

**friendly:** Indicates an amendment is approved by all sponsors of the draft resolution that is being amended.

**General Speakers List:** The foundational speakers list from which all other speakers lists branch, used for introductory remarks and comments; not to be closed until all council work is completed.

**hasty decision:** The result of a substantive vote taken before all pertinent information was presented, indicating a country wishes to change its vote.

**head delegate:** An informal position accorded to one member of a delegation; duties are determined by the needs of the team.

**in-order:** Denotes a motion that is properly proposed at the correct time and that is not dilatory. See also **order**.

**in-character:** See **character**.

**informal debate:** Any discussion that takes place during a moderated or unmoderated caucus.

**intel (JCC):** Information requested by the head of state of a cabinet from the JCC Coordinator. This can be information about the crisis, such as an investigation into who tried to assassinate a cabinet member. This can also take the form of super-secret information passed to the JCC Coordinator (e.g., "Turkey has decided to send 200 combat troops into Syria").

**interrupting motion:** An action that may be proposed at any time and does not require the chair to ask for points or motions to be proposed; these include procedural points, a Motion to Reconsider the Vote, and a Motion to Appeal the Decision of the Chair.

**introduction:** The formal presentation of a draft resolution or amendment to a council for consideration.

**introductions:** A plenary session activity allowing each delegate to introduce themselves prior to the Call to Order.

**item:** A matter of business to be considered by the body, such as a topic, resolution, amendment, or motion.

**JCC:** Joint Cabinet Crisis.

**JCC Coordinator:** The student facilitator of the JCC. The Coordinator determines the major events of the crisis, manages communication between all cabinets, and approves/disapproves of some actions taken. The JCC Coordinator is occasionally referred to as the "Higher Being," "Higher Power," or "JCC God" by cabinets.

**Local Coordinator:** Staff or faculty at the host institution responsible for the logistical coordination of the conference.

**majority:** The number of votes totaling more than but not equal to half, rounded up, referred to as >50%.

**member state:** One of the twenty-two countries of the League of Arab States, but not an observer state.

**mock debate:** A session to practice parliamentary procedure wherein students simulate real conference sessions.

**moderated caucus:** A type of informal debate wherein the chair recognizes speakers as they raise their placards rather than use a speakers list; may be used during a Suspension of the Rules.

**motion:** A proposed procedural action.

**National Council representative:** A staff person representing the NCUSAR at a conference.

**No with Rights:** A negative vote allowing a delegate thirty seconds to explain their decision after the vote, allowed only during roll-call votes; not recognized if the vote fails.

**objection:** This is called out if a delegate wishes to vote in any other way than affirmatively during a vote by consent.

**observer state:** A country other than one of the twenty-two League of Arab States member states that is represented; accorded all delegate rights and privileges with the exception of substantive voting.

**officer:** A member of the student staff, including the Secretary-General, Assistant Secretary-General(s), Chief of Staff, chairs, vice-chairs, rapporteurs, parliamentarians, and Chief Justice(s).

**opening ceremonies:** The gathering of all delegations at the beginning of a conference.

**operative clause:** An action to be taken by the League listed in the latter portion of a draft resolution.

**order:** The proper execution of the rules.

**order of precedence:** The order in which motions must be considered if proposed simultaneously.

**order of the agenda:** The order in which a council must address its agenda topics, set at the start of the first council session.

**original numbering:** The ordinal numbering assigned to agenda topics prior to the conference by which topics may be referred, not to be changed in the case of a change in the original order of the agenda.

**parliamentarian:** A student officer optionally elected by each council who is responsible for providing guidance on parliamentary procedure when requested by the Chair.

**parliamentary procedure:** The system of rules dictating formal debate.

**pass:** A voting option allowing a delegate to be skipped once and added to the end of a roll-call vote roster, after which the delegate must vote "yes," "no," or "abstain."

**placard:** A card indicating country name, used to gain the attention of the Chair for points, motions, or votes.

**placard vote:** The default method of voting wherein countries indicate how they vote by raising their placards; countries may vote "yes," "no," or "abstain."

**plenary session:** A special opening period moderated by the chair when certain matters must be addressed, including introductions, elections, Call to Order, roll call, and amending the agenda topics.

**plenary motion:** A motion allowed only during a plenary session, including the Motion to Add, Delete, or Amend a Topic, the Motion to Change a Topic's Assignment, and Motion to Adopt the Agenda.

**point:** The interrupting of procedural tools, including Points of Order, Parliamentary Inquiry, and Personal Privilege.

**point of information:** A question that may be asked to a delegate who has yielded remaining speaking time to points of information; not an interrupting procedural point.

**popcorn debate:** A type of informal debate allowed during a Suspension of the Rules wherein the current speaker chooses the next speaker; a motion must include speaking time and overall time limit.

**position paper:** A short treatise explaining a country's policies; used for delegate preparation, not required to participate.

**preamble:** The opening clauses of a draft resolution describing the problem, recalling past actions, and explaining the rationale behind the actions the draft resolution proposes; does not prescribe action; may not be amended after the draft resolution has been introduced.

**preambulatory clause:** The line of a preamble expressing a single thought or idea.

**present:** Called out by observer states during roll calls, indicating presence but not substantive voting rights.

**present and voting:** Called out by member states during roll calls, indicating both presence and substantive voting rights.

**presiding officer:** The officer currently moderating a session; most often, but not necessarily, a chair or Secretary-General.

**press release (JCC):** A public communication that will be sent to all cabinets and has the possibility of response from other entities.

**pre-written resolution:** Complete working paper written by a single country delegation prior to the start of a conference, which has been designed to pass in a council vote without debate or revision.

**procedural matter:** An item pertaining to a motion or other procedure.

**procedural point:** See **point**.

**procedural speech:** A thirty-second speech addressing a debatable motion; the chair takes up to two in favor and two opposed, in equal numbers if available, with priority going to the opposition. See also **speakers against and for**.

**procedural vote:** A vote taken on a motion.

**proceedings:** What constitutes the work and actions of the body.

**provisional agenda:** Topic language provided prior to the conference, unaltered and not amended. See also **agenda**.

**question:**   An action or motion under consideration by the body, as in Motion to Divide the Question.

**Question and Answer Session:**   Also known as a Q&A Session. A type of informal debate allowed during a Suspension of the Rules wherein delegate questions may be addressed by a specified delegate(s); a motion must include an overall time limit.

**quorum:**   The minimum number of countries required to enter substantive voting procedures, totaling half of all initially present countries.

**rapporteur:**   The student officer elected by each council responsible for assisting the chair and keeping speakers lists.

**recess:**   A break in the proceedings. See also **Suspension of the Meeting**.

**recognition:**   The recognition of the chair is required to address the body or make any non-interrupting motion.

**reconsideration:**   A procedure which may result in a re-vote; proposed immediately after the conclusion of voting procedures.

**Reply:**   A written statement in response to a formal speech insulting the national integrity of a country, read by the chair if acceptable.

**resolution:**   A council's response to a topic, written in standard formatting, passed by the council.

**resolution format:**   The guidelines dictating proper grammar and layout for a resolution.

**Right of Reply:**   See **Reply**.

**roll:**   Also called a **roster**. A list of League of Arab States member states and observers.

**roll call:**   A procedure used to determine which countries are present, and the majority and supermajority; countries not present for roll call must send a note to the chair to obtain speaking and voting rights.

**roll-call vote:**   A method of voting wherein the chair asks each country its vote in alphabetical order; countries may vote "yes," "no," "abstain," "pass," or "No with Rights."

**role-playing:**   To take on the persona and act out the ideology of real-world diplomats as accurately as possible.

**roster:**   See **roll**.

**round robin:**   A type of informal debate allowed during a Suspension of the Rules wherein each country is given equal time to speak on a specific topic; a motion must include a speaking time.

**Rules of Procedure, The:**   The complete body of parliamentary procedure, rules, and regulations described in the MAL Handbook.

**scope of debate:**   The broadness or narrowness of a given speakers list.

**second:**   A procedural requirement that a motion obtain verbal support from a second delegate to be considered.

**Secretariat:**   The student staff including the Secretary-General, the Assistant Secretary-General, the Chief of Staff, and the chairs.

**signatory:**   A country officially supporting the introduction of a draft resolution, but not necessarily its content.

**so moved:**   A statement made by a delegate obliging the presiding officer's request that a specific motion is made.

**speakers against and for:**   See **procedural speech.**

**speakers list:**   The order in which countries may speak during formal debate; restricted by the scope of debate.

**speaking time:**   The length of time a delegate may speak during formal debate.

**speech:**   Comments made by a delegate during formal debate via a speakers list.

**sponsor:**   The author of a resolution or amendment; draft resolution sponsors may determine if an amendment is friendly or unfriendly. See also **author**.

**Sponsor's Rights:**   Special speaking time accorded to a draft resolution's sponsors to discuss the draft after debate has been limited to it at the discretion of the chair.

**straw poll vote:**   A type of informal debate allowed during a Suspension of the Rules wherein the chair conducts a non-binding vote to determine a measure's current popularity.

**subsidiary item:**   An item narrower in scope, lower on the debate thread; for example, Resolution II/A is a subsidiary item to Topic II.

**substantive matter:**   An item pertaining to a draft resolution or amendment.

**substantive speech:**   A speech pertaining to the business at hand given via a speakers list.

**substantive vote:**   A vote taken on a draft resolution or amendment.

**summit session:**   A special closing period moderated by the Secretary-General when all draft resolutions passed in councils are confirmed by the body.

**summit format:**   The resolution formatting required for the summit session.

**summit motion:**   A motion allowed only during summit session, including a Motion to Read the Resolution and a Motion to Hear Speakers Rights.

**supermajority:**   The number of votes totaling two-thirds of all present countries, rounding up to the nearest whole number.

**Suspension of the Meeting:**   A break in the proceedings for an unmoderated caucus or a scheduled break.

**Suspension of the Rules:**   A timed period designated for various informal actions and debate styles.

**table (to table an item):**   To set an item aside in order to consider other business; to expand debate.

**table (on the table):**   An abstract place where items of business are listed for the body's consideration.

**team:** A group of students from a given institution who may or may not represent multiple countries.

**topic:** see **agenda topic**.

**threads of debate:** The concept that debate is organized into a series of connected speakers lists with debate moving down the thread to items narrower in scope by limiting debate and up the thread to items more general in scope by expanding debate.

**unfriendly:** Indicates an amendment is not approved by all sponsors of the draft resolution that is being amended.

**unmoderated caucus:** A short break in the proceedings achieved via a Motion to Suspend the Meeting.

**Upper Secretariat:** The student staff including only the Secretary-General and Assistant Secretary-General.

**vice-chair:** The student officer elected by each council who is responsible for assisting the chair.

**voting procedure:** The formal period when substantive voting takes place, beginning with the passage of a Motion to Close Debate (or similar) and ending with the announcement of the vote result.

**working paper:** The proper name for a draft resolution before it has been introduced to the body for consideration.

**yield:** An act of disposing of remaining speaking time.

# Works cited

D'Agati, Philip, and Northeastern University International Relations Council (NU-IRC). 2015. *NU-IRC Governing Documents*. Boston: Northeastern University.

Hätinger, Benjamin H. 2013. *The League of Arab States*. Norderstedt, Germany: GRIN Verlag GmbH.

NCUSAR. 2014. *Model Arab League Handbook*. Washington, DC: NCUSAR.

NCUSAR. 2015. Official website of the National Council on U.S.-Arab Relations: http://ncusar.org/.

Toffolo, Chris. 2008. *The Arab League (Global Organization)*. New York, NY: Chelsea House Publishers.

United States Department of State. 1947. "The Alexandria Protocol." *Department of State Bulletin*, Vol. XVI, No. 411, 18 May 1947. Washington, DC: Government Printing Office.

United States Department of State. 1957a. "Pact of the League of Arab States." *American Foreign Policy 1950–1955 Basic Documents*, Vol. 1, Series 117. Department of State Publication 6446. Washington, DC: Government Printing Office.

United States Department of State. 1957b. "Treaty of Joint Defense and Economic Cooperation Between the States of the Arab League." *American Foreign Policy 1950–1955 Basic Documents*, Vol. 1, Series 117. Department of State Publication 6446. Washington, DC: Government Printing Office.

# Index